Myths and Tales of the White Mountain Apache

Myths and Tales of the White Mountain Apache

GRENVILLE GOODWIN

With a New Preface by Tribal Chairman Ronnie Lupe
And a New Foreword by
Elizabeth A. Brandt, Bonnie Lavender-Lewis, and Philip J. Greenfeld

The University of Arizona Press / Tucson & London

The University of Arizona Press
Copyright © 1994
The Arizona Board of Regents
All rights reserved
Published by arrangement with the American Folklore Society
Myths and Tales of the White Mountain Apache was originally published in 1939 as
volume 33 of the Memoirs of the American Folklore Society.
Reprint copy of this book was provided by the Folklore Archives of the Department
of Folklore and Folklife, University of Pennsylvania.

⊛ This book is printed on acid-free, archival-quality paper.
Manufactured in the United States of America

99 98 97 96 95 94   6 5 4 3 2 1

Library of Congress Cataloging-in-Publication Data

Myths and tales of the White Mountain Apache / Grenville Goodwin, with
    a new preface by tribal chairman Ronnie Lupe ; and a new foreword by
    Elizabeth A. Brandt, Bonnie Lavender-Lewis, and Philip J. Greenfeld.
        p. cm.
    Originally published: New York : American Folklore Society, 1939,
in series: The Memoirs of the American Folklore Society ; vol. 33.
    Includes bibliographical references.
    ISBN 0-8165-1451-8 (alk. paper)
    1. Apache Indians — Legends.   I. Goodwin, Grenville, 1907–1940.
E99.A6M87   1994   94-2249
398.2'089972 — dc20   CIP

British Cataloguing-in-Publication Data
A catalogue record for this book is available from the British Library.

CONTENTS

PREFACE TO THE NEW EDITION

I am pleased to have been invited to write a preface to this republication of a collection of stories and myths of my White Mountain Apache people. This volume contains translations of Apache stories that reflect our distinct view of the world and our approach to life. These myths and fables have survived through untold generations because the truth contained in them is eternal and the moral lessons that they teach are still valid.

To gain an appreciation of these stories, you must travel in your mind to a different place. The setting is a limb-framed wickiup covered with dry branches and animal hides. A cold wind blows against the branches and slips through small openings in the walls. Only the fire keeps back the chill as you sit around the hearth with your relatives. Everyone's attention turns to a grandfather as he begins to instruct the children and remind the others in the wickiup of their relationship with each other and the natural world around them. The method is neither lecturing nor reading from a printed page but telling a story featuring Coyote or the Ant People or the Rabbit. As you listen, you see the characters spun out in the word pictures, you laugh at their antics — and you see yourself in similar circumstances and find the spiritual truths concealed in the fable. The story tells you how to act and why, a moral lesson is learned or reinforced. Often the story is shot like an arrow at a family member whose conduct has been inappropriate, and the person is guided back to the path of correct Apache behavior.

The richness of our White Mountain Apache culture is reflected in these stories, and the depths of our spiritual beliefs are often hidden in the story line and actions of the characters. Although many of the deeper meanings in these stories are lost in the translation from Apache to English, you can read these stories and catch a glimpse of how our ancestors observed nature, drew metaphors from everyday observations and happenings, and applied the lessons learned to everyday life. Read them and you will see how harmony with nature and the natural world is the goal of every Apache. Read them and you will see why the stories are eternal and why they set a standard of conduct and behavior that every Apache, every human, must try to reach to achieve the fullness of life.

As a White Mountain Apache, I am proud of the Apache philosophy and ideals inherent in these stories and myths, which have been passed down from my ancestors. Stories such as these have governed the life of my people for centuries. When you read them, I hope that they work on your mind and that you perceive new insights for guiding your life.

RONNIE LUPE
Tribal Chairman
White Mountain Apache Tribe

FOREWORD

Telling stories is one of the ancient ways members of a culture create and maintain their identity, their history, their sense of important knowledge, and their moral values. Myths and legends may be told in sacred contexts, sung in ceremonies, given as formal instruction, or used to entertain. Apache stories are used in all these ways. This collection is a part of the oral tradition of the White Mountain Apache group living primarily on the San Carlos Apache Reservation. Elders shared the tradition with Grenville Goodwin, an anthropologist, between 1931 and 1936.

The White Mountain Apache were the easternmost of the Western Apache subtribes, and they considered a huge area of Arizona their home, from the White Mountains in the north to the Pinaleños (Mt. Graham) in the south. They practiced seasonal agriculture, hunting and gathering, and also raided into Mexico in the prereservation period (Basso, ed. 1971; Goodwin 1942). Beginning in the 1860s, members of Western Apache bands were moved from their ancestral lands onto reservations in Arizona and were confined there by the U.S. Army. In 1871 the San Carlos Apache Reservation was established to control the movements of the Apaches who were being pressured by white settlement. The reservation became a kind of concentration camp, with more than 5,000 Apache and Yavapai Indians from different bands and subtribes. Ultimately it was divided into two reservations, Fort Apache and San Carlos, which today are the two largest Apache reservations in Arizona. Members of the White Mountain subtribe are found on both reservations, and there is also intermarriage between the two reservations. Apaches and Yavapais are also found today on small reservations near Camp Verde, Payson, Prescott, and north of Scottsdale. Apache populations on all the reservations number almost 18,000 (U.S. Census 1990).

This collection is entitled *Myths and Tales*, but this title gives a misleading impression of what some of these texts are and what they mean to Apaches. Storytelling is very important in Apache culture, as important as hunting, cooking, building a wickiup, praying, and conducting ceremonies. As an Apache medicine man once said to me (EAB), "Don't call these myths, because then white people will think they aren't true." These stories are a very important part of Apache culture, and they tell their truths in powerful ways. Ridington (1988:70–71) writes as a white man about the difficulties that non-Indians have in appreciating the myths of the Beaver Indians of Canada, a Northern Athabaskan tribe, but what he says is also applicable here:

> Stories are windows into the thoughtworld of Indian people. Their time is different from ours. . . . In our thoughtworld, myth and reality are opposites. Unless we can find some way to understand the reality of mythic thinking, we remain prisoners of our own language, our own

thoughtworld. . . . [T]he language of Western social science assumes an object world independent of individual experience. The language of Indians' stories assumes that objectivity can only be approached through experience. In the Indian thoughtworld, stories about talking animals and stories about the summer gathering are equally true because both describe personal experience. Their truths are complementary.

The stories in this collection contain a wealth of Apache knowledge and Apache ways of transmitting it. The *gaan*, or mountain spirits, that dance in these stories from the beginning of time still dance at girls' puberty ceremonies, which are being held for more and more girls, and at healing ceremonies, and you can still hear the haunting sound of their bells coming from far away and moving closer and closer. The long story of Changing Woman continues to be sung and performed in ritual drama in the puberty or Sunrise ceremony, *Naa'e'ees*, over and over again each summer season. These stories are true as any sacred text is true.

Apache oral tradition is much richer than the portion represented here. Some of the stories found here are incomplete or shortened versions of longer stories or cycles of stories and songs still told and sung today. The book provides a selection of stories that deal with the creation of the world and how to live in the world, and they show detailed knowledge of the places, plants, and animals found in this world. Most of the stories in this collection fall into the category called in Apache *godiyįhgo nagoldi'i*, literally "being holy stories." Apaches have other stories that are shorter and sometimes more entertaining, and some that are historical accounts of actual occurrences. Apache verbal arts are highly developed. Anna Price, who told some of the stories in this collection, tells us how sacred stories used to be told:

> In the old days when a person got ready to be told a story, from the time the storyteller started no one there ever stopped to eat or sleep. They kept telling the story straight through till it was finished. Then when the story was through, the medicine man would tell all about the different medicines. There would be a basket of corn seeds there, and for each line that was spoken, that person who was listening would count out one corn seed. This way there would sometimes be two hundred seeds. Then that person would have to eat them all. If he could eat them, then he would remember all the words he had been told. If you fell asleep during this time, then the story was broken and was no good. That's the way we used to do. (Basso, ed. 1971:29)

It is still the case today that, when stories are told or songs sung at ceremonies, no one eats until the medicine man and singers have finished all the songs that belong together, which may take five or six hours.

Apache stories (Basso 1990:116) are used "to enlighten, to instruct, to criticize, to warn, to entertain," and to provide a continuous link between the Apache and their land by telling the events that happened and the places where they happened. Apache place names are often complete sentences that describe a place so perfectly that it can be recognized from the name alone.

The name calls up a detailed mental picture of the place. The landscape, then, is rich in stories, not only sacred stories, but also historical tales of things that really happened at a particular place, creating layers of meaning. Apaches use these ties between a place and an event to create a hunting metaphor for storytelling. As Chairman Lupe says in his preface, they can be "shot like an arrow" to someone to redirect them to the Apache way. Basso (1990) has explored what it means to say this. A storyteller can target a particular person and relate a story that is a "telling" commentary on the target's misbehavior. Every time a person passes the place in the landscape that was mentioned in the story, that place "stalks" the person. In other words, the links among the person, the place, and the story are present again, potent reminders in the landscape. Nick Thompson provides the Apache view of this:

> This is what we know about our stories. They go to work on your mind and make you think about your life. Maybe you've not been acting right. Maybe you've been stingy. Maybe you've been chasing after women. Maybe you've been trying to act like a Whiteman. People don't *like* it! So someone goes hunting for you — maybe your grandmother, your grandfather, your uncle. It doesn't matter. Anyone can do it.
>
> So someone stalks you and tells a story about what happened long ago. It doesn't matter if other people are around — you're going to know he's aiming that story at you. All of a sudden it hits you. It's like an arrow they say. Sometimes it just bounces off — it's too soft and you don't think about anything. But when it's strong it goes in *deep* and starts working on your mind. No one says anything to you, only that story is all, but now you know that people have been watching you and talking about you. They don't like how you've been acting. So you have to think about your life. (Quoted in Basso 1990:124–25)

As a traditional aunt of mine told me (BLL), storytelling was done as a disciplinary action to our Apache children. Most of the animal stories, such as those in this book, have morals behind them. The storyteller would tell the children, "Now, don't be like Coyote" or, "Be like the Rabbit." There were no televisions, radios, or video games, so aunts, uncles, and mothers and fathers would take turns telling stories during the wintertime. Children would come to certain wickiups where they would be told these Apache stories. They would be told in the wintertime because that was when most of the animals hibernated, and out of politeness to the animals, they did not want them to overhear the stories. Today, stories can be heard at major ceremonies. Coyote stories may be heard at traditional wakes, for example.

These stories are still a vital part of Apache oral traditions on the San Carlos and White Mountain Apache reservations where they were originally told to Grenville Goodwin as he listened to Apache elders. Many of the people who shared their stories with Goodwin were well-known, thoughtful elders who were respected authorities on Apache culture. Some were spiritual leaders or medicine persons who were consulted for healing, for counsel in difficult situations, for protection, and for help in finding lost objects. These stories were told by Anna Price, Palmer Valor, Francis Drake, Bane (or Barney) Tithla, Charley Sago, and Alsus. Their descendants have become medicine persons, teachers, lawyers, council members, and other professionals, and many of them still live in the community of Bylas or other Apache communities.

Anna Price was the eldest daughter of Diablo, the most influential White Mountain Apache chief. She was a member of the *ʾiyaʾą́ą́yé* clan, blind and almost one hundred years old at the time she shared her stories with Goodwin. She was a widely respected cultural expert who also possessed two ceremonies. Such ceremonies gave her power, status, and special knowledge not shared with others. Goodwin's wife, Janice, who was formally presented to her after she married Goodwin, said that "she was like a queen." Some of her narratives dealing with the prereservation period can be found in *Western Apache Raiding and Warfare* (Basso, ed. 1971). Her stories were interpreted by Richard Bylas and Neil (or Neal) Buck from Apache into English. Palmer Valor, a medicine man and member of the *tʾiisłteedntʾin* clan, was ninety-five in 1932 and was known as a widely traveled and very knowledgeable man who had participated in prereservation life and had taken part in journeys to the Gulf of Mexico. Francis Drake was also a well-known elder and medicine man and was of the same clan as Palmer Valor. Bane Tithla, of the *nádits'oosn* clan, had learned many of his stories from his maternal grandfather and had a great deal of ceremonial knowledge, although he was a middle-aged man at the time these stories were collected.

The stories were taken down and interpreted from Apache to English by Richard Bylas, Neil Buck, Clyne Jose, and Thomas Riley. Mr. Buck died in 1965, and his obituary in the state's leading newspaper, the *Arizona Republic*, cited him as an authority on Apache history and mentioned his collaboration with Goodwin. Goodwin's widow, since remarried, says that Neil Buck was a principal collaborator who went everywhere with Goodwin. Apparently Goodwin collected these stories by listening to the stories in Apache, which he spoke and understood, then working with an Apache interpreter who helped him to write down and translate them into English. Goodwin then typed the stories in English. Goodwin created a dictionary for himself but was a little unsure of his transcription of Apache. He used a very rapid kind of shorthand to record materials verbatim, and he also sometimes used his typewriter in the field.

Grenville Goodwin was born in New York in 1907. He attended the Mesa Ranch School, a college preparatory school in Arizona, where he fell in love with the Southwest and began to study and learn anthropology. Goodwin became fascinated by the Western Apache and set out in 1929 to learn more. He lived for the better part of three years at Bylas on the San Carlos Apache Reservation, working at the trading post and visiting Apache camps, listening, watching, occasionally asking, and learning to understand and speak Apache (Spicer 1961:202). From this point on, he dedicated his life to learning what Apache people were willing to teach him. He studied anthropology briefly at the University of Arizona and engaged in field trips and extensive correspondence with professional ethnographers of the Apache, especially

Morris Opler (1973) and Harry Hoijer, who worked on the Athabaskan family of languages, to which Apache belongs. He also began graduate study in anthropology at the University of Chicago. By the mid-1930s, Goodwin had begun to publish articles on the Apache in the leading anthropological journals (1933, 1935, 1938) and had also begun to write and plan a series of books. This book was the first of that projected series.

The original manuscript of this book, which was first published by the American Folklore Society, is not in the Goodwin collection at the Arizona State Museum in Tucson, and members of the family do not know its location. At one point, Goodwin's wife, Janice, had produced watercolor illustrations to accompany some of the stories, and plans were made to reprint this collection in an edition produced by Goodwin's brother, but Goodwin did not like the illustrations and the publication plans ended. The only other sources of Apache folklore are the collections produced by Pliny Earle Goddard (1918, 1919, 1920), which are original texts in Apache with translations in English.

The stories presented in this volume are part of a much larger collection of ethnographic material contributed by Apache elders and interpreted and translated by them. The full set of materials can be found in the Grenville Goodwin Papers in the archives of the Arizona State Museum on the University of Arizona campus in Tucson. The collection also includes detailed field notes on a variety of topics. Especially important are materials on Apache religion and cosmology (restricted due to their sensitivity), an Apache dictionary, ethnobotanical material, and oral histories of prereservation life by the Apaches with whom Goodwin worked. Much of this material provided the basis for Goodwin's major work, *The Social Organization of the Western Apache*, which was published by the University of Chicago Press in 1942 after Goodwin's untimely death in 1940 of a brain tumor at the age of thirty-three. The work was reprinted by the University of Arizona Press in 1969 but is now out of print. Another set of Apache oral history materials was edited and prepared for publication by Keith Basso and published by the University of Arizona Press as *Western Apache Raiding and Warfare* (Basso, ed. 1971).

Goodwin's role in preserving these myths and in bringing them to a larger non-Apache audience is to be appreciated as a counterbalance to the literature on Apaches which earlier had created negative stereotypes. As Edward Spicer wrote,

> To Grenville Goodwin we owe most of what understanding we have of the way of life of the Western Apaches. Few have tried seriously to learn what that way of life was, and even fewer have written effectively about it. The abundant literature on the Western Apaches, inspired in great part by the spectacular forays of Geronimo and his predecessors, is largely a literature of the white men who fought the Indians and participated in the final relentless roundups. It is not a literature from which emerges a view of the values by which Apaches lived. But for the work of Goodwin, we would have lost almost all opportunity to participate in the Apache world. (Spicer 1961:201)

The quality of ethnographic reporting represented in Goodwin's collection of these myths and tales is certainly among the least appreciated in the history of anthropology. Goodwin was an excellent ethnographer, comparable to Malinowski in the scope and detail of his work. His was not a distanced view of the Apaches, it was a view from behind the counter of a trading post in the heart of the community and from the ground at night as he sat and listened to the old people's stories. It was personally very satisfying and pleasant. Although still framed from the outsider's perspective, as all ethnography is in some sense, Goodwin's view was one of a friend who also had some role in the community. Goodwin was no Victorian intellectual with an elitist curiosity about other cultures but rather a man with an immense liking and respect for the people, who were his friends. He named his only son for Neil Buck, one of his closest Apache collaborators. In communications with Morris Opler (1973:56), for example, he refers to Apaches as "My own friends, the W. Apache." In those same letters he combines feelings of excitement, awe, and eagerness with an almost joyful sense of wonder at each new piece of the puzzle as it falls into place in the process of ethnographic description and ethnological explanation.

Goodwin's work is respected not only by ethnographers working in the Southwest but also by the people he worked with. Goodwin's widow says that after Goodwin's death Neil Buck wrote her a very moving letter and told her about a ceremony they had had in Goodwin's honor (Mrs. Janice Massey, personal communication). Charles Kaut, who himself has done significant research on the Western Apache (Kaut 1957, for example) tells the following story:

> I was doing research in Cibecue for my dissertation in the 1950s and was having trouble getting a consistent set of kinship terms with respect to the patrilateral cross-cousins, for which there are a number of alternate terms (cf. Goodwin 1942:197–99). I decided to go to Calva at San Carlos where one of Goodwin's consultants, Neil Buck, was still alive to see if he could straighten the system out in my mind. During the interview with Mr. Buck, the terminology still seemed inconsistent and I made the mistake of saying, "The book says . . . " at which point Buck shot back, "The book is right," and refused further comment. (Kaut, personal communication)

The quality of Goodwin's ethnography stands among the best in the anthropological record and deserves wider and more public recognition than it has had. This new edition of these myths and tales should help to remedy the situation to some extent.

A second point is the fact that Goodwin anticipated today's concerns with voice, with subjecthood, with collaboration. He told us who provided the information and something about them. He told us who told the stories and who interpreted them. He gave credit where it was due. The Apache voice is here in the texts even though they are in English. The voices are found both in the traditional forms, such as myths and tales, in other personal narratives he collected of the warfare and prereservation period, which have been published in *Western Apache Raiding and Warfare,* and in the materials on cosmology and other aspects of Apache culture in his papers at the Arizona State Museum.

The multiple collaborators on this book have brought us some insights into Apache verbal arts, Apache tradition, and the Apache thoughtworld. These stories, which reach into the beginning, are also alive today and continue to teach, to warn, and to entertain.

ELIZABETH A. BRANDT
BONNIE LAVENDER-LEWIS
PHILIP J. GREENFELD

REFERENCES CITED

Boas, F., P. E. Goddard, E. Sapir, and A. L. Kroeber
  1916   *Phonetic Transcription of Indian Languages: Report of the Committee of the American Anthropological Association.* Smithsonian Miscellaneous Collections, vol. 66, no. 6. Washington, D.C.

Basso, K. H.
  1990   "Stalking with Stories": Names, Places, and Moral Narratives Among the Western Apache. In *Western Apache Language and Culture,* K. H. Basso, 99–137. Tucson: University of Arizona Press.

Basso, K. H., ed.
  1971   *Western Apache Raiding and Warfare.* From the Notes of Grenville Goodwin. Tucson: University of Arizona Press; reprint, 1994.

Goddard, P. E.
  1918   *San Carlos Apache Texts.* Anthropological Papers of the American Museum of Natural History 24, pt. 2. New York.
  1919   *Myths and Tales from the White Mountain Apache.* Anthropological Papers of the American Museum of Natural History 24, pt. 3. New York.
  1920   *White Mountain Apache Texts.* Anthropological Papers of the American Museum of Natural History 24, pt. 4. New York.

Goodwin, G.
  1933   Clans of the Western Apache. *New Mexico Historical Review* 8:176–82.
  1935   The Social Divisions and the Economic Life of the Western Apache. *American Anthropologist* 37:55–64.
  1938   White Mountain Apache Religion. *American Anthropologist* 40:24–37.
  1939   *Myths and Tales of the White Mountain Apache.* Memoirs of the American Folklore Society, vol. 33. New York: J. J. Augustin, Publisher. Reprint, Kraus Reprint Company, 1969, 1979.
  1942   *Social Organization of the Western Apache.* Chicago: University of Chicago Press.

Kaut, Charles R.
   1957   *The Western Apache Clan System: Its Origins and Development.*
          University of New Mexico Publications in Anthropology, no. 9. Al-
          buquerque: University of New Mexico.
Opler, M., ed.
   1973   *Grenville Goodwin Among the Western Apache: Letters from the
          Field.* Tucson: University of Arizona Press.
Ridington, Robin
   1988   *Trail to Heaven.* Iowa City: University of Iowa Press.
Spicer, E.
   1961   Grenville Goodwin: A Dedication to the Memory of Grenville Good-
          win, 1907–1940. *Arizona and the West* 3:201–4.
   1971   Grenville Goodwin: A Biographical Note. In *Western Apache Raid-
          ing and Warfare,* K. G. Basso, ed., 3–7. Tucson: University of
          Arizona Press.
United States. Bureau of the Census
   1990   *Arizona Reservations.* Washington, D.C.: U.S. Government Print-
          ing Office.

A NOTE ON WRITTEN APACHE

Goodwin had a good ear for Apache sounds, but he was using a phonetic writing system that had been developed by the linguists of the American Anthropological Association (Boas et al. 1916). He had just learned the system, and he made some errors. Goodwin gives a partial key to the meaning of the symbols in his introduction. Many of the symbols he used have changed, and linguists who work with the Apachean languages have settled on a system for writing all the related languages that comes from the system used in Young and Morgan's *The Navajo Language* (1980). This system represents the basic sound units but not always their exact pronunciation. The basic vowels /i e o a/ may occur short, long, or written as double vowels (aa or nasal ą, ąą). There are two tones: high and low, with the low tone unmarked. High is written with an accent over the vowel: á and áá. There are a number of consonants, with some pronounced similarly to English. These are t, k, b, d, g, gh, ch, h, l, m, n, s, sh, z, zh, w, and y. In addition, there is a consonant known as the glottal stop, /ʔ/, which can precede and follow vowels and modify the consonants /kʔ, tʔ, cʔ, tłʔ, and tsʔ/ (Greenfeld 1972, 1978). This sound is similar to the catch that one hears in *uh-oh*. Apache also has the barred /ł/, similar to the sound in the English *sl*. There are also several affricates, such as /dz/ pronounced like the *dz* in *adze*, /ts/ as in *tots*, and some lateral affricates such as *dl*, *tł*, and *tłʔ*. Goodwin sometimes ran words together, often wrote what he actually heard, and occasionally used the wrong symbol. The chart below summarizes the differences between Goodwin's symbols and the way they are written today. The practical orthography represents a nontechnical way of writing Apache.

Goodwin's Symbol	Goodwin's Intended Phonetic Value[1]	Contemporary Phonetic Symbol(s)	Practical Orthography[2]
c	voiceless alveopalatal fricative	š or ʃ	sh
ǰ	voiced alveopalatal fricative	ž or ʒ	zh
tc	voiceless alveopalatal affricate	č	ch
dj	voiced alveopalatal affricate	ǰ	j
ẋ[3]	voiceless velar fricative	x	h
γ	voiced velar fricative	γ	gh
°	indicates syllabic consonants		not used
·	indicates long vowel		double vowel

1. The AAA committee described sounds using terms that are in many cases now somewhat archaic. One of these is *sonant* to mean voiced. In the above table I have interpreted Goodwin's phonetic descriptions in contemporary terminology. In some cases I have also corrected apparent errors in his description. Thus he calls γ and x̣ palatals when they should be described as velar.

2. This is as used by Young and Morgan in *The Navajo Language* (1980).

3. In contemporary phonetics, a dot under a letter means just the opposite of Goodwin's description in the key. This symbol would be for a back velar fricative, not a fronted or palatal one. Since the convention at the time he was writing was similar to today's, this has to be viewed as a mistake on Goodwin's part.

ELIZABETH A. BRANDT

PHILIP J. GREENFELD

REFERENCES CITED

Boas, F., P. E. Goddard, E. Sapir, and A. L. Kroeber
  1916 *Phonetic Transcription of Indian Languages: Report of the Committee of the American Anthropological Association.* Smithsonian Miscellaneous Collections, vol. 66, no. 6. Washington, D.C.

Greenfeld, Philip J.
  1972 The Phonological Hierarchy of the White Mountain Dialect of Western Apache. Ph.D. dissertation, Department of Anthropology, University of Arizona, Tucson.

  1978 Some Special Phonological Characteristics of the White Mountain Dialect of Apachean. *Anthropological Linguistics* 20:150–57.

Young, Robert W., and William Morgan
  1980 *The Navajo Language: A Grammar and Colloquial Dictionary.* Albuquerque: University of New Mexico Press.

PREFACE

The White Mountain Apache of Arizona were the easternmost of the five distinct groups formerly composing the Western Apache.[1] These groups were based on recognized territorial limits and on a more subtle difference in speech and custom that the people are quick to point out themselves, but which ethnically is comparatively slight. All five groups spoke mutually intelligible dialects of Southern Athapascan and shared a hunting and wild food gathering culture, as well as agriculture to varying degree. Social practice and religion were equally similar.

The only published tales from the Western Apache are those of Goddard in the Anthropological Papers of the American Museum of Natural History, Vol. XXIV, parts 1 to 4, which came out in 1918 and contain a small collection of White Mountain tales and a slightly larger selection from the San Carlos Apache. Among those from the San Carlos all are duplicated in the present collection, excepting "The Sisters are Lured by a Flute" and "The Loaf, the Cloth, and the Hide," both of which also may exist among the White Mountain Apache. No tales from Cibecue, Southern Tonto, and Northern Tonto have been published. Those few taken down from the first two show nothing radically different from corresponding tales of the White Mountain or San Carlos Apache.

The following tales form a fairly complete collection from the White Mountain Apache. There are doubtless a few which have not been obtained and other versions are probably extant. All tales except those from Charley Sago and Alsus were taken down at Bylas,[2] on the San Carlos reservation, between March and July, 1932, and March and December, 1936. Those from Charley Sago were obtained in August, 1931, during travels in the mountains north of Bylas and the one from Alsus in July, 1936 on Cedar Creek. The work was done under the auspices of the University of Arizona, in connection with a general study of the Western Apache.

Tales are to be told during the night, at any time from dusk till dawn. The sun should not see you doing it. They are meant to be heard only during the cold months, from November to February.[3] In the spring, summer, and fall too much danger is abroad —

---

[1] The five groups were: White Mountain, Cibecue, San Carlos, Southern Tonto, and Northern Tonto. For limits of territory, interrelations between, and etc. see Goodwin, "Social Divisions and Economic Life of the Western Apache," American Anthropologist, Vol. 37, pp. 55—64.

[2] Bylas is an Apache settlement divided into two communities, one of White Mountain people, the other of San Carlos and Southern Tonto.

[3] Allowances were made in telling me the tales out of season.

snakes, poisonous insects, and lightning. For this reason people
wait till such evil things are absent so they will not hear themselves
spoken of and punish the narrator or his family.

Tales may be divided into two major and two minor cycles.
"Creation" and "Coyote" are the major ones. The minor cycles are
"Big Owl" and the "ga·n." There are also miscellaneous tales such
as "Vulva Woman," "Grasshopper Loses His Leg," "How Gila
Monster Got His Name," "The Man Who Visited the Sky With the
Eagles." European tales learned, as Apache themselves sometimes
admit, from captives taken in the Spanish and Mexican settlements
to the south, have been included at the end of this collection. Not
included are the brief clan legends having mainly to do with origins
and migrations of clans. These, curiously enough, are not classed
with the rest of the mythology and the general opinion is that they
may be told at any time of year. There is also the usual assortment
of adventure stories, — episodes in the life of actual individuals.
Though several of these have become almost classic, they are sharply
distinguished from true myths.

The Creation is embodied in several tales: "He Goes to His
Father, Slaying of Monsters, na·ye'nezɣane Wins His Wife Back,
and na·ye'nezɣane Obtains Horses." It is interesting, in comparison with Navajo mythology, to note that the emergence tale
does not play an important part and is seldom heard. All stress is
placed on na·ye'nezɣane and his doings.

Various episodes included by one narrator in a tale are often told
as entirely separate tales by another. This is particularly true of the
principal tale of the Creation cycle. When telling it all narrators
invariably put in the parts dealing with the birth of na·ye'nezɣane
and t'uba' tc'istcine, the journey to the sun, the trials of na·ye'nezɣane there and his return to earth where he proceeds to slay the
monsters. But certain parts that come after can be told as separate
tales, some narrators acknowledging them as belonging with this
principal myth, others saying that they are independent. Examples
are: "Obtaining Bow and Arrows," "Grasshopper Loses His Leg,"
"How Gila Monster Got His Name," "The Man Who Visited the
Sky With the Eagles."

Every tale does not have a title, though many are referred to by
names quite widely known among White Mountain Apache. Some
tales are known or alluded to only by sentences descriptive of the
main event in them and these may differ from person to person, as
do titles at times. Where possible, titles were secured from two
sources, John Rope, a Western White Mountain man, and Francis
Drake. Titles from the Apache are marked by asterisk.

Inquiries as to an accepted order of events and sequence of myths
disclosed their absence. One old man admitted my question had
started him thinking about this for the first time. He made an
effort to regiment the tales he knew, but with much hesitation. It

is usually admitted that the tale "The Earth Is Set Up" must be the first event, but order of following tales is purely conjectural and opinions differ. Absence of a strict sequence is indicated by the mixture of tales from different cycles which may come to the narrator's mind. However the order of events in a given tale is recognized, and epochs of one which can be told as separate tales may retain their sequence.

Tales are of two classes: altogether holy tales said by some to explain the origin of ceremonies and holy powers, and tales which have to do with the creation of the earth, the emergence, the flood, the slaying of the monsters, and the origins of customs. Any of the latter class can be told to persons regardless of sex or age, even though some of them are holy in part. They are often used to entertain children. Only one tale in this group is generally withheld from women or children, and usually taught to men when they are acquiring the supernatural power said to be based on it. This is that part of the main tale of the Creation cycle which has to do with na·ye'nezɣane and guⱡiⱡ'isi. This tale is the acknowledged basis of gambling power used to disable an adversary in a game where heavy betting occurs, and the power is considered very dangerous to the uninitiated and to the women and children. The Creation cycle also contains certain tales and parts of tales which are the basis of an important cycle of songs called "go̜jo̜ si̜'", used in the girl's puberty ceremony and on other occasions. These are: "The Earth is Set Up" and two parts in the main tale of the Creation cycle: "He Goes to His Father" and "na·ye'nezɣane Obtains Horses." "The Emergence" is considered to be the basis of the ant ceremony and songs. The majority of tales in the first class are intimately associated with the ceremonies and powers to which they pertain and are most often known in full to the person who has the ceremony based on them. "He Who Became a Snake" is considered by some to be dangerous for women and children, because of the power in it. Snake shamans, in telling the story to their children, placed a pinch of pollen in the mouth of each in order that they might retain it. It was usually withheld from children who were not the shaman's close blood kin, as a man wanted only his own children or grandchildren to have it. "She Who Became a Deer," "He Fell Down With Bear," "The Talking Horse," are all tales of this first class. Some of them are told in full in the words to songs of the ceremonies said to originate from them.

Three important White Mountain tales are not included in this collection: "The Gambler Who Secured the Water Ceremony," "The Man Who Visited the Sky with the Eagles," and "He Who Became a Snake." All are holy, the first accounting for the origin of the Water Ceremony, the second for the Hawk Ceremony, and the third for the Snake Ceremony. Goddard has recorded them in "White Mountain Apache Myths and Tales" (Anthropological

Papers, American Museum of Natural History, Vol. XXIV, part 2).
There is reason to believe that "He Who Became a Snake" is not
given in full, as a wealth of detail in the songs of this ceremony is
omitted from Goddard's version.

Stories are told inside the dwelling about the fire. Almost everyone
knows the more common such as "He Goes to His Father" and "The
Slaying of the Monsters," and the Coyote episodes. Of all the tales,
those concerning Coyote seem to be the most popular, particularly
with children. They are full of the ludicrous behavior of Coyote
and the listeners always laugh heartily at his pranks. Older children
would sometimes say: "Let's go to that old man (usually someone
in the maternal grandfather class) and get him to tell us stories."
So at dark, they went to the old man's camp and asked him to tell
them tales half the night. Those containing holy power or recount-
ing its exercise appealed more to grown men than to children.

The characterization of animals is a curious mixture of animal
and human. To the question: "How do you think of the animals
when you are telling or listening to one of these stories? Was Coyote
like he is today, or did he look like a man?" John Rope's answer
was: "I think of him as being just like a man when I tell about him,
with face, hands, and feet like a man. They say that all the animals
were people in those days. That is why I think about them in this
way." To the same question, Francis Drake answered: "The old
people used to say that Coyote wore clothes in the stories, but that
he walked on all fours and had the body of a coyote. So that is the
way in which I think of him. I guess all the animals had clothes like
him, but were in the shapes that they are now." There apparently
is more than one concept. Two animals have their personalities
sharply drawn: Coyote and Big Owl. Coyote's doings were both
good and bad. Without his help and initiative, the people would have
lacked many of the important things in life, but at other times his
actions outlawed him. In talking of him, narrators call attention to
this. His duplicity and cunning are well brought out, but often he
falls for the simplest of hoaxes. Coyote never follows a middle
course. Big Owl is a very different person. He is large and blunder-
ing, sensuous and slow-witted. His thoughts and doings are all
destructive.

na·ye'nezɣane, with exception of the sun, is the most important
male being in White Mountain Apache religion. His actions are
above criticism except in one case, "The only mistake he ever made,"
the Apache point out bitterly.[1] All that he did was for the good of
the earth and people on it. Without him no human could have survived. He is everything that is good, holy, and manly. 'isdzana·dlẹ·-
he is the most important of female beings and benefactress particularly of crops. Sometimes she is the mother of na·ye'nezɣane,

---

[1] His failure to choose certain things offered him by the sun, thus forfeiting
cultural superiority to Europeans.

and again she is spoken of as his maternal grandmother. The ga·n are a class of supernaturals living inside the mountains and certain caves and who may be equated with the Pueblo kachinas. They were a people living on this earth long ago, but went away never to return. If invoked properly, their help may be obtained, or if slighted or trespassed upon, they may do harm. Their ceremony is one of the most important.

Though myths are primarily used for amusement or conveyance of ritual knowledge, yet many have a moral of which the narrator is well aware. This is particularly true of the Coyote tales, and parents or grandparents after telling these to children, often gave a short lecture to the youngsters: "Don't do like Coyote did in the story. He did a lot of bad things for us long ago such as marrying his daughter and stealing. But because he did these things, don't you do them! You see, Coyote married his daughter and for this reason some people still do it. But you must not do as he did. It is very bad."

Some men and women are noted as good story tellers. Gesture with the hands and arms and posture of the head and body are frequently used to illustrate a story. This usually follows a regular, though extremely simple, pattern, as in the gesture for the shooting of an arrow, etc. There is also a definite sense of the dramatic in the good story teller and he will model the fine points of his tale in order to get the best out of them. This is principally done where humorous or dangerous and awesome situations arise. The narrator then strives to create a growing sense of the ludicrous or awe-inspiring till the climax is reached. Though these Apache may not use the grand climax so common in our own stories, it would not be correct to say that they lack or avoid climax in story telling. True, many tales lack marked climaxes, but others, especially the longer ones, contain a series of high points. That these are climaxes is indicated by the fact that some story tellers in reaching them, raise the voice as in humorous incidents, or lower it and not infrequently talk with the lips compressed and from the back of the mouth giving a peculiarly restrained and mouthed sound to the words when mentioning dangerous, holy, or sinister things. A like practice is found among certain individuals in singing or chanting holy songs. The variation of voice in story telling can be very evident, though not all make use of it to the same degree. "na·ye'nezɣane traveled over a big mountain," can be said in two quite different ways; one in a matter of fact voice, the other in a deep constrained tone, which for the Apache and even for the White can bring out with identical words the great towering dark mass of the mountain with its ridge on ridge piling up and away to a distant and mysterious summit. The voice is decidedly more important and more used for emphasis than gesture, which at times may be totally absent.

Besides the formal beginnings and endings for tales, there are two other style forms which should be mentioned. The first is the

use of the word 'ak'ogo' which may be equated with our "then."
It signifies *the next thing that happened* at the beginning of every
important sentence. In many places, it has been omitted from the
text to avoid monotony. Its retention in others is to preserve
something of original form. The second, djindi·, is a phrase which
has been left out entirely except at beginnings of tales. It comes at
the end of every sentence or group of related sentences, and means,
"they say," or "it is said," and implies heresay. Both expressions
may be used in conversation as well as story telling. Of folklore,
they are an integral part.

The Apache have a great love of humor and the mysteriously
powerful, and their folklore is full of instances in which these elements occur. Often other Apaches than the narrator were present
during the recording of tales, and this offered an opportunity to
observe their reactions to various parts. Those parts of tales which
appeared especially funny to listeners have been indicated. Many of
these incidents are things which might occur in daily life and the
thought of their happening among animals is an added amusement.
Apache folklore is or has been till recently a very living thing. Where
new traits were added to the culture, the folklore was built up to
account for them. The horse, of course, was introduced possibly two-
hundred and fifty years ago among these people, and is now definitely a part of the culture and mythology. The raiding of Spanish,
Mexicans, and Whites in earlier days is explained in mythology as
a part of the culture, and Coyote's efforts to read a letter written on
paper is, in a way, an expression of the modern. However, the
reflection of European contact is decidedly small in comparison to
the great mass of native material.

Like other folklore, that of the White Mountain Apache contains
certain motives which are found in more than one tale. These are:
Turkey and Bear shaking out foods, making dried meat from snot,
planting cooked corn, the hero who enters Spider Old Woman's hole
and is helped by her, traveling by magic flute, use of holy hoops in
changing a person back to human form, the hero coming from a
distant place unknown to the widely traveled birds who are asked
about it. Lapse of time is neatly shown in some tales when the hero
returns to find that the hair of his relatives, clipped in mourning for
his supposed death, has grown long again.

Much information concerning the economic life, material culture,
society and religion is to be found in tales, and it is important to
note the tales besides incorporating such information, are used by
the Apache themselves to convey knowledge. Moreover, the fact
that certain ideas or phases of life are stressed, when reasonably
interpreted, cannot fail to mean that they are of significance to the
Apache and therefore important in any study made of them. At
the same time, it would not be correct to say that all culture phases
not stressed are unimportant.

For the greater part of the yearly food supply, plant foods were relied upon. Meat secured by hunting game, both large and small, was used to a slightly lesser degree. Probably two-thirds of the total plant food consumed was from wild plants, the remaining portion from domestic crops. In the following tales, one cannot help noticing that wild food plants and the gathering and preparation of them are frequently mentioned. The greater part of tale 7 is given over to a description of various wild foods. Again, agriculture receives attention, and some idea of its importance among these people may be had when we find it referred to in eight tales. Hunting is most often mentioned in connection with deer, and naturally so for the deer was the most important large game animal. The territory of the White Mountain Apache is sharply divided into various life zones, because of the marked changes in elevation from north to south. These zones offered a diversity of economic supplies and using all of them as they did, the Apache were on the move much of the time during the growing season. Something of this round, from farm to wild crops, to hunting is brought out, especially in tale 7. Considerably less is to be found on material culture; utensils, tools, weapons, and clothing are not described minutely as names are sufficient to bring to the native mind all their familiar attributes.

Social structure was built primarily on the family cluster, composed of several house units. Matrilocal residence was the most common condition, though patrilocal residence was not infrequent. The average family cluster was made up of an older couple with one or two married daughters and not infrequently a married son. Strongly developed matrilineal clans were present. The closest bonds and obligations were with the maternal relatives. Several family clusters within a given area were commonly united into a larger unit, the local group, over which one man known as "chief" had considerable authority. Chieftainship depended to great extent on strength of character, wisdom, family backing, wealth, and generosity. Wealth was one of the principal criteria of success and social position. Ordinarily, it was not inherited but was built up by work and achievement, and only lasted as long as the individual was physically and mentally capable of maintaining it.

Data concerning kinship may be drawn from the myths. The maternal grandparent is mentioned time and again, either as an actual grandparent or as someone who helps an individual in need. The paternal grandparent figures not at all. This is quite typical, as in life the maternal grandparents are very important to children, instructing them, caring for them when the mother is busy, and playing with them. Though paternal grandparents may live close to children, be fond of them and show them considerable attention along the same lines, they never occupy an equal place in Apache thought. The cooperation of brothers in tales is also the normal pattern. In one tale, we find mention several times of the maternal

uncle or sister's child. This relationship and the obligation it entails
is one of the most important in the entire social structure. Siblings
of the father are by no means as important as siblings of the mother.
The most often mentioned kinship term is that for cross-cousins. In
life, the relationship between cross-cousins (distantly related) is an
outstanding one in that it may entail a joking relationship which
permits of the greatest license. The rough practical jokes cross-
cousins play on each other are endless. In tales, Coyote always
addresses individuals by the cross-cousin term. He is continually
thinking up ways to trick these same characters who reciprocate
with the term, because they expect such conduct of him.

In only four tales are clans mentioned. In view of the fact that
clan is the most common method of identification and that it plays
a very important part in extension of kinship terms and obligations,
it seems curious that it is not mentioned more frequently. However,
it is decidedly less important than blood kinship on the maternal
side and the Apache is far more likely to think in terms of the latter.
Considering the fact that there are clan legends and that after all
clan is mentioned in a few tales, it would not be safe to draw infer-
ences from this alone that the clan was of later adoption, though
such a conjecture might be quite valid.[1]

The number of times courtship and marriage are mentioned is
striking. From these references, a fairly complete picture of marriage practices may be drawn. Marriage was an outstanding social
event and the negotiations and the exchange of gifts between the
families involved often continued over several months. The fact
that one must have property to make a good marriage is well brought
out. Matrilocal residence is mentioned several times in tales,
whereas patrilocal residence occurs not more than once or twice.
At marriage, which is a distinct change of social and physical status,
the term "girl" is almost invariably changed to "woman."

Religion is so much emphasized in folklore that, perhaps, it needs
less attention here than other phases of the culture. First, the personification of earth, water, lightning, other elements and natural
phenomena, and of animals and birds is extremely important in
Apache religion. Secondly, the holy power that these sources contain and the way in which it is used in helping or punishing man
occur also in religious belief. Thirdly, the contacts through which
man may acquire these powers for himself and use them are well
described. The great holy experiences told in certain tales which
purport to be the origins of various ceremonies were paralleled by
similar holy events in actual individuals' lives. Some of the most
important people in Apache culture were the men possessing holy
power and a ceremony, and those who had curing rights were con-

---

[1] For a description of White Mountain Apache Clans, see Goodwin, "The
Characteristics and Function of Clan in a Southern Athapascan Culture,"
American Anthropologist, Vol. 39, (1937) pp. 394—407.

tinually called on in times of sickness. They were respected and
some of them feared because of their power. The part shamans and
their holy power play in folklore is best illustrated in the tales.[1]

Rather amusing and quite enlightening data as to the Apache
attitudes and beliefs concerning Europeans (both Spanish-Ameri-
cans and Anglo-Americans are included here) are to be found in
several of the tales. The types of Europeans with whom they have
come in contact have influenced these considerably. Thus the rich
man is described as driving elegantly about in his buggy, with a
man to hold the horse for him when he wishes to stop. He owns many
cattle and horses, as well as a saloon and a store! He dresses in fine
clothes and has plenty to eat. To the Apache, these things mean the
acme of prestige in European culture. On the other hand, some
signs of enmity and contempt for Europeans are shown in the mention of their greed for gold, and the way Coyote, who is thought of
as allied with the Apache, when jailed by the Whites, easily outwits
them at almost every following encounter. Again the man who
works for the Devil in "Magic Flight" is definitely Apache and
manages to win out in spite of the Devil (a white man). A comical
imitation of the self-important white official at his desk, reading a
paper, which Coyote gives in reading the letter at Sun's house, is
unmistakably applicable to what the Apache sees when he visits the
government agency.

In the European tales, we find interesting evidences of Apache
ideas. Thus though the number three occurs in several of the tales,
not uncommonly it is shortly followed by the Apache four. The
dragon which the hero slays outside the city in one tale is described
as one of the mythical monsters which na·ye'nezɣane slew, and
after he is killed his meat is distributed among the populace in true
Apache fashion. A magic ring is interpreted in terms of supernatural
power and the question asked concerning the owner of the ring,
"Where does he get his power?" is typically Apache. Again, a
sulphur wheat bush is pulled up and entrance to an underworld is
gained through the hole it leaves. The hero who works for the Devil
resting his head in the Devil's daughter's lap so that she may de-
louse him, is merely one more Apache motive.

The myths in this collection were told by Palmer Valor, Francis
Drake, Bane (or Barney) Tithla, Anna Price, Charley Sago, and
Alsus. They were taken down with the aid of interpreters, Richard
Bylas, a White Mountain man about forty-seven years old, Neil
Buck, also of the White Mountain group and approximately the
same age, Clyne Jose, who is of the San Carlos group and about
twenty-seven years old, and Thomas Riley of the Cibecue group,
some sixty years of age. All interpreters lived at or near Bylas,
except Riley who lived at Canyon Day, near Fort Apache.

---

[1] For a description of the religion, see Goodwin, "White Mountain Apache
Religion," *American Anthropologist*, Vol. 40, (1938) pp. 24—37.

Palmer Valor was of the Western White Mountain band and t'i·słednt'i·dn clan, originally coming from near Canyon Day. He died in the spring of 1933 at Bylas, approximately ninety-six years old. He knew a great deal about the old culture and was a shaman having several ceremonies, but known chiefly for his deer power. Richard Bylas interpreted for him.

Francis Drake is of the Eastern White Mountain band and t'i·słednt'i·dn clan, but has spent the greater part of his life on the San Carlos reservation. An elderly man and well versed in myths, he is also a shaman with a reputation. Richard Bylas and Neil Buck interpreted for him.

Bane Tithla, from whom many of the tales come, was of the Eastern White Mountain band and na·dots'usn clan, and had lived on the San Carlos reservation most of his life. He was a man of about fifty years, when he died in 1937 and though too young to have taken an active part in the life of his people in pre-reservation times, he knew a great deal about that period from older relatives. He had considerable ceremonial knowledge as some of his tales show, and said that many of those he told were acquired from his maternal grandfather, between 1893 and 1897, when he was learning holy power from him. Richard Bylas interpreted some of the tales, but most of them were interpreted by Clyne Jose.

Anna Price was of the Eastern White Mountain band and 'iya'-'aiye' clan, originally coming from the East Fork of White River, near Fort Apache, where she spent more than a third of her life. Since then, she had lived on the San Carlos reservation. She was an old woman close to one hundred years when she died in the spring of 1937. Her father was the most influential White Mountain chief of his time. Because of her great age, her knowledge of the old culture was complete. She possessed several curing ceremonies. It is interesting to note that almsot all her tales include a wealth of detail concerning certain cultural traits and practices, more so than those recorded from any other person. They deal especially with womens' work and marriage, and it may be that they are a type of tale peculiar to women. Richard Bylas and Neil Buck interpreted for her.

Charley Sago is of the Western White Mountain band and na·-ɣudesgijn clan, but has lived most of his life on the San Carlos reservation. He is about fifty and has ceremonial knowledge and a good understanding of the old culture. Richard Bylas interpreted for him.

Alsus is of the Western White Mountain band and biszą·ha clan, and has lived most of his life in the vicinity of Cedar Creek, west of Fort Apache. He is about eight-five and apparantly well-informed concerning the old culture. Thomas Riley interpreted for him.

Besides those who told and interpreted the tales and whose patience and painstaking hours of effort made this work possible, I am indebted to the Southwest Society of New York and to Miss Mary C. Wheelwright for their generous help with its publication. Thanks are also due Dr. Elsie Clews Parsons and Dr. Ruth Benedict for suggestions and aid in preparation of the manuscript. Finally I wish to express my gratitude to Dr. Byron Cummings and Mr. and Mrs. Robert Knowles for their help and kindly interest.

The phonetic system used is described in Smithsonian Miscellaneous collections, Vol. 66, no. 6. The symbols used are:

- · indicates lengthened vowel
- ‘ indicates aspiration
- ’ glottal stop
- ˶ under a vowel indicates nasalization
- ˳ under a consonant indicates it is syllabic
- γ sonant palatal spirant
- ł voiceless *l*
- c is like English *sh*
- tc is like English *ch*
- dj is the voiced equivalent of *tc*
- x̣ voiceless palatal spirant
- tł lateral voiceless affricative
- dl voiced equivalent of *tl*
- + at the end of a meaningless exclamation or imitation of a sound, indicates excessive length.

Tone accents have been omitted to facilitate printing.

1. *THE EARTH IS SET UP[1]

Four people started to work on the earth. When they set it up, the wind blew it off again. It was weak like an old woman. They talked together about the earth among themselves. "What shall we do about this earth, my friends? We don't know what to do about it." Then one person said, "Pull it from four different sides." They did this, and the piece they pulled out on each side they made like a foot. After they did this the earth stood all right. Then on the east side of the earth they put big black cane, covered with black metal thorns. On the south side of the earth they put big blue cane covered with blue metal thorns. Then on the west side of the earth they put big yellow cane covered with yellow metal thorns. Then on the north side of the earth they put big white cane covered with white metal thorns.[2]

After they did this the earth was almost steady, but it was still soft and mixed with water. It moved back and forth. After they had worked on the earth this way Black Wind Old Man[3] came to this place. He threw himself against the earth. The earth was strong now and it did not move. Then Black Water Old Man threw himself against the earth. When he threw himself against the earth, thunder started in the four directions. Now the earth was steady, and it was as if born already.

But the earth was shivering. They talked about it: "My friends, what's the matter with this earth? It is cold and freezing. We better give it some hair." Then they started to make hair on the earth. They made all these grasses and bushes and trees to grow on the earth. This is its hair.

But the earth was still too weak. They started to talk about it: "My friends, let's make bones for the earth." This way they made rocky mountains and rocks sticking out of the earth. These are the earth's bones.

Then they talked about the earth again: "How will it breathe, this earth?" Then came Black Thunder to that place, and he gave the earth veins. He whipped the earth with lightning and made water start to come out. For this reason all the water runs to the west. This way the earth's head lies to the east, and its water goes to the west.

---

[1] Told by Palmer Valor. Also called "When The Earth Was Made". Compare Goddard, Myths and Tales From the White Mountain Apache, Anthropological Papers American Museum of Natural History, Vol. XXIV, part 2, p. 119.
[2] This is the usual color-direction circuit.
[3] Personification of the wind of the east.

They made the sun so it traveled close over the earth from east to west. They made the sun too close to the earth and it got too hot. The people living on it were crawling around, because it was too hot. Then they talked about it: "My friends, we might as well set the sun a little further off. It is too close." So they moved the sun a little higher. But it was still too close to the earth and too hot. They talked about it again. "The sun is too close to the earth, so we better move it back." Then they moved it a little higher up. Now it was all right. This last place they set the sun is just where it is now.

Then they set the moon so it traveled close over the earth from east to west. The moon was too close to the earth and it was like daytime at night. Then they talked about it: "My friends, we better move the moon back, it is like day." So they moved it back a way, but it was still like daylight. They talked about it again: "It is no good this way, we better move the moon higher up." So they moved it higher up, but it was still a little light. They talked about it again and moved it a little further away. Now it was just right, and that is the way the moon is today. It was night time.

This is the way they made the earth for us. This is the way all these wild fruits and foods were raised for us, and this is why we have to use them because they grow here.

VARIANT[1]

naɫk'ide·la·djindi· (long ago they say).[2] There was only God[3] living above at that time and there was no earth at all. God had twelve people working for him then, so he talked to them. "I am thinking about making a sky and earth," he said. So they all said, "Good" and talked about it. Now God thought how he would make earth and sky. Then black water, blue water, yellow water, white water, they created to make the earth of. There were four whirlwinds, little ones, going around it. This way he (God) put it up. Then Black Wind, Blue Wind, Yellow Wind and White Wind ran against it from four directions and blew against it.[4] This way God tried the earth to see if it was strong, but it shook. Then Black Gopher got four kinds of rope, and with this he tied the earth up in thirty-two places.[5] But still the earth shook. It was no good this way, they said. Then from the east side Black Metal shot into the earth, from the south side Blue Metal shot into the earth, from the

---

[1] Told by Bane Tithla. Compare Goddard, ibid pp. 119—120.
[2] The conventional opening. The listener should reply "ya‘" (meaning assent or confirmation).
[3] White Mountain people recognized a non-Christian supreme being. His twelve workers are talked of collectively, but seldom if ever mentioned by name.
[4] The winds of the four directions.
[5] Four, twelve and thirty-two are the holy numbers.

west side Yellow Metal shot into the earth, and from the north side White Metal shot into the earth.[1] Then the earth was good and stopped moving about. It only shook a little bit. It was still not quite strong enough. So over in the east Black Metal made his moccasins, put them on his feet and stepped on the earth; from the south side Blue Metal did the same way and stepped on the earth; from the west side Yellow Metal did the same way and stepped on the earth; and from the north side White Metal did the same and also stepped on the earth. Now all four had stepped on the earth. After this big black cane[2] on the east side covered over the tracks of Black Metal where he had stepped. Then on the south side was big blue cane with blue metal leaves growing up inside. Then on the west side was big yellow cane with yellow metal leaves growing up inside. Then on the north side was big white cane with white metal leaves growing up inside. Now he made dew all over the earth to make it wet. Then Black Wind from the east ran against the earth (blew a great wind); then on the south side Blue Wind ran against the earth; then from the west side Yellow Wind ran against the earth, and then from the north side White Wind ran against the earth. Now when they did this the earth did not move any more.

Then on the west side was made big yellow cane with yellow metal leaves, growing up on the earth's back. On the east side he made black cane with black metal leaves, growing up between the earth's horns. The leaves from the plant grew down from the earth's head like whiskers. The earth's horns they made of black metal and they were round (like knobs). Then around the horns they put big black crystals. Then they made black metal, blue metal, yellow metal, and white metal, and these four kinds of metals they put in the earth. This way they made the earth with all these kinds of metals and many plants. There were thirty-two kinds of ripe fruits. Then he made clouds over the earth and made it rain a little, and the plants grew from this rain. This way he made these foods just for our people, but the different kinds of metals he made for the white people. Then all kinds of animals and birds he made to live among our people, and these, like bear and horse, he made for our people.

ci xuck'aṇ dasdja· (My yucca fruits lie piled up).[3]

2. * HE GOES TO HIS FATHER: SLAYING OF MONSTERS[4]

When the Sun rises up he passes overhead. One time a maiden spread her legs apart and let the Sun shine inside her. After that

---

[1] The word "metal" originally applied to obsidian and sometimes to churt and ritually still does. "Metal" (obsidian) is personified by the four colored metals.
[2] A species of wild cane.
[3] The conventional closing.
[4] Told by Palmer Valor. Compare Goddard, ibid 93ff., 115ff., 120ff,

she became pregnant. Then this girl had a baby. This was na·ye'-nezɣane (slayer of monsters). Now this girl went and lay under where water was dripping and spread her legs apart. This way she became pregnant again and soon had another baby. This was t'uba'tc'istcine (born from water). No one had seen this girl lying with the Sun or with Water and they did not know who the fathers of these two boys were. That is why some girls are still doing this way, hiding down behind bushes with boys.

When na·ye'nezɣane got a little older, he started off for his father's home (the Sun's home). He came to Sands Boiling Up. It was moving back and forth and he could not get across it. Then the boy called: "Yellow lightning,[1] strike downward on his (na·-ye'nezɣane's) breast!" and he went over the sands safely. After a while he came to a place where lots of xucntca·gi (a cholla cactus) covered with spines of black metal were growing thickly over the earth. The boy could not pass through here, and so he called to Black Wind Old Man. Black Wind Old Man came and twisted a path through the cactus. The boy passed through. Then, later on he came to two mountains all covered with mosquitoes with bills of black metal. The boy went up close to them, but he could not get by. Now Black Thunder made it rain female rain.[2] The mosquitoes got their wings all wet so they could not fly. Then the boy put his hands under his arms and passed through safely. Pretty soon the boy came to Black Metal Mountain[3] where there were two mountains together, and no one could go through or close to them. Then on top of them yellow lightning struck. Then the boy passed through safely. Now he could see where the Sun was living, with black water in four parts around that place.

The boy was walking through lots of black grama grass. While he was walking over this he stumbled on something and nearly fell down. Because of this he turned and walked back a little way. He tripped on something again and almost fell. Then he started back once more, the way he had been going, and almost fell again when he tripped on something. He turned back and looked at the place to see what it was. There at that place, Black Spider Old Woman had a little hole in the ground. Now Black Spider Old Woman began talking to the boy, "cixwi·ye'[4] (my daughter's son), what are you going after?" "I am going to my father, at the Sun's house," the boy said. The old woman said, "Don't you know that no one

---

[1] Personification of lightning of the west.
[2] Black Thunder is the personification of the thunder of the east. Female rain is gentle, drizzling rain; male rain is pelting, with thunder and lightning.
[3] Black, the color of the east, is often used in association with another word in ritual and myth. Because first mentioned in the color circuit it implies extreme holiness or power.
[4] Individuals are mentioned as addressing each other as grandson and grandparent in various tales. Almost without exception this implies maternal grandparents or daughter's children.

can go there ? Don't go there, my grandson!" The old woman told the boy to go in her hole. "You can go and visit the Sun tomorrow, but stay here with me tonight." "How will I get down in your hole, it looks too small ?" the boy asked the old woman. "My grandson, it is a little hole, but it will stretch. Come in, don't be scared, walk straight in!" The boy tried two times and backed off. Then he closed his eyes and went down in the hole all right. Inside he saw it was like a big wickiup. He could see lots of Spider girls lying together. The Spider girls had no clothes on.

The boy was wearing a cotton belt with tassels hanging from it.[1] The tassels were hanging down in back. The old woman said, "Something is hanging from your belt, my grandson. Give it to me!" "Where; what do you mean ?" the boy said. "That one that moves as if the wind were blowing it, that's what I mean," the old woman said. The boy took his belt off and gave it to the old woman. There was a lot of soft dirt in there. The Spider girls were lying in it with no clothes on. The boy said, "How can I lie down and cover over ? It is too cold in here." "My grandson, it is warm in here," the old woman said. Now they went over there and put things in their hands and rubbed them back and forth. The next morning they found lots of cloth there, in all kinds of colors. The old woman had woven it. The Spider girls dressed up in this cloth so they looked nicely. The old woman went out to look around. The boy knew the sun was rising, but he was not all up yet. When she got back all the people in the house were like the boy's family.[2] Then the sun was a little higher. "Now that's he," the boy said. The old woman gave the boy a turquoise and also a white shell bead.[3] "After this, what you ask for you will have," the old woman said.

Then the boy started to where Sun was living and came to the edge of black water. There he blew on the turquoise and it went under the water and up on the other side. Then he talked. Then he blew on the white shell bead and it went under the water and came up on the other side. Where Sun was living it was all black, sharp stones sticking up. Sun was living in among these. Then the boy said to the turquoise, "Go to the top of Sun's house." After turquoise got up on top of the house, it said, "That's what I am here for, I am up here." Then the boy said to the white shell bead, "Go over in front of the house, 'isdzana·dlę·he (Changing Woman)."[4]

---

[1] Not of Apache manufacture, but sometimes described as the Pueblo type. These were obtained in trade from Zuni at times.

[2] They had become acquainted.

[3] White shell and turquoise are holy and possess holy power. The first stands for females, the second for males.

[4] Changing Woman, so called because she can change from a baby through the forms of girlhood and womanhood to old age and back, is the mother of na·ye'nezɣane and t'uba' tc'istcine. White Shell Girl, the personification of white shell, though not the same supernatural, is closely associated with her.

White shell bead went over in front of the house where that woman (Sun's wife) was living. Then the woman said to the boy, "What are you doing here? Where are you from? No one is allowed to come here." The boy said, "This is me, I have come to see my father." Then the woman started to cook some food for the boy. As soon as it was cooked, he ate it up. When he had eaten he went over to one side where some hides were lying. He lay on them and they rolled around him.

Right in the middle of Sun's bed is a hole through which he climbs up to the roof of his house. Along about dark the boy heard Sun talking down under this hole. Now Sun was coming up. When he got to his house he asked his wife, "Who has come to my house here?" Then his wife said, "You know that no one can come here." "Anyway someone came here. I saw his tracks going over the four mountains, Dew Mountain, Rain Mountain, Ripe Fruits Mountain and Pollen Mountain, and going into my house."[1] "Anyway no one is allowed here," said his wife. Now Sun started to eat. His wife said to him, "You have always told me that when you traveled you never did anything wrong, but this is not so, because your son came here today." "Where is he?" Sun said. "Over there he is, rolled up in those hides." Sun got up and shook his boy out of the blankets.

On the east side of the house was burning black metal fire. Sun took the boy and threw him into this fire. Then he stirred the boy around in the fire with black lightning. The boy held in his mind the fact that he still had the turquoise and white shell bead and could wish on them. Then he wished that he might rise upward like a downy eagle feather. This way he did and came right back to Sun. Then Sun took him to the south side of the house where blue metal fire was burning. He threw the boy into it and stirred him around with blue lightning. But the boy held it in his mind about wishing. He wished that he might rise up like a downy eagle feather, and he did. Then he came right back to his father. Now Sun took him to the west side of the house where yellow metal fire was burning. But the boy wished he might rise like a downy eagle feather, and he did. Then he came right back to Sun. Now Sun took him to the north side of the house where white metal fire was burning. He threw the boy in this and stirred him with white lightning. But the boy wished that he might rise up like a downy eagle feather, and he did. Then he came back to Sun. Then Sun said, "hęhę.[2], that's right, you are my son."

Then Sun took the boy on the east side where black houses made

---

[1] Dew, rain and pollen are holy, hence their inclusion here. Dew, like the breath, is the essence of a thing; pollen is continually used in ritual and may also be the essence or holy excretion of an object.

[2] An ejaculation, used by an individual as an expression of vengeful satisfaction.

of black pointed metal were above. He threw the boy up into this.
There he was cut to pieces by the sharp metal. But he wished,
"Black lightning strikes with him." Then he made a noise like ze·,
ze·, ze·, ze·, like metal clinking on the way down. Then on the south
side Sun took the boy to where there were blue houses made of blue
pointed metal. Here he threw the boy up into this. The boy was
cut to pieces by the sharp points. But he said, "Blue lightning
strikes with him," and he was raised up and came down making
a noise like ze·, ze·, ze·, ze·. Then Sun took the boy to the west side,
where there were yellow houses made of yellow pointed metal. Here
he threw the boy up into this and he was cut to pieces. But he said,
"Yellow lightning strikes with him" and he was raised up. As he
came down, he made a noise like ze·, ze·, ze·, ze·. Then Sun took
the boy to the north side, where there were white houses made of
white pointed metal. Here he threw him up into this, and the boy
was cut to pieces in it. But he said, "White lightning strikes with
him" and he was raised up and came down making a noise like ze·,
ze·, ze·, ze·. Then Sun had done this to him four times.

On the east side of Sun's house was hanging a sack of black
tobacco. When any person smoked this, it killed them (choked
them). Sun went and took down the tobacco and started filling a
pipe for the boy.[1] The boy still had the turquoise and white shell
bead, and now he wished on them. There were thirty-two persons
all around him (thirty-two little winds). Then he said, "Little winds
will smoke this, but not I." Sun handed him the pipe. He took it
and pretended to put it to his lips. In one puff the tobacco was
gone. Then Sun said, "Surely."[2] On the south side of the house
was hanging blue tobacco sack. Sun went to this and made a
smoke for the boy. Right around the boy were the thirty-two little
winds. "Little winds will smoke this for me," said the boy. Sun
handed him the pipe. In two puffs, the tobacco was gone. On the
west side of the house was hanging yellow tobacco sack. Sun went
to this and started to fill a pipe for the boy. There were still thirty-
two persons around the boy. "Little winds will smoke this for me,"
said the boy. When Sun handed him the pipe, four little winds
smoked it for him and in three puffs it was all gone. On the north
side of the house was hanging white tobacco sack. Sun went to
this and started making a smoke for the boy. The thirty-two winds
were still around the boy. "Little winds, you will smoke this for
me," the boy said. Sun handed him the smoke and in four puffs the
tobacco was all gone. This way the boy never smoked any of it.
"hęhę·, you are my son all right," Sun said.

"Now I might just as well make a sweat bath for you," said Sun.
He made the sweat bath all ready. Then Sun went on the east side
to black metal fire and took out some hot rocks and carried them

---

[1] Tubular clay pipes are the common form.
[2] An expression of assent about the boy being his son.

to the sweat lodge. They went inside and sang one song for the boy
and then they came right out. Then Sun went to blue metal fire
and carried some hot rocks to the sweat lodge and put them in. He
sang one song for the boy in the lodge. "Now you will have to stay
in the sweat lodge," Sun told the boy. Then Sun went to the west
side where yellow metal fire was burning and took out some rocks
and carried them into the sweat lodge. Now it was getting too hot
for the boy. He said to the turquoise and white shell bead, "Little
wind, it is getting too hot here. Go a little further down between
the earth and the sky." And little wind came a little lower. Sun
sang one more song for the boy. Then he went to the north side
where white metal fire was burning and took out some hot rocks
and carried them to the sweat lodge. Then he sang four times. Now
four songs had been sung for the boy.

During this sweat bath Sun worked on the boy. It was just as if
he had cooked the boy and made his body soft so he could work on
it. The boy had a head like a round piece of mud. He had no hair
or features, no fingers, no toes, and no finger nails or toe nails. While
he was in the sweat bath Sun worked on him and made his eyes, nose
and mouth and ears. Then he pulled the hair out on the boy's head
so it hung down to the ground. This was too long, so he broke it off
to come to the middle of his back. Now he made fingers on his
hands, and toes on his feet. For finger nails, he set in little pieces
of white flint. He did the same for his toe nails. Now he was like
other people. When they came out of the sweat bath Sun told him
to line up with his other two sons. The boy stood in the middle and
they were all three alike.

Sun had a bow in his hand and he gave it to the boy. He gave him an
arrow also, but there were no feathers on it. Then Sun set up some
sticks a distance off and told the boy to shoot at them. The boy shot
the arrow with no feathers. It twisted and never hit the mark.
Then he put on one feather and shot the arrow again. This time it
shot a little better. He tried again and put on four feathers. When
he shot, the arrow was too heavy and dropped right down. Then
he took off two feathers and shot the arrow with two feathers. This
time it went pretty close. Then he put on one feather so that the arrow
had three. This time the arrow went right in the middle of the mark.

"Now let's go in the house," Sun said. They went in the house.
Sun took a gun, some blue pants, a black shirt, a black hat, and
long boots and laid them on the east side of the fire. "Would you
like these?" Sun asked the boy. The boy put all these clothes on
and put the rifle over his shoulder and marched back and forth. The
clothes made a noise as he walked, and were heavy. Then on the
west side of the fire Sun laid a quiver of mountain lion skin, a pair
of moccasins and a tsigijintc'a'.[1] The boy went and tried them on.

---

[1] A cap with bunches of small turkey feathers on it, and in the middle of them
two eagle tail feathers.

He put the quiver over his back and the moccasins on his feet and the cap on his head. Then he walked back and forth and these clothes felt good and light. It was night time now and Sun said, "We will decide about all this tomorrow." Then they went to sleep. That night the boy could not sleep at all. The next morning Sun asked him, "Why didn't you sleep at all last night?" "I tried to, but I could not," the boy said. "All right, I will make you sleep well," Sun said, and he put his hand up to his head, picked something off there and threw it on his son's head. This was louse. Then he picked something off the skin on his arm and put it on the boy's body. This was gray louse.[1] "Now you will sleep all right," Sun said. That night the boy slept all right and did not wake till morning.

In the morning Sun said, "Here are the things in two parts, there is the rifle and there is the bow; which do you want?" The boy said the rifle was too heavy and that he would take the bow and arrows as they were light.

Then Sun set up two mountains, one on the east and one on the west. The one on the east side was brown and barren. The one on the west side was covered with plants of all kinds and ripe fruits. "Which one do you want?" Sun asked the boy. The boy went up on the mountain to the east, but he found it all barren ground. Then he went up on the mountain to the west and found lots of ripe fruits and good things to eat. "Which one do you want?" asked Sun. "That one to the east has nothing on it and I would get hungry. I will take this one to the west," the boy said. Then Sun said, "All right, there is nothing fit to eat there, but you will have to eat it anyway. Those grasses are no good to eat, but you will have to eat them just the same." The boy's father moved the hill to the west to one side and the hill to the east he moved over that way. From the hill to the east came lots of horses, mules, burros, cattle, sheep, goats, all such animals. They were on that hill.

After this, Sun said to his boys, "Come on, let's fight, let's see you two fight!" One had a rifle, the other the bow and arrows. When the boy with the rifle started to shoot, the boy with the bow ran away. "All right, my son, now you will have to do this way from now on. When you are in danger, you will always save yourself by running away."[2]

After this, the boy with the bow and arrows went down on the earth and killed all the monsters there. For this he was given the name of na·ye'nezɣane (slayer of monsters). They all came together and talked about how they would call this boy. They talked about it for four days and then they sent for the old man who was the father-in-law of the boy. This old man was Old Gopher. When he got there he said: "Why is it that you can't find a name for him?

---

[1] This often elicits expressions of disgust from listeners.
[2] Apache warfare was commonly surprise attack and ambush, then skillful retreat, but seldom face to face combat.

You ought to be able to find a good name for him right off. Call my son-in-law na·ye'nezɣane, because it was he who killed all the bad monsters."

Big Owl[1] was the son of Sun. It was he who had been killing all the people on the earth. On account of this the boy had gone to his father and asked permission to kill Big Owl. He said, "Big Owl is no good, and he is killing lots of people. For this reason I want to kill him." "Why do you talk this way? He is your own brother," Sun said. The boy wanted to kill his own brother, and because of this our people did the same way. They still kill their own relatives sometimes. "All right, go ahead and kill him then," Sun said. So the boy went ahead and got ready to kill Big Owl. Over to one side there was water. Big Owl used to come to this water always at noon to drink. So the boy went to this place at noon and waited there. At noon Big Owl came to the water, but a little way from it he stopped and stood there on one leg. Behind, in the other leg he had a nerve twitching in his calf.[2] This meant that there was danger ahead of him. Sun had made this happen to him. Sun had told the wind to do this. Big Owl came to the edge of the water now, and stooped down on his hands and knees to drink. Right then Sun threw blood into the water, and that meant bad luck. Big Owl started to drink and while he was drinking the boy shot two arrows into him, but it did not happen as it had before. (?) As soon as Big Owl was killed his feathers spread out all over the earth, and that is why you can hear owls calling wherever you make your camp.

Then na·ye'nezɣane was the younger boy, and his older brother was tʼubaʼtcʼistcine. The older one would go out hunting and when he came back he would be all covered with blood on his hands and feet, but he never brought back any meat with him. So the younger brother said to the older that he was going along with him the next time he went hunting. He got ready and made his arrows out of tɬʼoʼtcʼiji·jeʼ (grass it breaks off)[3] and then the two started out to hunt. About sunrise the older brother killed a deer. Then the younger boy built a fire right there. But the older told him, "Hurry up and get rid of the deer right now, so that no one will see we have it." The older brother kept his bow in his hand and did not sit down at all. Then the younger said to him, "What's the matter? What are you afraid of?" and he took the deer meat and started to cook some in the fire. "Why don't you sit down here?" he said to his older brother again. But the older brother did not sit down or lay his bow down. Instead he kept looking around all the time. It was right then that a great man came there. This was be·chastį· (Metal Old Man). When they saw him the older brother left there and ran

---

[1] Big Owl (mbuʼtcoʼ) is sometimes called ye·ʼiʼ.
[2] A common omen of danger.
[3] A species of grass. Its use for arrows here is humor, for the brittle plant is totally unfit for shafts.

away. na·ye'nezɣane called to him to come back and asked him why
he was running away, but all the same the older one kept on running.
While the younger was cooking the deer meat over the fire, Metal
Old Man came up to him. When he got there he said, "This meat
is mine," and he reached over and took it. But when he did this,
the younger boy reached over and took it back, saying "This is my
meat." This way they kept on taking the meat from each other.
Metal Old Man said, "What's the matter, this is mine, this is my
meat." Then Metal Old Man grabbed up his (the boy's) bow and
arrows and mashed them all up. Then he took them and wiped his
back side with them and threw them away. The arrows of Metal
Old Man were made of the trunks of yellow pine trees; the feathers
on them were of black metal. But all the same the boy went over
to them, undid his gee string and stood there to rub his back side
up and down against them. "Now come on and let's fight each
other!" the boy said. Then Metal Old Man told the boy to stand
sideways to him and raise up one of his arms. The boy did this, and
just when Metal Old Man was going to shoot, the boy called on
something: "Yellow lightning with him it strikes," and when Metal
Old Man shot he raised up and the arrow went underneath him. It
went beyond and struck a hill behind, passing right through it.
Then Metal Old Man told him to turn around and raise the other
arm. The boy did this, but again when Metal Old Man shot his
arrow it went under the boy and passed right through a rocky
mountain behind. After this it was the boy's turn to shoot. Metal
Old Man was all covered with black metal and his body did not
show through it at all. Only under the arms was there a place that
was not covered with the black metal. The boy told him to stand
sideways and raise up his arm. Then he took his arrow and blew on
it, praying to it that it might go right in under the arm, where the
skin showed. He shot and the arrow went right in under the arm.
He told Metal Old Man to turn around and raise up the other arm.
When he did this, the boy shot again and the arrow went in under
the giant's arm as before.

Then Gopher Old Woman came to him and said, "I have made
thirty-two holes in the earth for you, one below the other. The last
of the holes at the bottom is a trail in adobe. If you go down into
it you will be safe." So na·ye'nezɣane went down into the bottom
hole. As soon as Metal Old Man was killed with the arrows, he
started to fall and as he fell the metal on his body started to sound
"zi +", and it flew off in pieces all over the earth, trying to find
na·ye'nezɣane and kill him. But he stayed down under the ground
in the holes that Gopher Old Woman had made for him. He was in
the lowest hole. When the metal was just about one hole above him,
almost to him, it stopped. That was how na·ye'nezɣane was saved,
by going down into the deepest hole which was so deep that the
metal could not get to him. This is the reason that there are different

kinds of metals all over the earth now. This is why we have money now. If na·ye'nezɣane had not done this there would be no metal.

3. OBTAINING BOW AND ARROWS.[1]

One time a boy was living with his grandmother near tse·dałtł'a'- 'o'ai'. Then all the birds were talking like people. Coyote was this way also. This boy started to think about what would be the best way for him to get ahead in the world. One day he said to his grand- mother, "cixwi·ye' (maternal grandparent), where is the bow wood growing?" She answered, "It is growing a long way off, and it is very hard to get. I don't want to hear you talking about it any more." The boy said, "Your vulva is dangerous," and he started off.[2] He traveled a long way and came to a mountain where the bow wood was growing. Right there a bear came after him. The boy said to him, "My grandmother, I am going to be your wife." The bear started to laugh, and he fell down on the ground. The bear asked him what he was here for and the boy said that he had come after wild mulberry to make a bow with. "All right, go ahead and get it," said the bear. The boy got the bow wood and took it back to his camp. There he worked on it and cut it down fine and fixed a good bow.

Then he said to the old woman, "My grandmother, where is cane growing?" His grandmother answered that the canes were growing a long way off, were very hard to get, and that she did not want to hear him asking about them again. The boy called to her, "Your vulva is dangerous," and he started off. He traveled a very long way and finally came to where the canes were growing. But right in front of the canes were two big rocks which moved together every time he tried to get through. The rocks kept on moving together and apart. He could not get by them, so he started to cry. Then Gopher came out of the ground, right by him, "What are you crying about, 'icǫ· (archaic term for boy)?" he asked. The boy answered that there were lots of canes growing there, but he did not know how he was going to get them. Gopher told him, "Go close by the rocks and stand there. I will cut the canes for you and every time the rocks move apart, reach through quickly and grab one of the canes." So the boy did this. Now Gopher burrowed a hole under the rocks and came to where the canes were growing. He started in to cut them right at their roots. The boy reached in and picked them out. Gopher kept cutting the canes till the boy had a big bundle of them tied up. Then the boy went back to his camp.

---

[1] Told by Francis Drake. Though this tale and the same episode as it occurs in Bane Tithla's version are really parts of the"Slaying of Monsters," yet it apparently is often told as distinct from the other monster slaying episodes and therefore has been given a title of its own.

[2] He was being impertinent.

After a while he asked his grandmother where he could get sinew. His grandmother answered that sinew was a long way off and too hard to get, that she did not want to hear him talking about it again. Then the boy said, "Your vulva is dangerous," and he started off. He traveled a long way over a big, flat, open country. Far off he saw something lying on the ground. This was bide·nte·li· (broad horns),[1] who used to kill and eat people. Everyone was afraid of him. The boy sat down and cried. Broad Horns could see him crying. Then Gopher came up out of the ground and asked, "Boy, what are you crying about?" He said, "There is that animal lying there and I don't know what to do." Gopher said, "Stay here, I am going to go under ground to Broad Horns. I will make four tunnels to him, one under the other. The boy sat there, and Gopher started off. He went to Broad Horns and back to the boy two times till he had made four tunnels, one under the other. These holes came up right under Broad Horns. Then Broad Horns got up. Gopher went to the mouth of one of the holes right under where Broad Horns was standing. Gopher spoke to him, "Lie down again. My children are cold and I want some of your hair." So Broad Horns lay down again. Then Gopher came back to the boy and said to him, "You go down in my tunnel and travel along till you come up under Broad Horns. Then stab him with your knife and go right away into the lowest hole." The boy had an obsidian knife. He started into the tunnel. When he came up under Broad Horns he could feel the animal's heart beating, where he was lying over the hole. The boy took his knife and stuck it into Broad Horns. Then he ran down into the lowest tunnel. He had stuck his knife right into the heart of Broad Horns. Broad Horns got up and with his long horns he plowed up the first of Gopher's tunnels. When he got to the end of it, he turned and came back, plowing the second tunnel up. When he got to the end of it, he turned back and started to plow the third hole up. He got half way on this and then fell dead. When Broad Horns was dead Gopher said, "All his hair will be mine." The boy skinned Broad Horns and took sinew from the back legs and the front legs. He took the stomach and filled it with the blood. Then he started back to his home with the sinew, the hide, and the stomach full of blood. That was all he took. He got back all right.

After a while he asked his grandmother where he would go to get feathers. His grandmother said that they were a long way off and very hard to get, that she did not want to hear him asking about them again. "Your vulva is dangerous," the boy said, and he started off. He had the hide of Broad Horns on him, laced down the back. On his throat he had smeared some of the blood. The rest of it was in the stomach, which he had inside the hide, against

---

[1] This term is also used for a large buck antelope.

his chest. He was traveling over a great open, level country. Pretty soon he heard a sound up in the sky above him. He lay down on the ground on his back. He could see some eagles coming. An eagle swooped down and tried to pick him up, but the eagle claws just scratched over the skin. The eagle tried again, and this time he picked up the boy and flew away with him. The eagle flew off with the boy to the top of tse·daɫtɬ'aᵒo'aiᶜ where the eagles had their home. Right here there was a sharp point of rock against which the eagles would throw all the things that they caught, to kill them. The end of this rock was all covered with blood. The eagle threw the boy against this sharp rock, and all the blood broke out of the stomach he had inside the hide. The eagle sat down close by. He had some young children there. The boy was not dead but he just lay there as if dead. One of the young eagles came over to him to try and eat him, but the boy said cd cd to it. The young eagle went back to its father, and said, "That dead body said cd cd to me." The father said, "That is only muscular twitching. Pretty soon the big eagle went off to hunt. Then the boy got up and killed all the young eagles but one. He asked this one little eagle, "When does your brother come back home?" "He always comes home when it is ni·cokijn (a kind of rain)." Pretty soon it started to rain this way, and in a little while the brother eagle came flying, carrying a litttle boy. He flew up and threw the boy against the pointed rock. Then he started to land. Just before he landed, the boy with the young eagle grabbed a stick and hit him on the neck and killed him. Then he threw him over the cliff. Then he asked the young eagle when his sister came home. "She always comes home when it is hiɫtsạ·natsuge (yellow rain)"[1] was the answer. Pretty soon yellow rain started and after a while the sister came, carrying a young girl. She flew to the sharp rock and threw the girl against it. Then just before she landed at the nest, the boy took a long stick and hit her over the neck and killed her. He kicked her over the cliff. Now he asked the young eagle, "When does your mother get back?" The young eagle said, "She always returns when female rain comes." Pretty soon female rain started and the mother eagle came flying with a woman in her claws. When she got there, she threw the woman against the sharp rock. Just before she alighted the boy hit her with a stick over the head and killed her. He kicked her over the cliff. Then he asked the young eagle, "When does your father come home?" "He always returns when male rain comes," said the young eagle. Pretty soon male rain started and the father eagle came flying home with a man. When the father eagle got there, he threw the man against the sharp rock. Then just before he alighted at the nest the boy killed him with a stick and kicked him over the cliff as he kicked the others. Then he said to the young eagle, "You

---

[1] When a rain storm in the distance with sun shining through it, has a yellowish tinge.

will always fool little children." This was after the young eagle had told him that these were all, that everybody had returned. Now the boy changed the young eagle into an owl. He flew off and alighted behind a rock, where he sat hooting like an owl.[1]

The boy looked down at the foot of tse·daɫɫʼa°oʼaiꞌ now, and there he saw są·ɫtsʼi·lisa·ni (Old Woman Bat) playing with her grandchildren. The boy hollered down to her, but she could not hear him and kept on playing. The boy hollered again, and after a while the old woman heard. She called to her grandchildren, "Stop making all that noise, you bastards![2] I hear a voice somewhere." Then she came around the end of the bluff, where she could see the boy way up above. The boy called to her to come up and carry him down to the foot of the cliff. The old woman said, "Lie down where you are and do not lift your head and look while I am climbing." The boy lay down on the flat rock and the old woman started up. As she came, the boy could hear her singing "'iɫtcʼąʼ tse·binahoctɫʼį·le ntɫʼį·ꞌ ntɫʼį·ꞌ ntɫʼį·ꞌ ndje·d ndje·d(back and forth I stick (climbing) to the rock, she sticks, she sticks, she sticks, she sticks, she sticks)." It was a long way up and it took the old woman quite a while to get there. When she got there, the boy saw she had a burden basket.[3] The band she carried this basket with looked about the size of a hair. The boy said, "Grandmother, what kind of carrying-strap is that you have on your basket; it looks as though it would break." "I carry my grandchildren in this basket with it," the old woman said, "and it never breaks." Then the boy told her to put in a heavy rock and dance around with it. "Let's see if that string won't break," he said. The old woman did so and danced around, but the string never broke. As she danced the string made a twanging noise: ndǫʼ ndǫʼ ndǫ. Then the old woman said she was ready and told the boy to get in the basket, "But don't look out to see where you are on the way down," she said. The boy got into the basket, and the old woman covered him over with a blanket and started down the cliff. She kept telling him not to lift the blanket and look while she was carrying him. On the way down she sang her song again. It was a long, long way down this great rock. The boy started to think, "Why did the old woman keep telling me not to look? What did she mean?" Then he lifted up the blanket and looked. Right away he and the old woman fell to the ground about fifteen feet below. The old woman was hurt and she cried. "Why did you look, I told you not to," she said. Then she called to her grandchildren to go and look for some są·ɫtsʼi·liʼize· (a medicinal herb, brown foot).

---

[1] "Owl will carry you off," is a common threat to silence crying children.
[2] This usually causes laughter, for it is amusing to think of an old woman bat saying such a thing.
[3] In former times the conical, twined burden basket in continual use for gathering wild foods, was an almost inseparable part of an old woman.

3

Then the boy gave the old woman all the small feathers off the eagles. The big feathers he kept for himself. He said to the old woman, "Do not walk under any tree or among sunflowers while you are carrying the feathers in your basket." The old woman started off carrying the feathers. She forgot and walked under a tree. Then do'+ tcid tcid tcid, the feathers all flew out of her basket and turned into the different kinds of birds that live all over the world now. The old woman took her basket quickly and turned it upside down on the ground to hold the feathers in, but only one feather stayed in the basket.

The boy went on back to his camp. When he got there, he made four arrows. On the first arrow he put one feather, on the second arrow two feathers, on the third arrow three feathers, on the fourth arrow four feathers. Then he set something a way off and started to practice shooting. He shot the first arrow and it swung around. Then he shot the second arrow and this was no good. The third arrow he shot went straight into the mark. The fourth arrow fell before it got there, as it was too heavy. This way the boy chose the arrow with three feathers. It was the best.

Then he had a bow and arrow and he went out to kill deer to make his living. One time when he was out hunting, he saw an eagle feather drop out of the sky. It was a white feather and it fell behind a rock. The boy went over to where he had seen the feather fall. When he got around a tree by that rock, he saw a girl standing there. She was all dressed up and looked nice. When the boy saw her, he was embarrassed.[1] He said to her, "I thought I saw a white eagle feather drop out of the sky and fall down here." The girl answered, "Yes, that's right, the white eagle feather is I." The boy took her back to his home. This is as far as I know this story.

4. *HE GOES TO HIS FATHER: OBTAINING BOW AND ARROWS: *VULVA WOMAN: SLAYING OF MONSTERS: HOW GILA MONSTER GOT HIS NAME: TURTLE SAVES HIS COMRADE: *na·ye'nezɣane WINS HIS WIFE BACK: na·ye'nezɣane OBTAINS HORSES.[2]

Long ago they say. A girl was wandering about by herself. She met nobody on her way. Then someone from above told her to go and lie under the water, where it was dripping. She did this and from the water she became pregnant. Then after this she had a baby and near the dripping water she left it. Next day she went

---

[1] Youths and maidens were very bashful and restrained in each other's company; particularly was this true of the former.

[2] Told by Bane Tithla. "na·ye'nezɣane Wins His Wife Back" is also called "At gułil'isi·'s Home." It is the basis of the supernatural power used against an opponent in card games and in hoop and poles. Excepting this incident which may be told as a separate story, the whole tale is called "The Doings of na·ye'nezɣane." For na·ye'nezɣane Obtains Horses, compare Goddard, ibid 98ff., 118ff.

back there and now the baby was all smooth and clean. The mother went home and stayed all night. The next day she went back again and now the baby was sitting down. Then she went home and stayed all night. In the morning she went back and this time the baby was crying and there were tears on its cheeks. Now the mother went home and stayed all night, and in the morning she went back and found the baby walking about. Then she made a little bow and arrow and gave it to the baby. She took the baby home with her. Then he started to shoot the bow and arrow. This way the baby went around with the mother.

They lived this way for a long time and then the woman got word again from someone to go up on a little hill and there build a tipi with four poles, just where the first rays of the sun would strike in the morning. On each of the four poles was a long zigzag line, the same as they make in the girl's puberty ceremony now. On the east pole black lightning struck down in zigzag line, on the south pole blue lightning struck down in zigzag line, on the west pole yellow lightning struck down in zigzag line, and on the north pole white lightning struck down in zigzag line. Then where the poles met above was tied narrow lightning. Now the woman went inside and lay there.[1] Then as Sun came up she pulled up her dress toward Sun and spread her legs apart, so that Sun shone between her legs. When Sun came up one of his beams went right into her, a red one. Then she got her menstrual period and the blood started to come. After that she became pregnant. After a long time she was ready to give birth, and so she went aside to a place and bore her child. From there she went home and spent the night at her camp. The next day she went back to her new baby, and she found it good and clean and smooth, with its eyes open. After she had seen it she went home. In the morning she went there and this time she found her baby sitting, so she left it and came home. The day after that when she went back she found the baby crying. She came home again. The next day she went back to the place once more and this time the baby was walking about. Then she made a little bow and arrow and gave it to the baby. When she took him back with her, he shot the bow and arrow as he was following behind her.

The first child that the woman had was called tꞌubaꞌtcꞌistcine (born from water) and the second one was called biɬnaꞌnoꞌɬtɫꞌi·je [with him marked down in zigzag line (on him)]. Then that woman had two children. The father of tꞌubaꞌtcꞌistcine was tꞌohastį·hn[2] (water old man) and from his father this one got his power. The father of the other boy was Sun. The first boy grew up tall and the

---

[1] The tipi in the girl's puberty ceremony is called the tipi of Changing Woman. It is supposed to be a replica of the above mythical one, the lightning being painted on the poles. The pubescent girl undergoing the ceremony is likened to Changing woman, the first to have this ceremonial tipi.

[2] The supreme personification of water.

younger one grew up, but not quite so tall as the first. Then the older one used to go out hunting deer. The younger one was about seven or eight years old and he was smart. Then this younger one began to reflect. He had no fingers, no toes, no hair, no ears, no nostrils, only holes there, and he had no eyes. This way they lived on there together. Then one time the younger boy asked, "Where does my father live?" "Where it is dangerous to go," said his mother. "I want to see my father," the boy said. "No, he lives far off where you can't go," the mother said. So the boy said no more about it. But after some time he said again, "I want to go and see my father." "No, he lives where you can't go," said his mother. This way they all stayed on there, and the older brother kept on hunting deer. After a while the younger one said again that he was going to his father, because he wanted to see him. He kept on thinking about his father. So again he said to his mother, "I want to go and see my father." He had heard from above that he was to go in search of his father and that was why he kept on asking about going. The boy had asked his mother about going four times now and each time she had put him off and lied to him, so the last time that he asked her and she lied to him, he said to her, "Your vulva is dangerous," and then he went off toward the east.

(From this point on the myth runs about the same as the version given by Palmer Valor. First the boy comes to Trembling Sand and when he cannot get across narrow lightning goes over it with him. Next he comes to Five Mountains Together and he cannot get over it, because it keeps moving toward him and then away from him whenever he gets close to it. He cannot get on to it. Then narrow lightning helps him across. After this he comes to xucntca·-gidiłxił (big cactus black), xucntca·gidutł'ij (big cactus blue), xucntca·giłitsuk (big cactus yellow), and xucntca·giłigai (big cactus white), all growing in four directions. There is no way for him to get through them. Then black wind, covered with black metal thorns, goes in front of him so that a way is cleared to go through. The next place he comes to is Crevasses in Stone which he cannot get by. Then Big Black Inchworm with striped back humps his back over it and the boy goes across on him. The next place he comes to is Black Metal Mountain with mosquitoes on its sides in front of him in four places, so that he cannot pass. But female rain comes on them and wets their wings. This way the boy gets through. When he gets by this last obstacle he comes to the waters around Sun's house, and the story goes on in full from there.)

Then he had come close to Sun's house, but in front of him was black water flowing, encircling, resting there. He could not get across it so he stopped. Then little turquoise talked four times and crossed over the waters. Then little turquoise was in front of Sun's house. Then little turquoise talked as a chief and entered. Then little turquoise talked as a chief and went around inside. Then little turquoise went on top of the house and talked there as a chief. Then to the top of the house went yellow warbler chief. Chief of birds (yellow warbler)[1] spoke as a chief[2] (on the top of Sun's house?), then small black water rested there. Thus it happened on top and a light rain fell there.

Then Black Sun had a trail along the ground, and from there on top it went. From the top there were four ladders going down, the first of black jet, the second of turquoise, the third of red stone, and the fourth one of white shell beads.[3] Then the boy went down to where Sun's wife was sitting. When Sun's wife saw him she said, "How did you come here?" The boy answered that he had come to his father's home. Sun's wife said, "No one ever comes here."

Sun went only till noon on his way, then another one took his place and went on from there and Sun turned back home.[4] So now it was noon and Sun was coming home. For this reason Sun's wife hid the boy and wrapped him up in black water. Soon there was a noise at the top of the house. Then the ladder from the top made a noise dję·j, dję·j, dję·j, dję·j, and when Sun was a little way down he said, "Where is he?" Then he came all the way down. (From here on the story proceeds much like the version of Palmer Valor. Sun says to his wife that he has seen the tracks of the boy going over the four different mountains, and that some one has come to his home while he has been gone. His wife says no, that no one has been here and she keeps on saying this to Sun who insists that someone has been here. Finally the woman admits it and the boy is brought out. Sun has thirty-one sons and with this boy he has thirty-two. He tells his sons to go and make a sweat bath in the shade, and while they do this, Sun tests the |boy out. On the east side of the house there is a tobacco sack, swinging where it hangs. On the other three sides of the house there are tobacco sacks in the same way. Also in each of these four places there is a pipe. Each pipe has thirty-two holes in it. Sun fills the pipe on the east, then holds it up and it lights itself, and he hands it to the boy to smoke. There are twelve little winds all around the boy, etc. Now the boy is tried out on each pipe in turn. After the tests they go to the sweat bath and inside Sun works on the boy, making his hair of black water and his fingernails and toenails of white metal, etc. Then they come out of the sweat bath and Sun has made the boy so like himself that it is almost impossible to tell them apart, so now the boy is a real son of his. After this Sun places two outfits in front of the boy. In one is a pair of moccasins, buckskin leggings, buckskin shirt,

---

[1] Yellow Warbler is often called the chief of birds, also the Sun's bird, as is oriole. The same term is applied to all yellow warblers in the region, distinctions between species not being made.

[2] Talking as a chief means to talk with authority, with power.

[3] Turquoise, black jet, red stone and white shell are the four sacred jewels. All have power and directional association by color.

[4] Daily Sun's helper goes on for him from noon till sunset.

and tc'ałba·ye (gray hat),[1] all these being painted yellow. Along with these are a mountain lion skin quiver[2] with four arrows it it, and a bow. In the other set is an outfit of White man's clothes and a rifle. The boy selects the first outfit. Now Sun makes two hills in front of the boy. On the first of these are growing all kinds of wild foods, like thistle, etc. and on the other there is nothing on the surface, but inside there are all kinds of metals and everything else that the White man has. Sun tells the boy to choose one of the hills, and the boy makes a mistake and chooses the first hill. Next Sun has one of his other sons, who is a white man, try out in combat against the boy. The son who is a white man puts on the white man's outfit and takes up the rifle. As he walks he makes a noise (his clothes do). Then he and the boy start to fight. The boy gets scared of the noise of the rifle and runs away, etc. While the boy is there Sun gives to him dark metal shield, dark metal spear, and dark metal xał.[3] Now the boy has received these things from Sun, as well as the hill and the outfit that he chose, and with all these things he goes back on the earth to his home. When he comes to the earth again he kills all the monsters that are destroying the people and it is on account of this that he is called na·ye'nezɣane (slayer of monsters).)

Then he was living with his mother, but he called her his maternal grandmother. Then one day he said to his grandmother, "Where does wild mulberry grow?" (From here on the story proceeds as in the myth told by Francis Drake "Obtaining Bow and Arrows." The boy goes to get the wood for the bow and while looking for it he meets Bear. Next he goes out to get sinew. Gopher helps him to kill du'ilgid[4] by tunneling up under the monster and gnawing the hair away from over the heart, as he lies there. Gopher takes this hair away to his children to make a bed for them, and that is why Antelope still has no hair under his front legs, over his heart. The boy stabs du'ilgid in this place and kills him, etc. As soon as the monster falls over dead, from all over the earth all the different kinds of birds that build nests come and pull the wool and hair out of the monster's body to make their nests out of. They leave the monster all bare, smooth, and red. Now the boy takes out the brains and all other parts, even the kidneys. Then after he is through butchering, he packs the meat in the hide and starts off home with it. Out of the sinew that he gets from du'ilgid he makes a bow string, etc. On top of tse·yi'nagole· [stone in he made (a place)] Eagle is living. The boy needs feathers for his arrows, and so he

---

[1] A buckskin cap with a small bunch of eagle feathers on it. It is the warrior's cap.

[2] Though quivers were made of other animal's skins, those made of mountain lion skin were the most highly prized.

[3] xał, a mythical sword-like weapon.

[4] A monster sometimes described as a giant antelope and identical with Broad Horns in tale 2.

makes ready to get them. He takes the brain of du'ilgid and ties it on his head, and inside he has turquoise xał. He goes to the foot of the place where Eagle is living, and lies down there. Eagle swoops at him three times and misses, but at the fourth swoop he gets his talons into the hide and carries him off and dashes him against the rock. When he strikes the rock the brains burst out and all the guts as well. In the nest, when the young eagles go close to the boy, he makes them jump from him by saying c, c, but the mother eagle says no, that he is not alive because all his brains and guts have been dashed out. While the old eagles are gone he kills three of the young eagles, and leaves one alive. Then he says to the young eagle, "When will your sister get back?" "When ni·cokiji (a kind of rain) starts." Soon the sister comes back with a young boy and dashes him against the rock. Next the brother eagle comes carrying a good young girl and kills her also by dashing her against the rock. Then the parents come, etc. When he is about to get rid of the last of the young eagles, he says to it, "All right, from this time on whenever a baby cries an owl will come after him. So you will be called owl from now on. Go over on the other side of that rock there and say tcu'ici·ni· (?)." Now he lets the young eagle go. It turns to an owl and flies over behind the rock. To this day owl still says this at night. Now the boy stamps on the rock and each time he stamps on it, it goes down. But when he stamps on it the fifth time it won't go down any more, and he is stranded. Then Bat Woman comes and gets him down. They have a fall, but when the bat medicine is boiled and the old woman eats it she gets well right away. After the boy gets home from this adventure, he goes after canes for his arrows. He cannot get to them. Gopher cuts them for him so that they fall over the rocks and he can get them, etc.).

Then there was only one thing that he still needed, and that was hardwood foreshafts for his arrow tips.[1] So he set off for the mountains to get these. When he got there he found where the wood was growing and started to break some off. Just then a woman came to where he was. This was djuc'isdza·hn (Vulva Woman) and between her legs she had teeth. If she lay with any man, she would bite off his penis this way. When she came to him her vulva was making a gritting noise, like ką' ką' ką', and before he could get away she caught hold of him. He tried to get away from her, but he could not because she kept hold of him. "Go ahead and do something with me," she kept on saying. But he could not even get near her because of the teeth between her legs. So he told Vulva Woman to wait a little while, that he would be back. Then he went off. First he got a piece of k'į·ntc'i' (a bush with very hard wood); then he got a piece of tc'idnk'ų·je (a species of sumac); then a piece of k'į· (a bush with very hard wood), a big piece; last of all he got a

---

[1] Arrows were generally made in two pieces, a cane shaft and a hardwood foreshaft.

piece of k'isnda·zi (mountain mahogany), also a big one. Then with these four kinds of wood he came back to the woman. "All right, let's start!" he said to her. He held the four sticks in his hand so that the woman did not see them. Then the woman lay down, all the time holding on to him, and got ready. "Go ahead!" she said and so he took the piece of k'į·ntc'i' and stuck it into her. "γaz, γaz, γaz," her vulva said, and it chewed the stick all up. Next he stuck the stick of k'isnda·zi in and again came the sound, "γaz, γaz, γaz," and the stick was chewed up. After that he put in the stick of tc'idnk'ų·je and still it sounded "γaz, γaz, γaz," and the stick was chewed up, but this time only half of the stick was eaten and he could feel her vulva grating on it as if it could no longer chew it and had almost quit. Then last of all he put in the stick of k'į· and now the stick was not chewed at all. When he saw this he picked up a rock and with it he broke off all the teeth that were between that woman's legs, just leaving one there that is called biγo'its'o·se (her tooth narrow). This is why women are the way they are made today. Before this time Vulva Woman had been going around and finding men and asking them to lie with her. This way she had been killing them. After this he went home and took all the foreshafts that he needed for his arrows. Then he had all the things that he wanted and so he went ahead and made his arrows. When he had made them he put some poison on their points.

At this time Big Owl was going around on the earth killing people. Big Owl was really a son of Sun also, but he was doing bad things. On account of this he (na·ye'nezγane)[1] went to see his father, the Sun. When he got to Sun's house, he asked that he might kill Big Owl because Big Owl was destroying the people on the earth. But Sun said no, that he could not do this, so he came back on the earth once more.

Then tse'da'tc'e'iłta·ɩn [rock over (down) he kicks] was killing people also, by kicking them off the edge of a cliff as they went by. This creature was the same as dibe·tco' (mountain sheep). Then he (na·ye'nezγane) was coming along with his dog, gray fox. Inside his shirt he had yellow snake (a rattler). Pretty soon he came to where tse'da'tc'e'iłta·ɩn was. A trail went by here. When he got close, tse'da'tc'e'iłta·ɩn told him to pass by, that he would not do anything to him. But when he got close the monster drew back his leg as if to kick, and so he (na·ye'nezγane) stepped back. Each time that he went close to him he did this way. Then he told his dog, gray fox, to go by him. When gray fox did this tse'da'tc'e'iłta·ɩn kicked at him but he jumped over him and was not hurt. Then he (na·ye'nezγane) took yellow snake out of his shirt and threw it at tse'da'tc'e'iłta·ɩn. When the snake came by him the two wrestled

---

[1] In relating tales in which na·ye'nezγane is a participant, his name is not often mentioned. In this tale it has been put in in parenthesis at times to avoid confusion.

together and while this was going on he (na·ye'nezɣane) took his turquoise xal and with it cut the monster's head away from the rock it was fastened to, and threw the monster down the cliff where it had killed so many people by kicking them off. Then he (na· ye'nezɣane) went home.

He (na·ye'nezɣane) was going about on the earth then. He still hated Big Owl. On account of this he went to see Sun once more. At that time he had a kind of little fly that went along with him and told him what to do. This kind of fly has fur on it. It does not live here any more. It lives way up on top of the mountains. When he got to Sun's home, he said to his father, "Big Owl is making lots of trouble on earth and I want to kill him. I want you to let me kill him." "No," Sun said, "he is your brother and you cannot kill him. I treat you just the same way that I treat him." "Then did you tell him to go around killing people on the earth and to eat them up ? He has eaten my friend and killed him." When Sun heard this he was mad and so he sat down and thought about it. At last he said. "It's all right to kill Big Owl, but I don't think that you can do it."

After he had the right to kill Big Owl, he started back to the earth. When he got there he made things ready to go after Big Owl. First he dressed himself. Then around his feet he made big hail running wherever he stepped. Then black lightning, lightning going together helping each other, with it he tied his buckskin leggings (like the Navajos use).[1] He had black metal shield, and he held it on his arm. Then black ice, four (ply), his body over it, his shirt he put on. He put it on so that he could go after Big Owl. He also had turquoise xal. He took this with him. He knew where Big Owl lived, so he went there. Big Owl lived close to where there was water. He knew where Big Owl came to drink. He went to that place and waited for him. Soon after he got there Big Owl came. When he got to the edge of the water, Sun shone red on the water and Big Owl saw it. "hehe·," he said, "I never saw Sun that way before." Right there he (na·ye'nezɣane) was going to cut off Big Owl's head, but now Big Owl walked away and he just stood there. Big Owl went into his house. When he got inside his wickiup he dressed himself in a set of clothes like those of na·ye'nezɣane. He had a xal also. He had all these things, because he was also a son of Sun and a brother of na·ye'nezɣane. When he had gone to see Sun about killing Big Owl, Sun had said to him that if he should kill Big Owl, he wanted him to give him his hat. That was the only thing that he wanted. Then Big Owl came out after he had put on the clothes, and he (na·ye'nez ɣane) could see that he had on the same kind of clothes as himself. When he saw this he stopped right there and watched him. He became a little frightened. For this reason he went off home.

---

[1] Two different kinds of lightning.

He kept on thinking about how he could kill Big Owl. After he had thought it over a while he decided to go to Black Thunder for help. So he went to Black Thunder and asked him to help him kill Big Owl. "All right," Black Thunder said, "I will help you." There were four Thunder People.[1] Then the blue one, the yellow one, and the white one came down like sunbeams to the top of Big Owl's wickiup and stuck on it. When this happened Big Owl's wickiup was made to rise up with him. They did this all night and all the next morning. Big Owl did not know what was happening to his house and so he came out by himself. When he came out na·ye'nez- γane started to fight with him. He took his turquoise xał and stuck it into Big Owl's breast, but Big Owl did not fall down at all. Big Owl had strong medicine. When na·ye'nezγane fell down Big Owl took this medicine and blew it on him and he would get up right away. na·ye'nezγane had this medicine also and when Big Owl fell down as if dead, he took out the medicine and blew it on him. Then he would get up right away. While they were fighting this way, right there he killed Big Owl. When Big Owl fell dead his feathers blew out and scattered all over the earth. These feathers became owls and that is why there are owls all over the earth. Then he (na·ye'- nezγane) took Big Owl's cap to his father as he had promised to do.

(Now comes the story of the fight and doings with Metal Old Man, just as in the creation myth told by Palmer Valor.)

Then he (na·ye'nezγane) was traveling around on the earth. There was one man who was going around killing people. This was one who was called tsi·'its'inyeiγa·ni (Head That Kills). He had an enormous head. There was another one. He was killing lots of people also. He was called binda·yeiγa·ni (Eye That Kills). He had one great eye like a moon, and it was with this eye that he was killing the people. The first one, tsi·'its'inyeiγa·ni was going around at night and butting his great head against the people's wickiups and knocking them over. binda·yeiγa·ni went around at night also, killing the people with his eye by looking at them. Then he (na·ye'- nezγane) went to where all this trouble was happening. He still had the 'itc'i',[2] the liver and other parts and the guts that he had taken from Broad Horns when he had killed him. He had also 'ici·diltc'ił (salt that bursts out), a kind of salt. When he got to that place the people there told him how this one man was going around at night killing people with his head. When all the people went to sleep at night, tsi·'its'inyeiγa·ni would come and with his head he would knock the wickiups over. He was still doing this when he (na·ye'nezγane) got to that place. That night, when he had gone to bed, but before he had gone to sleep, he heard one of the wickiups being knocked down. He always carried his turquoise xał with him and right then he heard one of the wickiups close by being knocked

---

[1] Personifications of the thunders of the four directions.
[2] An internal organ attached to side of stomach. It is quite long.

down. He saw tsi·'its'inyeiɣa·ni doing it, so he took his turquoise xaɬ out when he saw the wickiup fall and got ready. Then tsi·'its'-inyeiɣa·ni came to the wickiup that he was in and tried to knock it over. Right there he went to him and in front of the doorway he cut his head off. For the rest of that night all the people slept well.

The next day the people told him that binda·yeiɣa·ni would come there at night also. They all went to sleep. But he (na·ye'nezɣane) got ready and built a fire in front of the wickiup, when he saw that one coming with his eye shining like a moon. Then binda·yeiɣa·ni had come close to where he was sitting by the fire. He looked at him from where he sat by the fire and said, "Why are you looking at me?" But binda·yeiɣa·ni did not answer him and just stood there and looked at him. This was because whenever he looked at a person with his eye they would die right away. But now he was looking at him and he did not die. Pretty soon there came another one of these monsters, and after that lots of them came. It was this first binda·-yeiɣa·ni who had summoned these others, because when he looked at na·ye'nezɣane he did not die. Then all of them looked at him, but he did not die. He had with him the 'itc'i' of Broad Horns. He filled it with the salt. Then he said to the binda·yeiɣa·ni, "What are you looking at me for? I am just going to roast 'itc'i', that is why I have made a fire." Then one of the binda·yeiɣa·ni stepped back a ways and said, "He is saying something that is wrong. That is why he is telling this to us." Then he (na·ye'nezɣane) put the 'itc'i' on the fire to roast. When he did this the salt inside the 'itc'i' got hot and all burst out. As soon as this happened the eyes of all the binda·yeiɣa·ni standing around there were burst. Then as they were stumbling around trying to fix their eyes, he took out his turquoise xaɬ and cut all their heads off. Only the one who had stepped back from the fire first of all got away. So he followed him.

After binda·yeiɣa·ni had gone a way he stopped and built a fire and in it he put one tse'ni·zi·ɬ (heated rock). From the fire he saw two men had gone on. Still he kept on following the binda·yeiɣa·ni. After a while he came to where the binda·yeiɣa·ni had stopped again and built a fire. Here they had put in the fire two heated rocks and from that place three binda·yeiɣa·ni had gone on. He knew this because he saw the tracks and found where they had built the fire. Still he kept on following them. Then in a while they built a fire again and this time they put in four heated rocks. From that place four binda·yeiɣa·ni had gone on. But he kept on following them from where he had seen the four tracks going from the last fire. They went on a way and then they stopped and built another fire and this time they put in a lot of the stones. Right at that last fire he caught up to them. From the fire lots of tracks went on; the tracks of men, women, boys, girls, and small children. All these tracks went on from that place to where nit'egotci· (bare ground on edge of water)[1] is.

---

[1] Near old San Carlos.

He started back to the north where he had come from in chasing them.

When he got back he met Gila Monster and said to him, "Let's go to nit'egotci· There are lots of 'inda· (enemies) living there." Gila Monster was his cross-cousin, so when he answered him he said, "All right, my cross-cousin, let's go there!" So they started off. There was a town at nit'egotci· then.[1] This side of it a little, they killed one 'inda· woman. Then they took all her clothes off. Then Gila Monster said, "There is something that comes together between her legs." Then he (na·ye'nezγane) said, "My cross-cousin, that thing that you have just said will be your name," and from that time on Gila Monster was called łe·nenlai (two coming together). Then they went back home where they had started from.

When they got back they met Turtle. They told Turtle, "There are lots of 'inda· living down by nit'egotci· Let's go there!" Turtle said all right and so they all started off for that place. On their way Turtle said to them, "When we get to this place if these 'inda· start to chase us, you two get inside my shell." "All right, we will get inside your shell if any trouble comes," they said. They kept on till they got close to nit'egotci·. There at that place lots of 'inda· came out and ran at them. This way the 'inda· chased them up the San Carlos River to where Rice is now, and on from that place toward bitc'iltł'ehe.[2] All the 'inda· who were chasing them were shooting at them. Then na·ye'nezγane said that he was all in, so Turtle said to him, "Get under my shell." na·ye'nezγane got under his shell, and Turtle went along with him this way. All those 'inda· kept on shooting at them, but the missiles just glanced off Turtle's shell. Turtle was almost all in, but he got to bitc'iltł'ehe all the same. When they came to this place na·ye'nezγane got out from under the shell and said to Turtle, "You got to bitc'iltł'ehe all right and so from this time on this mountain will be called bitc'iltł'ehe (towards it he runs)." Then when they got to the top of this mountain the 'inda· got tired and went back home.

Later on na·ye'nezγane was staying with his grandmother. There were no people living in the region. So he started out to travel around in the mountains. One girl from some place knew that he was living on the earth. When he went off in the mountains this girl came to his home. Then she went away again. When he got back he saw her tracks and he saw the marks of the jingles on her dress. He asked his grandmother who had been there, but she answered him that no one had been there, no one at all. So he sat down and thought. The next morning he went out again in the mountains, and while he was away the same girl came once more to where he was living. There she was with his grandmother and talked with her. Just before he came back she left. When he got back he said, "Some one

---

[1] Prehistoric Pueblo ruin, said to be inhabited at the time of this story.
[2] The Apache Peaks north of Globe.

has been here again. I saw the tracks." "No one has been here.
There are no other people living here," the grandmother said. "Well
I saw the marks of the jingles on her dress where she sat on the
ground. You have nothing like that on your dress to make such
a mark," he said to her. Now the old woman had sores on her back
side. They made a sort of mark where she sat on the ground. So
she told him that it was these that made the marks on the ground.
These sores are called xuc. The next morning he went off in the
mountains and the girl came again, and was with his grandmother
the same as before. When he got back that evening he saw the
same tracks and the marks of the jingles where this girl had sat on
the ground. Then he said to his grandmother, "You have been
lying to me before. Someone has been here and has sat on the
ground. I can tell by the tracks." But the old woman just said,
"I have sat by myself here and when I moved the marks from my
sores look like the marks of jingles."

As he went off he was thinking about this, and wondered where
these other people were living. Then he went toward where they
were living. When he got close to their home he stopped and sat
down. That girl knew in her mind just where he lived. That was
why she used to go there to his home every time he was away. While
he was sitting near the home of that girl, she came out for water,
close to where he was by the spring. She brought a t'us[1] and a cup
dipper. When she got to the spring she set the t'us down by the
water and was just about to dip some water up in the cup when he
took out his flute and blew on it. When she heard it she stopped
with the cup in her hand and she waved it back and forth gently.
As she did this there were two butterflies flying about the cup as
she swung it. She kept on moving the cup to make the butterflies
go away. When they were gone she got ready to dip up the water
again, and was just about to do it when he blew on his flute and
right away the two butterflies came back and flew around the cup
so she could not dip up the water. She had to move the cup around
to chase them away. Finally they went off and she started to dip
up the water once more. Again he blew on his flute and the two
butterflies came back and flew around the cup. She moved the cup
and the butterflies flew away. Then she started to dip up the water.
He blew on his flute so the two butterflies came back and flew about
the cup just as before. All that she could do was to move the cup
back and forth till the butterflies went away once more. Then the
girl went ahead and dipped up the water and the butterflies did not
bother her any more. She filled the t'us and went back to her home.
When she got back the girl did not tell anyone about what had
happened at the spring. She thought that the butterflies had just
been flying about her cup for fun.

---

[1] Basketry pitched water bottle.

He went back home and stayed there all night. The next day he came to the same place and sat there. After a while the girl came to the spring to get water as before, with the t'us and the cup. When she was just about to dip up the water he blew four times on his flute. The two butterflies came there and flew about the cup. The girl moved the cup and in a little while they went away. Then she got ready to dip up the water once more. Again he blew on his flute and the butterflies came and flew about the cup. The girl moved the cup around. In a short while they went away and she started to dip up the water. Once more he blew on the flute and the butterflies came. Then the girl began to think there was something wrong, so she looked all around. Then she saw him sitting there a little way off. That is the way na·ye'nezɣane made love in the beginning, and that was how he set the custom of doing this. That is why our people make love this way.[1] When that girl saw him, she went to him. He spoke with her and told her that he wanted her to go home with him. "That's why I have come here," he said. Now he took the girl with him to his home. When the two got there, the old woman, his grandmother, called the girl, ca·'iɣe' (female relative-in-law other than sibling-in-law and married to a male relative), and now that girl lived with them.

Then t'uba'tc'istcine (born from water) was living far to the west. To the place he was living he had taken all of the good girls and women and there he was keeping them. That old woman (grand-mother of na·ye'nezɣane) had a nice patch of corn and squash growing by the edge of the water where they lived. na·ye'nezɣane and the woman[2] and the old woman lived there at their home together for quite a while. The woman was now her daughter-in-law.[3] na·-ye'nezɣane had butterflies all around him, all over his legs, on his shirt, hat, and on his shoulders. t'uba'tc'istcine, living far to the west, was just the same way, with butterflies all over him. These two looked exactly like one another. Then one day the old woman said to her daughter-in-law, "Go and get some squash blossoms in the patch, and bring them here so that we can boil them." So the woman went for the squash blossoms. While she was gone for them, gułil'isi (he walks on tiptoes)[4] came to her.

It was just about sunrise when the woman had gone for the squash blossoms. Then it was afternoon and she had not come back yet.

---

[1] Young men courting girls play to them on flutes.

[2] After marriage a girl is no longer called "girl", but is referred to as "woman".

[3] Ordinarily she would call the girl by a sibling-in-law term, being the husband's grandparent. The variance here may be due to the maternal relationship of Changing Woman to na·ye'nezɣane In this tale it does not mention the identity of the old woman.

[4] Another name for t'uba'tc'istcine. It seems to be used for him only in this part of the creation myth. Some say that gułil'isi is not the same man as t'uba'tc'istcine. The above name was given because he stole (tiptoed up to and off with) so many people.

So the old woman set out to look for her, as she thought that something must be wrong. When she got to the patch she found the woman's tracks among the squash plants but she was not there and had gone off some where. They did not know where she had gone to. When guɫiłʼisi had come to her she thought that he was na·yeʼnezɣane, because the two looked alike. She thought that this man was her husband. On account of this she had gone off with him. Then someone went to her family to tell them about her and how she had disappeared. They said that she was not with them. All the people knew that guɫiłʼisi had been doing this way before, taking girls away with him, so everyone said that it must be he who had done this. Then na·yeʼnezɣane made up his mind to follow and get his wife back. So he started off and went to where the woman had been taken from. From that place guɫiłʼisi had gone off to the top of a mountain, and from there to a second mountain. From this second mountain he had gone to a third mountain, and then on to a fourth mountain. After he had gone from one mountain to another four times he reached his home. His home was at yanadoḷkǫ· (foot of the sky) and there he lived in the middle of a great rock, where there was no way to get in from either top, bottom, or any side. That is where he took that woman. When na·yeʼnezɣane came to the place where guɫiłʼisi had stood with her among the squash plants he stopped and blew on his flute. Immediately he went to the top of the first mountain. There on the top of this mountain he saw where the two had stood. Then he blew on his flute again and immediately he got to the second mountain. He saw their tracks just as before. There were lots of poppies growing here and he saw where the two had been picking these flowers and throwing them at each other in fun.[1] Now he blew on his flute and immediately he got to the third mountain. At this place he saw their tracks together where they had walked among the flowers. He could see the tracks very plainly. Then he blew on his flute and immediately he got to the fourth mountain. On this fourth mountain there were grasses and flowers all over and he could see the marks on the ground where the two had lain down together. From there the two had gone on to his (guɫiłʼisi) home. They got there just at sunset.

Then na·yeʼnezɣane had come close to where there was a spider's hole, but he did not know that it was there. He stumbled on the spider's web and fell down. He did not know that there were any people around here, but pretty soon Old Woman Spider came to

---

[1] The butterflies about the girl's cup at the spring and those covering the bodies of the two brothers are connected with love making and love power. It is said a man by using love power may make a girl's mind like a butterfly flitting to flowers which attract it, without apparant control over its self. He may draw the girl to him. The mention of the poppies being picked and thrown also indicates love.

him. When she got to him, she said, "citco· (maternal grandparent-grandchild term), you live far off. How did you get here? You passed by here with your wife not so long ago. Why do you come back here?" "That was not I who passed by here, but I want to find that one who passed here," na·ye'nezɣane said. "citco·, you cannot go to gulil'isi. There is no way to get to where he lives. Come in my hole here!" Old Spider Woman said. Then he went in her hole. In there there were lots of her children. On his belt he was wearing something and now the old woman saw it. "citco·, give me what you have on your belt. All my children will freeze because I have nothing to clothe them with." "This is small and it would not be enough for all your children," he answered. "Anyway, if you give me that cloth there will be lots," she said. So he gave it to her and she took it into another place and there she wove it into cloth and made it like calico. There was lots of cloth now, all kinds, even silk. All the spider children were dressed in it. After this he talked with the old woman and told her how gulil'isi had gone off with his wife and that he wanted to get her back. "You cannot get to where gulil'isi lives. But if you do go to him, get him to gamble with you at all the different kinds of games," the old woman said to him. This way she helped him out and gave him luck to win the games. Then she said to him that there were some people living over in that direction; so he started off and came to the place where these people were living.

When he got there he asked where the chief was living. "There in that wickiup, below," they said. Eagle was the chief, so he went to his camp and sat down there. Then the chief said to him, "Where are you from, and why did you come here?" Then he answered, "I left gutalbakǫ·wa꜀¹ (camps by dance ground) this morning." The chief said, "We have been all over the earth, but there is no place like gutalbakǫ·wa꜀ that you speak of." But he said, "I was living there with my grandmother at gutalbakǫ·wa꜀." Then the chief sent for Red-tailed Hawk Old Man. He was very old and had traveled all over the earth. When he got there they said to him, "This man says that he came from gutalbakǫ·wa꜀." Then the old man said, "I have been all over the earth, but there is no gutalbakǫ·wa꜀." After that they sent for Goshawk Old Man. He had been all over the earth, so they thought that maybe he would know of this place. When he got to the chief's place they said to him, "This man says that he came from gutalbakǫ·wa꜀." Then the old man said, "I have been all over the earth but I have not heard of that place." Raven Old Man had been all over the earth and so they sent for him. When he got to where the chief was, they said to him, "This man

---

¹ This is the oft mentioned mythical abode of the Western Apache immediately prior to their occupation of their historical territory. The White Mountain Apache place it somewhere to the north or northeast of the White Mountains.

says that he came from gutaḷbakǫ·waʻ today." "he·! That gutaḷbakǫ·waʻ, I know it. It is very far off. This man could not have come on foot. Long ago I left here and started for gutaḷbakǫ·- waʻ and it was at sunset on the twelfth day that I got back here. That was when I was young and strong and even then I got tired and sweated a lot. This man must be brave and smart to come here from gutaḷbakǫ·waʻ, not traveling on foot," the old man said. Then the people asked him to tell them why he had come there. So he told them that guḷiḷ'isi had run away with his wife and he had come after her. "guḷiḷ'isi is a bad man. He has taken lots of girls away. There are not many left now," he said. Then those people told him that guḷiḷ'isi liked to gamble a lot and that he had gambled with them for girls many times. He had won lots of girls from them. "There are not enough people here any more on account of this," they said. Then they told him how guḷiḷ'isi always came out from his home about mid-morning and played at all kinds of games. "He plays hoop and poles and whenever he plays this game he always starts first. His poles are made of cane and the hoop that he plays with is bull snake. It is not good that way. It is bad," the people told him.

Then he started to think over all he had been told. He was think- ing about making a set of hoop and poles that night; so he went to the east and there he cut a pole. Then he went to the west and cut a pole from a tree. This was female wood. Now all the people came together and worked on the poles. (Here there is a song that they sing when they are making hoop and poles.) They made the poles well and finished them. Then they made the hoop, turquoise hoop. The beads on the hoop they made of the windpipe of dibe·ndi·ye (a bird, one of the flycatchers). In the middle of the hoop they made the yo·tcoʻ (big bead) of turquoise. Now they counted the beads both ways. On the edge of the hoop they cut eleven notches.[1] Then they tied the three parts of the poles together.[2] The first part was called nigustsaṇ nayidiḷgohn (?), the middle part was called 'iḷtc'ą' nḷi·hn (it goes both ways from), and the end part was called yut'anadiguce (?). Now all was finished and the men said, "Let's go to sleep," so they all went to sleep. Early in the morning they said, "Let's eat," and they ate. Pretty soon guḷiḷ'isi would be coming. When they finished eating it was sunrise.

---

[1] Across the diameter of the hoop is a strand of cord wrapped with another cord. Each encirclement of the wrapped cord is called a "bead". In the center of the strand is "big bead". The "beads" and eleven notches are used in the scoring. The wrapped cord and the birds trachea have somewhat the same ringed appearance.

[2] The poles are made in three pieces, assembled by tieing together with sinew when used. The game was one of the most popular and important among these people. Because of the dangerous gambling power let loose on each other by opponents, women were not allowed to see it played as they are too vulnerable. The frequent arguments over scoring were usually averted by getting a third man to count.

4

Old Spider Woman had told him (na·ye'nezɣane) that if he should
see the end part of a pole (for this game) sticking out, he should
blow on his flute. If it happened this way where he was staying he
was to do this. So when the end section of the pole came out and he
saw it, he blew on his flute. This way gulil'isi came out. There were
lots of girls and women following him. That man's (na·ye'nezɣane)
wife was coming right behind gulil'isi. Then they all went to the
hoop and poles course. When they got there, gulil'isi said, "Let's
play hoop and poles," and he went on the course and started to play
by himself. na·ye'nezɣane was standing behind him, so he did not
see him. This way he stood for a long time and watched him playing
by himself. The people there had told him that if he should play,
he was to bet twelve girls. That was all the girls left among these
people. He remembered this and now he got ready to play. Then
he said to gulil'isi, "ce"ile· (my gaming opponent),[1] let's play together!" He had hidden his set of hoop and poles in the grass near
by, so gulil'isi did not know that he had any. "All right, ce"ile·,
let's hurry up and play right away!" gulil'isi said. He had his own
set of hoop and poles in his hand. "All right, hurry up, let's play!
There are only twelve girls left here and I will bet them all," he
said. Then the two stood together and took up the poles. The poles
were red racer snake and the hoop was bull snake. The red racer
pole had its tongue darting in and out on the end, and both it and
the hoop had eyes. Then gulil'isi said, "I am going to do the counting." But na·ye'nezɣane said, "No, I am going to do the counting."
"No, I will keep count and score," gulil'isi said. "No, if you don't
give me the hoop first, I will not play," na·ye'nezɣane said. So
then gulil'isi gave him the hoop. He held it in his hands and when
he felt the eye of the hoop, he flicked it out with his finger. Right
away the hoop turned into bull snake and ran off to a tree. It had
felt smooth (like a snake) in his hand. Then he took the pole and
he flicked out the eye with his finger, and right away the pole turned
to red racer and ran off. "he·! What did you do with my hoop and
poles?" gulil'isi asked. "That kind of hoop and poles you had here,
are not to play hoop and poles with," na·ye'nezɣane said. Then he
went and got his own set. He gave one of the poles to gulil'isi,
saying, "This is the right kind of pole, the real one, not like the one
that you had." Then he had turquoise hoop inside his shirt. He
took it out and gave it to gulil'isi. "This is the real kind of hoop,
but the one that you had was not," he said. After that gulil'isi did
as he said, and they started to play. First they played to the east.
na·ye'nezɣane rolled the hoop and they both threw their poles.
gulil'isi said that the hoop fell on his pole, but it really fell on the

---

[1] This term, "gaming opponent," is used between two people who continually
play against each other. It denotes a rivalry and a man will use it to stir
such a rival into gambling on a contest with him.

pole of na·ye'nezɣane. He won all the beads on the hoop.[1] This way guɬiɬ'isi lost twelve girls to him. Then he said to na·ye'nezɣane, "I will bet you for those twelve girls that you have now." This time they played to the west. Again guɬiɬ'isi said that the hoop fell on his pole, but it fell on the pole of na·ye'nezɣane. He won again by making all the beads fall over his pole. Then guɬiɬ'isi said that he would bet him for all that he had won. They played again, this time to the east. It was the same way. All the beads on the hoop fell over the pole of na·ye'nezɣane, and he won. Once more guɬiɬ'isi said that he would play him for all that he had. They got ready and played to the west. When the hoop fell, guɬiɬ'isi said that it fell on his pole, but it did not. It fell on the pole of na·ye'nezɣane, with all the beads over the wood, and he won. Then na·ye'nezɣane had won lots of the girls, but still guɬiɬ'isi had many left.

They stopped playing hoop and poles. Then guɬiɬ'isi said, "Let's play some other game! ce"ile·, let's play tsiɣogo·hi (wood against)! Come on, I will play you for all that you have." So they bet all the girls that he had won, and got ready to play. There was a big post in the ground. They were to run against this and knock it down with the shoulder.[2] Old Spider Woman had told him that she would help him in this game. She helped him by cutting away the roots at the bottom of the post and putting in their place black metal for roots. This was for guɬiɬ'isi to try to knock over. When all was ready guɬiɬ'isi said that he would be the first to run at the pole, but na·ye'nezɣane said no. "All right, you be the first to run at it," he said, but again na·ye'nezɣane said, "No, you go first!" guɬiɬ'isi had played this game before and whenever he struck the pole it always fell down. He never had any trouble in knocking the pole down. For this reason he was sure that he could knock the pole over, so he did not mind running at it first. Then he ran at it and struck the pole with his shoulder, but he did not knock it over. When this happened he felt badly, because he had always knocked the pole over before. When guɬiɬ'isi ran at the pole, the roots all turned to black metal. This was why he could not push it over. It was Old Spider Woman who had done this. Then na·ye'nezɣane ran at the pole. When he hit with his shoulder he knocked it down easily. This was because Old Spider Woman had cut all the roots for him.

"Well, I cannot help it, you have won, ce"ile·. Now let's play tsiɣanano·łɣe·de (hair it goes across)!" said guɬiɬ'isi. So na·ye'nezɣane said all right, and they got ready to play. This time guɬiɬ'isi bet the wife of na·ye'nezɣane. Both of them had the same kind of hair, and it was good and long. Both had the same kind of clothes, too, and

---

[1] To score the hoop must fall across the butt of the pole, and the number of beads lying over the pole are counted. In this case all the beads lay over his pole so he won the game in a single play.

[2] The game is mythical. It was never played within the memory of old people now living.

both carried turquoise xaɫ. Then they ran to the bank of the river
and stopped there. The game was to let their hair down, and let it
trail out over the surface of the water. The one whose hair reached
out the farthest was the winner. When they got to the river, guɫilʼisi
said, "You go first, ceʼʼileꞏ!" But naꞏyeʼnezɣane said, "No, you go
first, ceʼʼileꞏ!" "All right, I will go first," said guɫilʼisi. He went to
the edge of the water and let his hair down so that it floated out
over the top of the water, but it only floated out as far as the middle.
It caught in some cockle burrs and stuck there. Then he walked
aside, and said, "Now you try, ceʼʼile.!" So naꞏyeʼnezɣane ran to the
edge of the water. His hair fell down and spread out across the top
of the water, all the way over. This is how he won.[1]

guɫilʼisi was he who had been born first, and he had always had
good luck wherever he had gone. He had gone far off to the west,
to earth's edge, and there he stayed at the camp of tʻohastiꞏhn
(Water Old Man) who was his father. From his father he got his
luck (power). The other one, naꞏyeʼnezɣane, got his help (power)
from his father, Sun, so he had lots of luck also. That was how he
was able to come to earth's edge. It was how he had come to this
place and had shown tʻubaʻtcʼistcine up as nothing. After this last
game they had another contest, and now it was to be for their lives.
It was to be a race and the one who won was to kill the other. guɫilʼisi
had a dog and this was jack rabbit. The dog of naꞏyeʼnezɣane was
gray fox. guɫilʼisi in his travels had married Big Owl's daughter.
He had been doing bad things and stealing girls and women. This
was the reason that the people called him by that name, guɫilʼisi.
Everyone called him by this name now. Then they got ready for
the race. naꞏyeʼnezɣane had killed Broad Horns some time ago
and he had kept the kidneys, stomach, daʼguɫtciꞏʼeʻ (part of the
stomach), liver, and the heart. He had these things with him there.
In case he got in trouble, he could use these to help out. Way
off on a ridge, there was a small juniper tree. They set the race for
around this tree and back again. "You start first, ahead of me.
Hurry up!" naꞏyeʼnezɣane said. He said this because he thought
that he was going to win the race. So guɫilʼisi started to run for the
juniper tree, and the other waited behind. They had told the people
that guɫilʼisi was to come out on one side of the tree and that naꞏyeʼ-
nezɣane would come out on the other side. The race was to be in
a great circle. After guɫilʼisi had been gone for quite a time, the
other started. naꞏyeʼnezɣane thought surely that he was going to
beat, so he did not mind starting behind. As he ran along he could
see the tracks of the one ahead and on them it was raining a little.
Then both of them had made the turn about the tree and were on
their way in. They were running where it had rained and guɫilʼisi
was only a little way ahead. Pretty soon they were running almost

---

[1] This game has no counterpart in the culture; is mythical.

together. Then na·ye'nezɣane said, "I have not started to run yet ce"ile·, so you better run." But gułil'isi answered, "I have not started to run yet either, so you better start to run, ce"ile." Then na·ye'nezɣane thought that the other was going to win, so he took out the heart of Broad Horns and threw it down in front of gułil'isi. Immediately there were a lot of ridges in front, where there had been none before. gułil'isi had to run over these, but na·ye'nezɣane ran on level ground. Even with this handicap he caught up to him again, so na·ye'nezɣane took out the liver and threw it down in front of gułil'isi. Immediately there were lots of rocks in front of him over which he had to run, but na·ye'nezɣane ran on level ground. Even that way gułil'isi caught up to him in a little while and they were running together again. Then na·ye'nezɣane took the stomach and threw it down in front of gułil'isi. Right away there were lots of ridges running ahead in different directions. gułil'isi had to run around these, but na·ye'nezɣane just ran straight ahead. After a while gułil'isi had caught up to him again, and so he took the kidneys and threw them down in front of him. Right away there was a big rock that gułil'isi had to run around, but na·ye'nezɣane ran straight ahead. In spite of this he caught up to him in a little while. Then it was only a short way to the finish. na·ye'nezɣane took out the da'gułtci·'e' and threw it down in front of gułil'isi. Right away gułil'isi was running in small mountains but na·ye'nezɣane was running on level ground. He was way ahead now, but he came out in the wrong place, below where he was supposed to, because he had made a mistake. There were lots of people waiting for the runners to come in. When they saw na·ye'nezɣane coming in on the wrong side they thought that it was gułil'isi, so lots of them were cheering for gułil'isi. Big Owl, the father-in-law of gułil'isi, was there. He said, "I know that my son-in-law will win. His brother could never beat him." Big Owl was dancing around and hollering because he felt good. But the people who were for na·ye'nezɣane all felt badly because they thought he was behind. When they saw that it was really na·ye'nezɣane who was coming in they started to holler for him. This was how he came in first and gułil'isi was way behind, coming in now. Then gułil'isi got in and he said to the other, "Kill me right away while I am still hot, ce"ile." Then na·ye'nezɣane made a mistake and grabbed the turquoise xał that belonged to gułil'isi. He stuck it into the side of gułil'isi, and because of this gułil'isi did not die. na·ye'nezɣane cut him into little pieces, but even after this he came alive again. Then na·ye'nezɣane cut his head off, but it came right back and joined on to the body again, even though he had thrown it away. It was because na·ye'nezɣane had the wrong turquoise xał that he could not kill him. "If he does not die there will be trouble," na·ye'nezɣane said. Then he cut off his right arm and then his left leg, both completely off. Still the man lay there alive.

Then na·ye'nezγane got his wife and said to her, "Let's go home!"
Then he blew on his flute, and right away they were on the first
mountain. He blew on his flute and then they were on the second
mountain. Then he blew his flute once more and immediately they
were on top of the third mountain. There was only one mountain
left. He blew on his flute, but nothing happened because his wife
was pregnant and was too heavy with child. They spent the
afternoon there.

Back where they had left him, gulil'isi had one arm and one leg
cut off, but he was still alive. Because of this he used one arm and
made a fire with a fire drill by using it against his cheek bone. When
he had the fire going he started to burn up the whole earth. There
was lots of smoke. It came out of the earth in great clouds. Then
gulil'isi got on one of the great smoke clouds and went up into the
sky. Where na·ye'nezγane was staying with his wife it became a
little dark. There was a big rock there, and tsido·'ḷγe·si· (he rolls
a stone; one of the wrens) who had his home under this rock, came
out from under it and talked to na·ye'nezγane. "It is dangerous
now, so I want you to come in my house with me, and stay there
all night," he said. Then above where they were there came a great
black cloud and gulil'isi was on this cloud. Then gulil'isi said to
na·ye'nezγane, "You must go to your home right away. Do not
try to spend a night on the way. Do not stay out tonight." He had
told him this also before he had been killed by him. tsido·ḷγe·si·
knew what was going to happen. That was why he had got na·ye'nezγane to go under the rock with him. Just about dark gulil'isi talked
to na·ye'nezγane and said to him, "You must not stay here tonight.
You did not use your turquoise xal to kill me, but instead you used
mine, my brother, and tried to kill me with it. If you stay here
tonight there will be all kinds of lightning that will strike this rock."
But all the same na·ye'nezγane stayed there all night.

The lightning struck all about the rock and broke off pieces
That wren had a t'ul.[1] Every time that the lightning struck the
rock and knocked great pieces off it, he took the t'ul and marked
with it on the rock. Immediately the rock would become whole
again. This kept up all night and the rock became small from having pieces knocked off. But when this happened Wren marked with
the t'ul on the rock and it got big again. When it was about daylight
gulil'isi said to na·ye'nezγane, "My brother, you did not kill me.
I am the one who made all this happen here on the earth. Now keep
on going to your home." And so na·ye'nezγane went on home. If
he had used his own turquoise xal he would have killed gulil'isi
forever. But because he did not use his own, gulil'isi is still alive.
This one had done wrong on the earth, so now he went up in the
sky and kept on doing wrong. He does so to this day. That is why

---

[1] This tool is mentioned several times in White Mountain mythology. It is
pointed and narrators say it is like an awl (flaking instrument ?).

lightning still strikes men and their homes, and all that lives on this earth.

(Now comes the tale, "The Man who Visited the Sky with the Eagles." It is not included in this collection.)"[1]

Then all the monsters on the earth were killed, and he (na·ye'-nezɣane) was living well among the people. Then he went to get something for the people again. He went to his father, Sun. When he got to Sun's home, he said to him, "My father, give me something good. The people on the earth do not have much. My father, give me a horse." "I have no horse. Do not talk this way, because we have no horses here. Where could I get a horse for you? What horse would I give you?" Sun said to him. But all the same Sun went off to the east where was Black Wind Horse. When Sun rode this horse the earth went down and the sky went up. "No, not that horse. I don't want him," na·ye'nezɣane said. Then Sun went to the south where there was Lightning Horse, and he led this horse back with him. But he (na·ye'nezɣane) said, "No, I do not want that one." "Then what horse shall I give you? These are all the horses I have," Sun said. Just the same he (na·ye'nezɣane) kept on asking. After a while Sun went off to the west and led back a black stallion. This seemed like a good one, so he took it off home with him. But this horse was not a good enough horse for him.

When he got back home with him, he tied him to a tree for the night. That night the horse kept running around the tree and making a great noise. He nearly pulled the tree down, and kept this up all night. So in the morning he went back to his father again and said to him, "That was a bad horse you gave me. He was nearly running away all night." Then Sun gave him a good, tame horse; the kind he wanted. It was a yellow mare. Now he said to him, "Take this mare with you back to your home and put her with the black stallion. If you do this, the stallion won't want to get away any more." Then he gave him a saddle, bridle, rope, and blanket, and told him, "When you get back home put the bridle to the east the first night." So when he got home he put the bridle to the east. The black stallion stayed where the bridle was all night and kept neighing. Sun had told him to put the saddle blanket to the south the next night, and he did so. All that night there were horses neighing at that place. When he went to where he had put the blanket the next morning there were lots of horse tracks all around the place. Sun had told him to put the saddle to the west on the third night, and he did so. That night he heard horses neighing all night long. In the morning when he went where he had put the saddle there were horse tracks all around the place. Sun had told him to put the rope to the north, and so he did this on

---

[1] Bane Tithla says that this man was na·ye'nezɣane, though others deny it. The episode may be told as a separate tale. See Goddard, ibid 132 ff. It is said to be the origin of the Hawk ceremony.

the fourth night. All that night there were horses neighing, also
colts, at that place to the north. When he went in the morning to
where he had put the rope, there were lots of horses, all kinds, black
ones, white ones, blue ones, and others. From that time on there
were horses on the earth.

(He ended the myth here. "There is just a little left," he said.
"It is about how na·ye'nezγane set up the customs of raiding down
into Mexico, and tells about the way we should lie in wait for pack
trains and wagons, and attack them. Also about how to live well
and not lie. That is about all.")[1]

*VARIANT (VULVA WOMAN)[2]

A boy was living with his maternal grandmother. He used to go
out and hunt and kill lots of deer for her. One time she said to him,
"My grandson, when you kill a deer, never butcher it under a white
pine!" The boy got to thinking about what his grandmother said.
Why had she told him this and what did she mean ? The next time
he killed a deer, he dragged it under a white pine and started to
butcher it. Pretty soon pieces of the bark started to fall off the tree
and made a sound just like bushes rustling. But the boy paid no
attention and kept right on butchering. Then he heard a sound
like a woman talking. She was saying, "ką' (husband), ką', ką', ką'."
She was coming through the woods saying this, and was getting
close to the boy. Before she got there the boy jumped up, grabbed
his bow and arrows, and ran away. He ran fast and reached his
grandmother's camp. "My grandmother, I butchered a deer under

---

[1] In a variant from Drake, not included here, the order of events slightly
differs. On the return of na·ye'nezγane and tʻubaʻtcʻistcine from their first
visit to the Sun, Metal Old Man is slain, following which the two brothers
again visit the Sun to obtain horses. After being offered two unsatisfactory
horses the Sun brought in a very slow horse, but at the last minute, "Wait,
my son. Don't take the horse. Take this instead," and he handed him a
large book with lots of writing and pictures in it. na·ye'nezγane took the
book and the brothers started home. When they had gone away, na·ye'nezγane said, "What is this book anyway ? It's too heavy. I don't want it,"
and he dropped it. tʻubaʻtcʻistcine, coming behind, picked it up. When they
stopped to camp na·ye'nezγane saw him with the book. "I threw that thing
away. What are you doing with it ? It is no good," he said. tʻubaʻtcʻistcine
was looking at it. "Come on, lets eat," his brother said. But he said "Wait,"
and looked at the book some more. He did this every time they stopped on
their way." The tale goes on about the choice between the two mountains,
after which the narrator remarks, "This way na·ye'nezγane missed his
chance to get the best things for our people three times. The first was when
he failed to choose the clothing with the rifle in the Sun's house, the second
when he threw the book away, and the third when he chose the wrong mountain. Then tʻubaʻtcʻistcine set fire to a patch of cane. From the burnt patch
came up many people and tʻubaʻtcʻistcine went off with them (origin of
Whites)."

[2] Told by Francis Drake. Also called "Vulva That Kills." This is an old
man's story. When old men get together they like to tell it.

a white pine and then I heard a woman coming after me, talking as if I were going to be her husband." "I told you not to do that way," his grandmother said. Then she dug a hole under the fire and put the boy in it. On top of him she put a łe·ts'a· (kind of basket) and over this she put back dirt and ashes.

That woman followed the boy to his camp. She asked his grandmother, "Where did my husband go?" "I haven't seen him any place," said the grandmother. The woman said, "I followed his tracks to this place." Then she squatted down by the head of the bed there. She said, "Whichever way my water goes, there will be my husband." She urinated and the water ran to the fireplace. "My husband is under the fire," she said. She dug in and found the basket and under it the boy. She grabbed him and pulled him out. "Come on, my husband, let us lie together," she said, and she lay down on the ground, drew her knees up and spread her legs apart. The boy looked between her legs. Her vagina was moving apart and together and there were teeth down each side. The boy said, "You will have to gather poles for a wickiup and set it up, as the only place I ever lie with a woman is in a wickiup." So the woman started off to gather poles. While she was gone the boy got a piece of hard k'į· (a shrub with very hard wood) and shaped it down to the right size. The woman came back and right away she had the wickiup poles set up. Then the boy said, "You must cover the wickiup well with spruce boughs. That is the only way I ever lie with my wife." So the woman started off to gather spruce boughs. While she was gone, the boy worked on a piece of k'į·ntc'i' (another bush with very hard wood) and cut it down to just the right length and shape. Then the woman came back and covered the wickiup over with spruce boughs. Then the boy said, "I have to have a bed of cactł'o' (a grass). That is the only way I ever lie with my wife." So the woman went off to get it. While she was gone, the boy worked on k'isnda·zi (mountain mahogany) and cut it down just right. Then he worked on tc'idnk'ų·je (a species of sumac, a soft wood) and fixed it. The woman came back and made the bed.

When it was done, she said, "We might as well lie down now, my husband." So they went in the wickiup and lay down. Then the boy took the k'į· and stuck it in between the woman's legs. "γaz, γaz, γaz, γaz" it sounded and ate the stick all up. Then he stuck in the k'į·ntc'i' and that was all eaten up. Then he put in the k'isnda·zi and it ate this up, but had a hard time doing it. Then the boy put in the tc'idnk'ų·je, but the vagina had stopped chewing now and was still. The boy took a sharp pointed rock and with the end of it he cut out all those teeth, all except one which he left, and that is called 'itsasa''a·ni. Then he lay with that woman all right.

5. THEY KILL GIRLS ASLEEP[1]

Long ago an old woman, 'isdzana·dlę·he was living. With her (their maternal grandmother) were living her two grandsons and two granddaughters. One night she told her grandsons, "I am going to get a bow for you each tomorrow." The next morning she went out and cut two staves of wild mulberry and brought them back to camp. There she pealed the bark off and set them outside to dry. When they were dry, she said, "I'm going to look for white flint to make arrow heads of." So she started off. When she got the flint she also got eight arrow canes. She brought back another piece of white rock which she worked on, making a groove in its center. This was for making the arrows smooth. It was a piece of rock about four inches long and two and a half inches wide. When she got back to camp and finished this arrow smoother, she set it in the fire to heat. Then she kept feeling it to see if it was hot enough. When it was hot enough she took it out and set it down. Then she straightened the cane shafts with it. She kept sighting along the shafts and working on them till they were straight. This is called yik'ą·s. Then it was evening. The next day she made the hard wood foreshafts for the arrows. Then she worked on the arrow heads, chipping them out from the white flint. This is called be·chisd'uk. When the points were made, she fitted them to the hard wood foreshafts. Then she sent her grandsons out. "Go to the creosote bushes and collect some gum and bring it to me," she said. This was to stick the feathers on with, she said. The boys went out and got some creosote bush gum, but it was not enough, and the old woman said she was going after some more and also some other things she needed. She started off and as she was going along she met Buzzard. He pulled one of his wing feathers out for her. Then Red-tailed Hawk pulled out a feather for her. Then Turkey pulled out two of his feathers and gave them to her. She brought these all back and started to work on them. The old woman fixed these feathers and stuck them on the arrow. That's why we still use three feathers on our arrows. She painted part of the shaft with creosote bush gum and then glued the feathers on with it. As she worked she kept sighting down the feathers to see that she had them straight. The two boys laughed at her. Then she bound on the feathers with sinew and put in the point and also glued it into the cane shaft with creosote bush gum. When this was done, she bound an arrowhead on to the foreshaft, and now the one arrow was complete. She started to work on a second arrow and finished it just the same way. When she finished the two arrows, she set them aside with the other unfinished arrows. Then her grandson looked and saw that all the arrows were finished. "My grandmother, you

---

[1] Told by Anna Price.

finished only two arrows, but now all eight are done. What does this mean ?" he asked. Then one of her granddaughters said, "I saw you put aside only two arrows and now there are eight. How can you do this ?" The old woman laughed and said, "Well, I just have good power I guess."

Next she started to work on the bows. She worked on one and laid the other by her feet where she was sitting. She cut the wood down and shaped it and made it straight. Then she put a sinew bow string on it. Then she finished it all. They saw that the piece of bow wood at her feet was all finished too, with a bow string. One of her grandsons saw this and said, "I saw you make no string for that other bow," and one of the granddaughters said, "I didn't see any string on that bow before. How did it get there ?" "Well, I put it on before and set it by my side here," the old woman said, but she was just fooling.

After the bows and arrows were finished no one bothered with them. "I'm going to put them at the head of the bed tonight," the old woman said. The next morning there were two quivers lying there with the bows and arrows. One of her grandsons said, "I thought you laid only the bows and arrows there last night." The other grandson said the same thing. Then the old woman took them out and showed them how to shoot. "This is the way to draw your arrow, always over the bow and straight back; never under the bow. This way whatever you see on your travels, if you shoot at it you will kill it. Never hold more than two arrows in your hand at a time. Don't bother about the other arrows in the quivers."

Then she sent the two boys out to hunt. After they had gone a little way they saw two little deer, spotted ones. This was because they could have anything they asked for. The youngest brother said, "I don't know how to shoot very well. You shoot it!" So the oldest brother shot one arrow and killed both the young deer. Their grandmother had told them, as soon as they had killed something they must come right home. So now they had to do this. They each packed one of the little deer home. When they got there the old woman said she was glad to see they brought home the deer. She told the girls to get some blue grass and lay it on the ground to put the deer on. The girls got the grass and spread it. Then the old woman made the boys lay the two little deer down on it, one one way and the other the other way, back to back. This meant that they would always have good luck in hunting. The old woman rolled back her sleeves and started to butcher. She told the girls to set the pot of black jet on the fire with water in it. When the water was hot the old woman put some deer meat in it to cook. Then she took out the stomachs of the little deer. These had milk inside and she sucked this out. The rest of the meat she cut up thin and dried it. Then she made two round hoops out of poles to stretch the deer skins on. She set them to dry. When the meat in the pot was cooked, they all started to eat. Then she told her grandsons, "My grandsons, don't go out again today, but tomorrow go out and a little beyond where you went today you will see something else." The girls asked their grandmother what kind of things these were that they were eating. The old woman said, "This is what I was raised on when I was a little girl, this stomach with milk in it. This deer is called 'ija·jelikije (white-tailed fawn) and the other 'ija·jetcu·he (black-tailed fawn). These two boys killed them for us, and from now on that's the way they will do." These two little deer together were called "spotted burden." The girls wanted to know what kind of deer they would bring in tomorrow. The two girls did not know the different internal organs of animals, and so the old woman told them. "These are the bowels, this is the heart, this one is the spleen, here is the stomach, and this the liver." All of them she showed. "The heart is what makes us breathe and live," she said.[1]

Next morning the two brothers started out to hunt again. After they had gone a little past where they had been yesterday, they saw a deer and killed it. They butchered this deer and started back to camp, each carrying half of the meat. One of them used the deer hide to pack with and the other used some brush to wrap the meat in and pack it. When they got home the old woman took the hide right away. She dug a hole in the ground and laid some grass in the bottom of this. Then she put the hide in and poured water over it and left it to soak. "I will scrape the hair off this hide tomorrow," she said. Then she skinned one of the front legs of the deer and got the lower leg bone out and cleaned the meat off it. With a rock she ground one end of this bone down till it had a sharp edge on it. This was to use in fleshing the hide. After this she went out and got a post to lay the deer hide over when she was scraping it. The next day she was working on the hide. After she had scraped all the hair off, she put water in that hole again and soaked and rinsed the hide out in it. Then she wrung all the juice and blood out of it, put fresh clean water in the hole and washed and wrung the hide out again till no more blood ran out of it. The two girls watched their grandmother working. They thought she was making medicine of some kind. The old woman had the deer brains boiling in a pot on the fire. She took these out and told the girls to spread some grass on a level place. The girls did this, and then the old woman laid the hide down on this grass and commenced to rub the brains into it. She had some kind of dry weeds that she rubbed on with the brains. When she was through, she set the hide to dry. All this time the girls were watching the old woman. "It looks as if you made that place level there. Why did you do that?" they asked. The old woman said, "This is all for today. By tomorrow

---

[1] Lungs are considered a part of the heart.

evening the hide will be dry. Then I will let it soak that night and the next day you will see what I do." The next evening the old woman took the hide and put it in łe·ts'a· (a kind of basket) to soak with water. In the morning she took it and wrung it out and then started to work on it. This was after they had eaten. She spread a cloth on the ground and put the skin on top of it. She worked and pulled it with her hands. The two girls kept watching her. When she was finished the hide was good buckskin and soft. The girls picked it up and looked at it. "You have done a good job," they said.

After this the brothers brought in more deer. The old woman tanned the hides. She taught the girls to cut meat the right way and also how to make buckskin. The next time the boys killed a deer, the old woman tanned the hide with the hair still on it, for a blanket. Then the brothers said, "We have lots of meat and there is no one using it, only us. So from now on we will hunt no more deer." The old woman said, "It looks to me as if you two were tired out from hunting deer. For this you will go out four days." Then the old woman sent the boys off with a carrying basket to gather food. She said, "I am going to soak up those four hides and make tc'ałba·ye (holy caps) for my grandsons." "Why do you do that for those boys?" the girls asked. After the four skins were soaked, the old woman cut one in half with a flint knife, while it was pegged on the ground. Then out of each half she cut a circle. These circles of hide she measured on her head to see if they were the right size. Then she cut them in half. The two halves she sewed together with a bone awl. After she had finished sewing on them she made a chin string for both. When the caps were all finished the old woman said, "I am going to set these caps out to the east here for four days. Then at the end of four days we will see how they look with something on top of them." "What do you mean, grandmother? We want to see this thing," the boys said. At the end of four days she sent one of the boys out to look at the caps to the east. In a little while he came back and said, "I saw something white and soft on top of those caps." That day the old woman went to wash at the river and it was when she came back that the boy said, "My grandmother, you must have put that soft white stuff on top of the caps." "No, the caps just got that way," said the old woman. She told the boys to leave the caps where they were. "Tomorrow morning we will take them down," she said. The boys wanted to know what the feathers were; what they meant. "They are called t'a'its'o·s (water down or forehead down) and all over the world these feathers know what is going on. They know everything. Leave them in the same place now and in four days you are going to use them."

Then the brothers talked together. The oldest said, "Our grandmother is making everything for us; moccasins, caps, bow and arrows. Now we have all, both of us. It must be that your mind travels other places, my grandmother," he said. But the old woman just laughed. It was evening when they were talking. "Yes, I am fixing all for you. You boys talk together about what you are going to do. That is the way you will get smart. Tomorrow I'm going to tell you about what I mean," their grandmother said. The next morning the old woman cooked up some ground na·djicyu·je seeds. That evening the brothers walked around outside the camp and talked together. "What is our grandmother going to do with us? It looks as if she is getting ready to send us off to far places," they said. A little later when they came back to camp, the old woman fed them the na·djicyu·je, but some she saved. That night the boys slept with their bodies stiff and straight all night from eating the na·djicyu·je. "Why did you feed us this na·djic yu·je?" they asked, "It made us lie straight all night." The next day the old woman worked on na·djiłba·ye seeds. Some of it she cooked and the rest she saved. After the boys had eaten the na·djiłba·ye, they felt badly. "We ate that na·djiłba·ye you cooked and that's why we don't feel good today," they said. What was left of the na·djicyu·je the old woman tied up in a little buckskin bag and gave to the boys. "These seeds will bring you good health and make you strong," she said. "I will give you this much when I send you to the end of the world. You will have to use this food on your way. It doesn't matter that there is only a little. It will never run out." The boys said that this wasn't very much food and that they would soon use it up. "No, I fixed it well and you will not run out of it," the old woman said. "Tomorrow I am going to talk to you just at sunrise. You must hold this food in your hands and stand there before me. Then I will say just four words to you."

By early morning, first dawn, all was ready for the brothers. The old woman woke them up. "You have a long way to go today, but nevertheless you will get there this evening," she said. After they had eaten the sun was just beginning to shine on the tops of the trees. The old woman told the boys to get out of the wickiup so they could start off. "Don't come in the wickiup again!" she said. The brothers stepped outside. They had their bows and their quivers, each with four arrows, and their holy caps were on. The old woman said, "I am going to send you way to the east, where the Sun rises. On your way we will be living here thus and that is why I am sending you. Before you get to where the Sun is you will meet some girls, not very far off. I know there are lots of people living near us. The first girls you meet you must stop and tell to fix up a bed so that you can lie with all of them in a row. They will offer you some food, but you must say, 'We do not eat that kind of food,' and not eat it. You will see and do lots of things." (As the story was told she tells them all they are going to do.)

Then the brothers started off on their journey to the east. After they had gone quite a way they came to where people were living. Here they met some girls. These girls were of the Piñon Jay people. They were busy gathering and roasting piñon nuts. They took some of the nuts to the brothers and wanted them to eat, but the brothers said, "This is not our food," and they would not eat it. There were eight of these girls, and that night the brothers told them to make a bed so that they might all lie in a row. The girls made the bed. Before they lay down that night, the brothers told the girls to let their hair down. In those days young girls used to do their hair up at the back of the head with a tsiɣeˑl (a hair ornament). The girls let their hair down. After they were all asleep the brothers got up quietly and tied all the girls together by their hair. Then they killed them all with sticks.

The next day they started off again. After a while they came near where the Coyote people were living. Here they met eight Coyote girls out gathering the fruit of Spanish bayonet. The girls offered this fruit to the brothers, but they said, "We don't eat this stuff at all. We only use this plant to wash our hair with." That night they told the Coyote girls to make a bed so they could all lie down in a row. Before they went to bed they told them to let their hair down. When they were all asleep the boys tied the girls' hair together and then killed them with sticks.

In the morning they started out again. After a while they came to where the djiˑlts'osˑeˑ (a species of jay) people were living. Here they met eight of the Jay girls out gathering acorns. They offered some to the brothers, but they said, "These are not our food. We only use this tree for wood." They told the girls to lie down on the bed that night, and in just the same way they killed them all while they slept.

The next morning they started off again, and after a way came near to where the Raven people were living. Here they met some Raven girls out gathering prickly pear fruit. They offered some to the boys, but they said, "This is not our food. We only use this to paint our faces." That night they did just the same with these girls and killed them all.

The next day they started off and came to where the Buzzard people were living. They met some Buzzard girls out gathering tcˀicoˑgiˤxuc ("buzzard cactus"). They offered some to the brothers, but the brothers said, "We don't eat this. We only use this for salt." That night they told the girls to make a bed so they could all lie together. After they were asleep they killed them in the same way.

The day after, they started out again and came near where the Red-tailed Hawk people were. Here they met eight Red-tailed Hawk girls out gathering something. They offered this to the brothers, but the brothers would not eat it. That night they told the girls to make a bed in the same way. Then before they went to sleep the boys said, "Where is the Red-tailed Hawk chief's house?

His daughter must be here; one of these girls here ?" "Yes, I am the chiefs' daughter, and he is living in a two story house over there," one of the girls said. That night the brothers killed all these girls just as they had done with the others. The next morning the older brother said, "We will go to the Red-tailed Hawk chief's house now, but first we will cut a strip of meat from the belly of his daughter and show it to him. I think he will know the meat and find out we killed his daughter." They cut out the meat and started off to visit at the chief's house. They carried the meat tied up in a bundle and slung over the back by the quiver. When they got to the chief's house, one of the boys handed the meat to him. "I have brought a little meat with me, and I want you to cook it for yourself and your wife," he said. The chief handed the meat to his wife and told her to put a pot on the fire and boil this meat so they could make soup. After the meat was cooking, the chief had a bed made for the boys and spread blankets on it for them to sit on. When they had left their grandmother's house the old woman had told these boys that if they killed Red-tailed Hawk chief's daughter, not to try and go to the chief's house afterwards.

Then they started to eat the meat. The older brother told the younger not to pick the meat up in his hands, but to hold it with weeds of some kind. The chief's wife bent over the pot. The steam from it went up her nose. She said, "This meat smells like my daughter and it tastes like my daughter also." Her husband said, "We told those girls to go over to łe·na·l k'id (two hills coming together) yesterday, and that is where they should be now." Then the chief sent some of his men over to see if the girls were still at łe·na·l-k'id. That evening the older brother said to the younger, "When we run out we will go through that window over there and get out that way." There was a window in one side of the house. Later on that night they heard the men who had been sent to look for the girls coming back, hollering as they came. They came to the chief and told him, "Your youngest daughter was killed over there and you have been eating her meat. Your daughter's meat is in your belly now and it will make a mark across your belly, this way."

That night the brothers got out through the window and ran away. Their grandmother had told them that if this happened and there was lots of brush as they ran, they could wish for no brush and the country would become level and open. There was lots of brush here. The boys wished for an open country and right away the country became that way, with no brush on it at all. Far off ahead the boys could see two white mountains standing together. They made for these. Red Tail Hawk chief had notified all his men about what had happened, and four bands of them were out chasing the brothers. The brothers looked back over the open country and could see the four bands following them in line, one behind the other. On their way the older brother said to the younger, "Make your mind good and strong and your heart also.[1] Don't cry, but be a man! We are going up on these two peaks. You go on this peak here and I will go on the other to the east. Don't you shoot first! I will shoot first." Then they went up on their two peaks and got ready. The four bands of the enemy followed them and surrounded the two peaks on which they stood. The enemy started to shoot. When they shot, the older brother said, "I am like the eagle feathers on my cap," and this way he rose up in the air and the enemy's bullets never hit him. As soon as they shot, he came down on the peak again, and his brother did the same way. Right away the older took one of his arrows and told it, "Go now and follow this people in a circle around the mountain and kill them all and come back to me!" Then he shot and the arrow followed the enemy all round the mountain and came back. This way all the first band of the enemy was killed. The enemy shot again at the boys, but they raised themselves up just as they had done the first time and were not killed. As soon as they came back to ground the older took the same arrow and talked to it as before. Now he shot it and it traveled all round the mountain and killed the second band of the enemy. Then it came back to him. The enemy shot at the boys again, but they raised themselves up as before and were not killed. As soon as they came down the older brother took his same arrow and talked to it as before. Then he shot it and it traveled all round the mountain, killing the third band of the enemy. Then it came back to him. This was power of some kind the boys were using. There was only one band of the enemy left. They got ready and shot at the boys. But the brothers raised themselves up as before and were not hurt. As soon as they came down the older brother took his same arrow and spoke to it as before. Then he shot it. It traveled in a circle about the mountain and killed the last band of the enemy then came right back to the boy. Now all the enemy were dead.

The older brother called to the younger and told him to come over. When he got there, the two talked together. The older said, "Our grandmother told us the truth. Whatever we have said, the eagle feathers on our caps have done for us, and these feathers know everything. That's how we were able to kill all these people. If we didn't have this power, we would be dead long ago." The younger said, "You killed all these men with only one arrow. I had four arrows, but I never shot one." "Here, this is the arrow I killed them with," and he showed his younger brother the arrow. They started to talk about what kind of weapons these enemy had been fighting with, as they had never seen this kind before. They went down to where the dead enemy were lying and looked at them. These enemies had been using guns, and the guns were lying on the ground beside the bodies. "When they shot these things at us they sounded

---

[1] The heart and head are the two governing centers of the body in Apache belief.

like 'idla₊ (imitation of noise)," the brothers said. Each of them took one of these guns, and off the bodies they each took a belt for themselves. The dead people also had two white belts they were wearing crosswise over their chests. On the ground around were lying lots of cigarettes. "We will take these guns home and show them to our grandmother. She will know all about them," the brothers said.

Then they started for home. It was a long way but they got there right away. Their grandmother knew they were coming before they got there. She woke up in the early morning and could hear voices, as if on the air. This was the brothers coming on their way. She woke the two girls up and told them to start cooking for their brothers. The girls ground up some seeds and corn and set it to boil on the fire. Their cooking was not finished when the brothers arrived. The old woman turned around and saw the boys coming. Then she was angry with the girls. "I told you a long time ago to start cooking," she said. She asked the boys what they had done. The brothers said, "We have done it all, just as you told us; all of it." "Those caps you are wearing, take them off and lay them aside," the old woman said. Then the boys told her all they had done (as told they rehearse all briefly). "Every time the enemy shot at us water's down (downy feathers on caps) raised and lowered us. Then the old woman said, "Yes, you have done as I said you would, and I am very well satisfied." Then the boys said, "We still have these seeds you gave us tied up here. We never ate or drank anything on all our journey and that's the way we have come home." The old woman told them, "From now on you will settle things all over this world and make open country without brush. You have killed these people over there, and they are the ones who have been killing us before. This way you have done well and now we are all living well and safely."

Then the old woman told the brothers, "Don't take a bath for four days! In five days we will talk about these guns here. Then we will know more about them." In four days the boys went down to the river and took a bath. When they came back their grandmother dug up some soap weed and washed their hair with it. The next morning she told the boys to go out and exercise. "Go out and run towards the four directions! It seems to me your bodies are not feeling good and that is why I am telling you to do this. This way you will be all right again." The boys did this and now they believed their grandmother. Before they felt badly, but now they were all right. "You have done well. Stay near camp now. I am going to think about these guns here, the ones which you brought. I want to lay them down here. Don't touch them, but just let me think about them. Take your bows and arrows now and go off and kill some rabbits and rats." The boys wanted to know how to handle the guns, but the old woman said, "No, I told you not to touch them.

Go and hunt the rabbits and rats." They went off hunting and killed lots of rabbits and rats and came back. "All the time we were out we could not put these guns out of our minds," they told their grandmother. She said, "I am going to think about these guns at night for four nights, then I will know how to use and handle them."

After four days had passed by the old woman said she knew about the guns, and she showed the boys how to use them. "You stand the gun up this way and put the powder down the muzzle, down to where the fire starts from. Then you put this round bullet in, down the barrel, and it is ready to shoot," the old woman said. She loaded the guns this way. Then she went over to a big pine stump and drew a circle on it. "If the bullet goes in the center of this it will be all right," she said. Then she told them to go ahead and practice. The guns had sights on them. "If it is so far, you set the sights so; if so far, then this way," the old woman said. Now the boys shot and the bullets went right in the middle of the circle. The next day they both used their guns and killed deer with them.

6. *THE EMERGENCE[1]

Long ago they say. Long ago they made the earth and the sky. There were no people living on the earth then. There were four places under the earth where Red Ants were living. These Red Ants were talking about this country up here on the surface of the earth, and they wanted to come up here. Among them was the Red Ant chief and he talked about coming here. "All right, let's go to this new place above!" all the Ants decided. There was a big cane growing in that place. This grew upwards toward the sky. Then all the Red Ant People started off from the bottom of this cane and traveled up it. When they reached the first joint of the cane they made camp there all night. The next day they traveled on from there, still upwards.

They spent many nights on their way, always making their camp at the joints of the cane. They kept on traveling that way, upwards, and then finally the chief told them to look around this place where they were. So all the people went out and looked around this new country and all of them said that this was a nice place. There were lots of foods growing all around. The chief said, "Bring in all those foods that are good to eat, to our camp." So the people brought in the different kinds of foods and fruits that were good. They went all over the country for these wild foods. This way they found lots to eat and they found good places to live all over the new land.

After that the chief told the people to look around, and then he

---

[1] Told by Bane Tithla. This myth is the basis of the Ant songs and ceremony. The name of the place of emergence, ha·tc'ono·ndai (coming up out of), is identical with that used for this tale. The place of emergence is vaguely somewhere to the north of the historic Western Apache territory.

sang a song. At every song that he sung all the people were to come together again. Then the chief was singing and in his song he said, "You can go off any place you want to, and when you find a place that is good, then stop there and settle." So this was the first place that people were living, and these were the first people, the Red Ants.

Badger and Porcupine were the first ones on this earth also. Then all kinds of birds started to live on this earth; Eagle and Hawk and all the other kinds. Then God had made man on this earth and everyone was living well. This is the story about how man first became.

My yucca fruits lie piled up.

7. *THE FLOOD: TURKEY MAKES THE CORN: HOW COYOTE SHOWED THE WAY TO MAKE A LIVING[1]

Long long ago people were living on this earth. Then Tanager[2] came to them and said that the ocean was going to come over this country and cover all their homes. Tanager came to where two boys were living with their mother and told them that they must build a great big t'us, so all three could go inside it when the ocean came and save themselves. He told them to weave this t'us out of brush and to pitch it all over outside, so it would not leak. So these people started in to work on the t'us. Tanager went among the other camps and told them to do the same way, to make a big t'us for themselves to get into. But they would not believe him and just laughed when he told them. "What's the matter with you that you want us to make t'us for ourselves to get in when the ocean comes? We do not believe the ocean is ever coming over here," they said. But those two boys went ahead and made a big t'us as Tanager told them. When it was finished they could stand up inside it and there was just room enough for them.

Then Tanager said to them, "I want you to gather some wood and put it inside your t'us. Also put some dirt inside and some food. Put in lots of yucca fruit and corn and sunflower seeds." So the brothers started to do as they were told. They ground up lots of sunflower seeds and lots of corn. It took them two days to get all this food ready. Tanager told them to make a flat rock to put over the mouth of the t'us, to seal it. So the brothers ground down a flat rock to just the right size. When all was ready the brothers got inside the big t'us. Then Tanager told them, "I want you to seal that rock on with pitch, over the mouth of the t'us so it won't leak. I will know when the water will be all gone again. When it is all gone I will pick up this t'us and carry it some place and set it down on the ground. Then you must come out of the t'us again."

[1] Told by Anna Price.
[2] Louisiana tanager.

The sea started to come to this place and was covering all the land. Then the brothers went in to their big t'us. When the water got to the camps of the people who would not believe Tanager, they saw the water and believed. They came running over to where the brothers were in their t'us and wanted to get in, but there was no room for them. Some of the women cried to the brothers to take their children inside and save them, but they could not do it. Then people climbed up into trees to try and save themselves, but the water kept on rising and some of the trees fell over. These people were all drowned and washed away.

Turkey was on top of a mountain, sitting there (Kelly Butte, near Fort Apache). Each time he gobbled, the water went down a little. But the water had come almost up to him and the foam from the water was right on the tip of his tail. That is why the end of Turkey's tail is white today. Mountain Sheep plowed in the earth with his horns and went into the water and swam. When he came out of the water his eyes were yellow. This is the way Turkey and Mountain Sheep helped those people in the big t'us.

Now the water started to sink into the ground and go away. When the water was gone, Tanager set the t'us down by the side of the river. The people inside it came out. All the earth was changed. All the mountains and trees and plants and rocks, everything had been washed away. At that place there was only level, sandy country with nothing growing on it at all. One boy cried to his mother, "What will we get here to eat ? There is nothing." The mother told him to go and look inside the t'us and see if any food was left. The boy found a little of their corn and a few acorns and yucca fruit. They took it out and divided it up equally. "Now where will we get fire ?" they asked. Their mother told them to go and look in the t'us again and get some white rock and some rotten wood powder. This t'us was like their house. They had everything in it. She told them to bring some wood from inside the t'us also. The brothers went inside again and found the white rocks and powder of rotten wood and wood and brought them all outside. There was no wood left in this country at all. They worked on the fire and started it up. Their mother told them, "We have some pots in there. Bring them out so I can make some corn stew."

They did not have much food left, and now they had cooked it and used it all up. They all felt badly about this and were sitting there crying. "What are we going to eat tomorrow ?" they asked. Then Turkey came to them and told them not to cry, that tomorrow there would be lots of food for them. The next morning Turkey came and told them to start a fire and put a pot of water on to heat. Then Turkey went off and shook himself. Out of his feathers and body dropped lots of gray corn. The people[1] went over there and gathered

---

[1] The story shifts here from the three occupants of the t'us to a group of people.

it all up. Then Turkey walked a little way further and shook out of himself lots of red corn seeds. They all went over and gathered the red corn seeds from the ground. Turkey went a little way further and stopped and shook himself again and yellow corn seeds fell out of him to the ground. This the people gathered up also. All the people who had corn went on one side, and what Turkey did next was for those who had no corn. He shook himself and blue corn seeds fell to the ground. This was for the people. The last time Turkey shook himself striped corn grains fell from him to the ground. Turkey shook himself four times, and that was enough.

Then Bear came there. "I hear you have had a hard time and are starving to death. That's why I have come. I have lots of food on me," he said to those people. He shook himself and out of him fell xuctco'; he shook himself again and out fell xucdilkǫ·he, then xucntsa·zi, then xucts'ise,[1] yucca fruit, piñon nuts. "Now I have brought lots of food for you people," Bear said. He shook again and out fell juniper berries, Gambel's oak acorns, Emmory's oak acorns, manzanita berries, tc'idnk'ǫ·je (a species of sumac), gadts'agi (a kind of juniper berry), na·djiłba·ye (an edible seed), and 'id'ą·diłkǫ (acorns of a species of oak). All these that Bear gave to us are the ones that are growing on the earth today.

"What are we going to grind these seeds on?" the people said. "Better go to Rock Squirrel Old Man and ask him. I do not think he will find a rock for us, but we better go there and ask him all the same," they said. So they went to Rock Squirrel Old Man and asked him to find them a rock to grind their food on. It was all level and sandy and there was not a rock anywhere around. Rock Squirrel Old Man was lying down when they got to his camp. They asked him to help them and get a rock. "You are just trying to make fun of me," he said. But the people prayed to him to help them. Finally he said all right. He got up and put his head band round his head and started off to look. Pretty soon he found a metate. It was a prehistoric one, and must have been washed there by the water. He brought it back and said, "Here is the one I have found for you people." When they got this metate they strated to grind their foods on it.

There was only a little water left in the t'us (not the big one) that they had brought with them, and so they went to Beaver Old Man to ask him to help them get water. When they got to where he was living, they found him lying down, and asked him, prayed to him, to help them get water. "Well, there are lots of you people here. How am I going to find water for you?" he said. The children were crying for water, they were so thirsty. "Well, give me a t'us and I will see if I can get some water for you," said Beaver Old Man. So they gave him a t'us and he started off. He was back right away

---

[1] All four are cactus with edible fruit.

with the water. He said he had found water in some pools on the rocks. With this water the people boiled some corn stew for themselves. The children also drank lots of water. But still the several tʻus of water stayed full. After a little while the children of Beaver Old Man came to where the people were and told them their father had lied about the water. "He did not get the water where he said he got it. He got it right at his camp where the springs are coming out. There are springs right there," they said. Beaver is the one that the people prayed to to get them water, lots of it, and he is the one who started the water flowing in Black River and Gila River and in springs and rivers all over the earth.

After the water had gone, it left the earth so bare that it did not look good, there was nothing growing. But now they planted the seeds of all those plants Bear had given them, and other trees and grasses; all the plants that are growing now like cottonwood, willow, tcʼilxe (a bush), jojoba, pines, cedars, manzanitas, oaks, all kinds. Bear gave them dziłkʼeºize·[1] (a medicine plant) and said, "These roots are good if you have sores on your legs." That was the kind he used.

Level, without mountains, it did not look well. So they set up mountains, and on them aspen and spruce and pine started to grow. Bear gave them da·sinexuc (a cactus), nadałbai (a mescal) and all the mescals and foods that we still eat today.

Then Slim Coyote started to sprout corn. He was going to make tʻułibai.[2] "I do not feel like eating. That is why I am going to drink tʻułibai, so I will feel good. I sprout it for four days and then I take it up and grind it right away. Next I boil it. When it gets sour I will give you each a cup. But this tʻułibai I am making for myself," that's the way Coyote spoke to them. Now he started to drink. "This is the way I do and now I feel good," he said. When I was a little girl we had tʻułibai.)

They had not eaten meat for a long time. When Turkey came along again he said, "Why don't you go out and hunt deer so we can eat meat ? But don't skin the deer too quickly. Be careful and skin it out, right to the hoofs. That's the way Big Owl does when he kills deer." Gray Fox spoke in the same way: "When I go along with you the deer all come together and I will make them easy for you to kill. But for doing this I want you to give me some meat." They went out hunting and got lots of meat and lots of hides to make into buckskin. "Before you start back home with your deer, start a fire with flint and steel[3] and cook a little meat so you will be strong," he told them. When they got back with the deer they divided up the meat. "We are all right now," they said, "but we don't know what to do with these hides." Coyote told them, "You have to scrape the hair off and after that wash them well." Coyote knew all

---

[1] Also the name of the Bear ceremony, in which the plant may be used.
[2] A slightly fermented drink made from corn.
[3] Term also used for striking two stones together to make fire.

about it. "Go and cut a post and peel all the bark off it so we can lay the hide over it to scrape it." "What will we use to scrape it with," they said. "How will we work on the hide?" "You have to sharpen one end of a front leg bone and scrape down with it. All that white stuff under the hair you must scrape off also. Where the hide is rough you will have done enough on it, but where it is smooth you must scrape it some more." After a while Coyote said, "Are you finished scraping these hides?" "Yes, we finished doing them in four days time," they said, "and now they are in water, soaking." Later Coyote said, "Did you put lots of brains on those hides?" "Yes, we put lots of brains on them," they said. "All right, now I am going to make moccasins for you," said Coyote.

"Get me some cow hide to cut my moccasin soles out of. I am tired of using the hide from the neck of deer, and it wears out too fast. Put your foot down on this hide and cut around it for the sole," Coyote said. Then the buckskins were made and Coyote took one and spread it out on the ground. Then he went to his camp for a long string of sinew. When he came back with this, he painted it red and with it he marked a line (by snapping the string, held taut at both ends) right down the middle of the buckskin. Then he cut the buckskin in half and started sewing on the halves for uppers. "While I am working on these you better put those hide soles in the ground to soften," he said. Coyote worked on the moccasins fast. He made tie strings also. He made moccasins that came up to the knee (ke·t'age). That's the way Coyote made a good pair of moccasins the first time. It was he who taught us how and we still follow this way.

Then Coyote showed those people how to make baskets and t'us and turkey baskets.[1] Coyote did a great deal for us long ago. It was he who won daylight and the sun and moon for us when he gambled at the time it was always dark.

Coyote showed them how to use the different kinds of foods. He showed them juniper berries and how they had to pound the berries in a rock with a hole in the middle, using a pestle. Then how they had to pat a cake into shape with their hands. "This is the way to make it," he said.

They did not know how to use 'iya' 'ai' seeds (a plant). Coyote went out and gathered the seeds of this and brought them back to camp. He pounded them on a rock and ground them up and made na'iltcil (a mush) out of them. Then he divided this up, among the people to eat. He gave some of this to the 'iya°aiye' ('iya°ai' people) clan to eat. "It seems to me that these people are eating themselves when they eat this food," Coyote said. That's the way he made fun of them.[2]

---

[1] Baskets to put young wild turkeys in. Young birds were occasionally kept as pets.

[2] This clan was named for a place where the plant grew in abundance, hence was considered related to the plant.

Then Coyote went out and gathered yellow juniper berries. He built a fire and with coals from this he parched the berries in a basket. When he was finished the children came up and wanted to taste this food. He gave it to them so they would know it.

They did not know how to use na·djicyu·je' either, so Coyote parched these seeds in a basket and then ground them. After grinding, it looked like flour and he gave it to the children. This is the way he showed them.

Next he showed them about tunas. "When the fruit is red you go out and gather it and bring it to camp. Then you have to peel it and sometimes you split it and let it dry in the sun. Sometimes you squeeze the juice out and drink it. He showed them just how to do all this.

Then Coyote showed them yucca fruit. They did not know about it. He built a fire and put some in to roast. When they were all done he took them out and gave them to the people. "There are lots of them over there. When they are ripe we will go and gather them," he said. "This tastes good," the people said. "When it is soft you can pick it, but when it is green don't use it," said Coyote.

"xucts'ise (a cactus) you don't have to peel. You just eat it plain. If you peel it the skin on your body will start to peel off also," he told them.

Coyote showed them piñons. He went and gathered a lot of cones. Then he built a fire and put these cones in it. When they were done he pounded out the nuts with two rocks. Then he started eating them. "This is the way you have to do with these. There are lots of them now and we will go and gather them, because winter will be coming soon and it will begin to snow," he said. He cracked a lot of nuts and separated the shells. The meat he divided among those people so they would know it.

After a while Coyote said, "You are gathering lots of tunas and yucca fruit now. I want you to store it away so you can use it again sometime. I want you to go with me now to where there are lots of piñons ripe, so we can gather them to use in winter. We will stay there till we have picked all the nuts." So they all started off for that place and got the piñons. They roasted lots of them in the ground in hitca· (small roasting pit). It did not take long to roast them (about one hour), and when they were done they took them out. He showed them also how they had to tie a piece of yucca string around their hair to keep it from getting in the piñon pitch. When they had shelled out all the piñons, they put them into buckskin sacks. Then they went home and started working on t'us to store their foods in.

They did not know how to make t'us, so Coyote taught them. He told them to put pitch only on the outside. Then the t'us were finished. Coyote told them to put all the foods they had gathered in these t'us and set them in wood rat nests so wood rat would cover them over and build his nest around them. In this way they hid their things in wood rat nests. "This is called no·laciltci·," Coyote said. "Put all your things in t'us in wood rat nests now, because I want you to go with me to where na·djiłba·ye (a plant) is growing." Later on he asked them if they had stored all their food away. "No, we haven't yet," they said. "Well, get ready and do it now because we are going to start for the place where pine trees are growing to gather na·djiłba·ye, before the season is over. Before we start I want you to fix your wickiups over well with bear grass, to keep the heavy rains out." Now all was ready and the foods stored away. They started off to gather seeds and foods. They were packing their bedding on their backs, and carrying baskets and their children. The men carried their quivers on their backs. Before they started Coyote told them to tie a slow match of bark to the quiver and light it from the fire, so they could start a fire in their new camp. Coyote was in charge of everything, and they did as he said. "We will go to where there are the most seeds," he said. When they got to that place Coyote told them to fix their camps up first, because it was liable to rain. "We will start to gather seeds tomorrow," he said. The next day they went out and gathered up the seeds and carried them back to camp in sacks. "Out of these seeds we will make t'a'da'hndiļ (gravy)." They stirred this with three sticks tied together by sinew. Coyote told them to put in salt. Coyote got his salt from ground around the edge of some springs. When the cooking was over, he told them to divide it up in a basket. Coyote wanted to know how they liked this food. "We like it well," they said. "Well, we will gather more and when we come back we will cook it. You have to grind it on a rock and then it is called łinestci·."

After they got through here, Coyote went to see how the sunflowers were. When he came back he said they were ready to harvest. "All right, now we will go and gather them. You have to break off the stems and pile them in a row with the flowers on. Then in four days they will be ready to work on." This is the way some of the poeple did and got the seeds out. After this they worked on na·dzisgid and brought its seeds to camp.

Then Coyote saw lots of mesacal somewhere in the mountains. "We might just as well go out and work on this," he said. "What will we cut the leaves off with?" they wanted to know. "Well, I have six sharp rocks to cut with, called be'ed'ạ·s," Coyote said. While the people were cutting the mescal, Coyote dug out a roasting pit, piled lots of wood in it and got lots of rocks. Then he gathered lots of weeds and grasses. They brought the mescal to this place to cook it. Before Coyote set fire to the wood in the pit he said, "I am going to light this fire from the sun. Fire which never goes out, Black Sun, his fire, he sets fire to it."[1] Then the fire was lighted.

---

[1] The last sentence is a prayer now in use when the mescal pit fire is lighted.

"Now you have to wait till the rocks are all white before you put your mescal in." When the rocks were all white they put the mescal in the pit and covered them over with the grass and weeds, and then put lots of dirt on top. "In two days we will come and take it out," Coyote said. After the mescal had been in the pit one day, Coyote told them to start and make a frame for spreading the mescal on. The people said, "I do not think we put very much mescal in that pit," but Coyote said, "It may not have looked like much, but there will be plenty. It is always that way." He set the men to cutting brush to lay on top of the frames. The next day they took the mescal out and worked on it all day. The women worked till their arms hurt. "How do we make ndu·lk'ane (sheets of prepared mescal)?" they asked. Coyote showed them how to pound it out so wide and so long, in sheets, and that's the way we still do. Turkey, Bear, and Coyote are the ones who helped us. The people did not understand 'ike·γa·j (a part of the cooked mescal). They got a rock and pounded this out till it was soft and made 'ike·γa·jndu·lk'ane (sheets made from this part). They finished doing this.

Coyote told them to store all their foods away again, as it was time to go back for the second crop of sunflowers. "We will go back to the very same place for the sunflowers," he said. So they went back there and started work again. Then he asked them if they were all finished. "Two days more," they said. "All right, fix everything up well because we are going to gather nadałtsuge (a kind of mescal) next, and you must work on that." Coyote knew all the mescals, nadałbai, nadałtsuge, nadałtce'e. In two days they were all finished, and they told Coyote that they wanted to gather nadałtce'e now. "We will be gone eight days," Coyote said. That's the way he planned and we still do that way.

They were working on nadałtsuge now. "Go and cut the mescal, but look out for its thorns. I'm going to dig a roasting pit for you," Coyote said. So they started in and carried the mescal to the edge of the pit that Coyote dug. Coyote got lots of wood and rocks and piled them near the pit. He fixed the wood and rocks in the pit. Then he got some grass. "I made tsidaskan here (piled up wood and rocks in pit). Tomorrow I will set fire to it." In the morning Coyote set fire to it. "This is the way you must set fire to it from the sun; just at sunrise. Fire that never goes out you must call it, and that way the mescal will always cook well. I want you to understand all this well, for in a few months I will have to leave you. For this reason you must understand everything I have showed you so you can do it for yourselves without me. I cannot be working for you and showing you all the time." When the stones were hot they piled the mescal in and put grass over it and then dirt. The next day they worked on a rack to prepare mescal on and split sotol poles for a frame. The second day they took the mescal out. It was all black and well cooked. They had made just enough to use this time. This they worked into 'ike·γa·jndu·lk'ane and pounded it and spread it. After they worked on it they had to wait two days to let it dry. After two days Coyote told them to be ready to start early in the morning. "If you have a heavy pack of mescal on your back, you must rest on the way," he said. In the morning they started off and after they had gone a good while Coyote stopped them for a rest. "We will rest only once more between here and camp. It's not far now," he said. When they got near home they stopped to rest again. Then from here they went on home without stopping. When they got to camp the old women fell on the ground because they were all in. "When I travel my knees hurt me, and now I am rubbing them," they said.

"We can't be traveling all the time. We will stay here in camp for a while now. I'm going to hunt deer in two days. I have got lots of food for you. I'm going to fix my bow and arrows and hunt deer over under that mountain there," Coyote said. He told his wife to cook some na·djicyu·je' for him while he was gone. Before sundown he killed a deer and brought it home. He gave a piece of meat to every camp and told them to make a stew of it. Next day the women said to him, "Thanks very much for this meat. We ate it all and slept well last night." Then Coyote told his children that he was going out to hunt rabbits. He killed lots of rabbits and gave them away to the people. "I don't want you to chase the rabbits before you kill them. Kill them with an arrow. If they get excited and run around their meat is no good."

Some time after this Coyote's children stole some piñons from the other people. They went to Coyote about it and asked him to talk with his children and teach them not to steal. "They stole some of the piñons that we worked hard to gather. We are living here with you and your family. While we go off to gather wood, you go and eat our food. It looks to us as if you were no good," they said. Coyote's children were bad and they stole. "We don't want to live with you. We may be going over to another place where there are some people living, because your children steal too much," they said to Coyote. When the women went out to gather wood, Coyote's children would go to their camps and rob them of their seeds and other foods. Because of this some of the families moved away and started living with other people. They told about how Coyote had been doing. Coyote went to other camps with his children to try and steal, but they chased him off and now Coyote had to live by himself.

One family went off and joined a new band of people. They told how they were afraid to live with Coyote any more because he and his family stole so much, and that now they wanted to live with these people. That's the way this family became members of the band.

These new people killed lots of deer and gave some of the meat to that family. The family said to the chief of the band, "We want to live with you because we have no other place to go." Then the chief said to them, "We are going to move from here now. Have you left anything back in your old camp that you want?" "No, only some mescal we left there," they said. "Well, we will come back for that some other time," the chief said. They heard that Coyote and his family had moved far off and were living in a distant country. The chief wanted to know if they had left their camp fixed up, and they told him "Yes." "All right, we will be back again some time," he said. "We didn't know before that there were other Indians living in this country, but now we know there are. We used to travel very poorly when we were living with Coyote, but now we live well with you," that family said. "We are going to move to the big mountain over there, and I want you to go with us so we can all hunt deer," the chief said. After all the people got to the mountain they killed lots of deer and gave some meat and hides to this family. They were going barefoot before, but now they made moccasins for themselves. "We have lots of meat so we might as well go home before it rains," the chief said. He had some horses and one of these he lent to the new family. "I want you to fix your camp well and make it thick on the sides and peak before it starts to storm. Then go and get the mescal you left in the old camp and bring it here, because we will be living at this place right along," he said. The place they were living must have been in the pine timber as the chief told them to cover their wickiup with pine bark and over this to lay grass. For the door they tied young juniper trees together in three parts. When they were ready to sleep they set this door up.

The next day the chief told them to go for their mescal. "Don't go alone, but four or five of you go together. That way you will be safe, but if you go alone some danger is liable to come to you," the chief said.[1] He loaned them a horse to take along. They started out and got to their old camp, where they stayed one night. The next day they started back, packing their mescal and some piñons. When they got back they gave some of their food as a present to the chief who had loaned them the horse.

Some time after this the chief came to the family's camp and spoke with the man.[2] "You have four daughters and I have three sons and a daughter. For that reason I would like your oldest girl to marry my son. That's why I have come here. I think you and your family have come to live with us for always. The horse that I loaned you, you better keep for yourself."[3] Then the man said, "Whoever

---

[1] Such simple bits of advice and instruction as the chief gives in this tale, are typical of the tenor of the talks which chiefs made to their people.

[2] The remainder of the tale contains valid marriage data.

[3] In asking for a girl in marriage, a gift must accompany the request. This gift was usually one or more horses, depending on the social status of both families. That it was not strictly a purchase price is illustrated by the attitude in these tales.

asks for my girl, I will give her to. I will not hold her back." In two days they came after the girl. The woman said, "I have come after my sister-in-law to take her back with me." That's the way she spoke of the girl. The girl's parents said, "All right." Then that girl started to cry.[1] They took the girl and started back to the chief's camp with her. There she stayed with the boy all night. In the early morning, before it was light, she came back to her parents' camp. In two more days the chief's family made a pair of moccasins for the girl, a buckskin skirt and a buckskin cape with a hole cut in the middle for her head. They brought them all to her camp. In two days more they brought a horse, saddled and covered with blankets, to the girl's camp. Now the girl's mother said to one of her relatives, "My relatives and close cousins, my girl has been going to that boy's camp for four days so I want you to help me this day to grind and cook lots of foods to give to his family." That evening they took the food over to the boy's camp, twelve of them carrying it. The boy's family divided this up among their close relatives and ate it all. Then the boy's mother said to her close relatives and cousins, "They have cooked for us, so I want you to help me cook lots for them." They did this and took it to the girl's parents in their camp. The parents divided it up in the family and ate it all. After they had eaten, the girl's mother started in to make a new wickiup for her daughter. They fixed it well and laid lots of grass on it. The girl's mother and the boy's mother brought blankets to the new wickiup made from the hides of animals. After that the new couple were living as man and wife. The girl's mother told her, "You have to cook and eat in that wickiup with your husband, so you must not be ashamed. That is the only way for you to do." She brought juniper berries to the camp for them and told the girl to eat with her husband. Also she gave them sunflower seeds and all the other kinds. The girl's husband started off deer hunting. He killed lots of deer and took all the meat to his mother-in-law's camp, to give to her. From then on they lived well. The girl's mother said, "We are traveling with a new people now, and my daughter is married to one of them. He is taking good care of her."

In the spring the young couple went to gather cactus, and this they brought back to the girl's parents. The husband killed some baby black tail and white tail deer to give to this parents-in-law.[2] Later they went out to gather acorns. They killed young deer at this time and gave it to the other people. The bones were still soft; the meat was as if still mixed with milk. They boiled the blood inside the stomach in a clay pot. Their acorns they gave away to the girl's mother and her relatives and also the boy's mother. After the

---

[1] Girls might cry from reluctance or sadness at bidding goodbye to their youth.

[2] Notice the stress placed on the man giving his hunting spoils to his parents-in-law. Such gifts and attentions were expected of him.

acorns were shelled and winnowed they stored them away in buck-skin sacks. They got tc'idnk'ụ·je (species of sumac) and walnuts for their mothers also. These they had to wash before they gave them away.

It was after this that the people all spread out and went to live in different places. One group would say, "We are going to live in such and such a place," another group in such a place and so on. From the places they settled they afterwards took their clan names.

8. TURKEY MAKES THE CORN: COYOTE PLANTS COOKED CORN[1]

Turkey made the food for our people. That was long ago when all the animals talked like people. A boy and his sister were living together. They were talking to one another about how they had no food. Turkey overheard them talking and came to that place. "What does your little brother want?" he asked the girl. "He wants something to eat, but we have nothing," the girl said. When Turkey heard this, he shook himself all over and all kinds of fruits and wild food dropped out of his body. Then they ate these up. Turkey shook himself again and big corn (a variety of corn) dropped out of his feathers. Then he shook himself again and yellow corn dropped out. A fourth time he shook himself and white corn dropped out of him. The boy and girl did not use up all of this corn. Some was blue corn, and they hid it away for seed.

Then Bear heard how Turkey was doing, and he came to that place. Turkey told him, "These two, my sister and my brother, over there, I am helping to feed them." Then Bear said, "You can only shake four times and make food come out of you. I have every kind of food on me from my feet to my head." Bear shook himself and out of him dropped juniper berries. He shook himself again and out dropped xucdilkọ·he. He shook again, and out dropped acorns. Then he shook out xuctco', then xucts'ise', then xucntsa·zi, then xucgaiye,[2] then Gambel's oak acorns, then blue oak acorns, then piñon nuts, then tc'idnk'ụ·je (a species of sumac), then manza-nita berries, then wild mulberries, then sahuaro fruit he shook out of his fur.

Then Turkey said to the boy and girl, "I have four kinds of corn seeds here for you. This is a good place to plant so you might as well plant your seeds." The boy and girl started to work on the planting. They cut digging sticks and with these made holes. In the holes they planted all their corn seeds. They planted all their corn in one day. The next day it had already come up and was about a foot and a half high. Then the girl said, "We still have some more seeds here to plant;" these were squash seeds. They planted these.

---

[1] Told by Anna Price.
[2] All those plant names beginning with "xuc" are species of cactus.

The boy and girl asked Turkey for more corn seed. "The corn looks good and is coming up nicely, so we want to plant more, and make another farm over there," they said. Turkey gave them the seed, and they started off to make the other farm. They left Turkey to look after their first corn and squash. When they came back they heard Turkey hollering down at the corn field, so they went down there. They saw Turkey dragging one wing along the ground on the side toward them. There were snakes on the other side of him and that was why he was doing this, to shield the boy and girl. The squash plants had young squash on them, and the corn was grown tall and had ears on and tassels. These corn tassels had pollen in them, and this was why the snakes were here; they were busy gathering the pollen out of the corn plants.[1] Turkey told the boy and girl to stay away from the corn for four days, till the snakes were through gathering the pollen. When they came back at the end of four days, the corn was all ripe. Now Turkey told them, "This first time will be the only time when the corn will come up in four days like this. Hereafter it will take quite a while." That is the way our corn grows and ripens now.

They gave seed corn to some of the other people. This made three times they had planted corn now. Then Slim Coyote[2] came to the people and asked for some corn. "The corn you planted is growing well, and the ears are coming out on it. I would like to have some seeds to plant for myself," he said. Coyote would have to do lots of work if he wanted to raise his corn, but he did not want to do this. "These other people here plant their corn and after it is grown, they have to cook it. Me, I'm not going to do this way. I will cook my corn first and then plant it so when it is grown I won't have to bother about cooking it." Here is where Coyote made a big mistake and was not as smart as usual. Coyote cooked his corn, ate some, and planted the rest. He planted quite a patch and after he planted it he felt pretty good. "Now I have done well for myself. You people have to cook your corn after you plant it, but mine will be already cooked," he said. After he planted, they all went off to gather acorns.[3] When they got back to their corn the place that Coyote planted had nothing growing on it at all. Coyote got angry. "You people must have taken the hearts out of the corn seeds you gave to me." "No, we didn't do that, but you cooked the heart out of your corn seeds before you planted. You ought not to have done that," they told him.

Coyote asked for some more seed corn. They gave him some and he planted them the right way this time. Now his corn grew up, and

---

[1] A common belief among White Mountain Apache.
[2] This is the name Coyote usually goes by in tales.
[3] Departure to gather wild plant foods after the crop is in and up, is the regular procedure which the great majority of families followed. Only a few old people were left to watch over the fields at the large farms.

he had lots of it. The day after he planted, his corn was up about one foot and a half. Coyote felt good.

The people who planted their corn right at first, were harvesting now and tying their corn up into łida·stł'un (bundles of ears). Coyote saw these łida·stł'un and wanted some. They got mad at Coyote because he was always asking them for corn. "I just want some green ears to feed my children. As soon as I get my corn ripe, I will pay you back," Coyote said.

The other people had all their corn in and stripped now, but their squash were still growing in the field. Coyote went to their field and stole their squash. Then the people all came to his camp and wanted to know if he was the one who was stealing their squash. Coyote pretended to get angry. "No I didn't steal your squash at all. You are always blaming me for stealing everything. There are lots of camps over there, but you have to choose my camp to come to and blame me." The other people said, "You are no good, Coyote. You are always thieving. From now on don't make your farm near us. Move away and live some place else!" "All right, there are several of you who are here whom I was going to repay with corn, but I will not do it now because you treat me this way," Coyote said. Coyote's family was living poorly then, and they never bothered to cook anything before they ate it. This is how it was.

9. *LOST WITH TURKEY[1]

Long ago they say. There was a young man living, about eighteen years old. He was living with his father and mother and sisters and brothers. This young man was a real gambler. He played all the time. This way he started in to play at hoop and poles with another fellow. First he bet his moccasins, then his leggings, then the rest of his clothes, and finally his hair. He lost everything and had to come home without anything. When he came home his father and mother got after him, also his brothers, and made trouble with him about losing everything that way. They said to him, "You have not done right. You lost your shirt, moccasins, leggings and all, and besides you lost your hair and had it cut off close to your head. So we don't want you to live here any more. You better go somewhere else." This man had a pet turkey, and that was all he had.[2] So now he left his people and started off, taking his turkey with him.

After the two had gone for a way, they came to a great river and stopped on its bank. Then this man thought, "What shall I do? All my relatives are mad at me. Where shall I go?" After a while he thought, "I will look for a log, a big dry one, and make a hole inside

---

[1] Told by Bane Tithla. This is the origin myth of the Hopi Snake clan or society.
[2] Sometimes young wild turkeys were kept as pets, but the domestication of turkeys was absent.

it and go in and plug the ends up with pitch and then roll into the water and let it carry me as far as it goes."[1] So he looked around and found a good big log. After he got this, he went out in the mountains and brought in a lot of pitch. When he had fixed the log all up, he rolled it to the edge of the river. Now he got inside and sealed the ends. Then Turkey pushed the log, with him inside, into the water and the river started to carry him off. The river carried him on and on, but after a long way he found he was at the end of the river. The water had taken him there. His log was washed up on the shore. Then he moved around and tried to roll the log, but it was not in water any longer and it would not move. So he broke a hole in the pitch and after a while he came out. Turkey was with him there also, and now the two walked around together.

They started traveling over the country. When Turkey shook his body, corn seeds fell from him, and that was the way they got their food. After they had gone some distance, they came to a good place to farm. Then the man said, "I might make a farm here, but I don't know where to get seeds to plant." Turkey knew what he was thinking about and he said to him, "Where you see good land you had better plant." Then the man said, "But where will we get the seeds to plant? We can't get any here." So Turkey said, "All that you want we have right here," and so the man started in to clear and level the land, also Turkey scratched up the ground and made it level. After they had it all cleared, Turkey shook his body and out from his feathers fell white corn, blue corn, yellow corn, brown corn, red corn, all kinds of corn fell to the ground. Also he shook out beans and squash seeds.[2] They planted these seeds in that ground, and Turkey helped fill in the seed holes with dirt. Turkey had given all these seeds and helped clear the ground and level it, and he had worked very hard. Because of this the man felt happy about Turkey and liked him. Later on when the corn was getting big, Turkey cultivated it and pulled out the weeds. Then the corn was getting good and big.

While the two were living like this, one night the man saw a fire a long way off to the west. He thought, "There must be people living over where that fire is. I think I will go and see them. I will go tomorrow," and then he said to Turkey, "I want you to stay here and take care of the corn and watch it. I'm going to where that fire

---

[1] The young man's desperation because of the attitude of his relatives toward him is quite typical of these people. When one's relatives no longer want one or cease to show signs of affection and fulfillment of obligations, no situation could be worse and it can easily end in a suicidal gesture or actual suicide. A case exists in which a young man committed suicide because his older brother refused him a drink at a party. The active disapproval of not only parents, but brothers as well in the above case, hints at the important part brothers may play in each others lives.

[2] Corn, squash and beans were the only aboriginal crops among white Mountain Apache.

is. I think there are people living over there. If there are, I might
not come back for quite a while." That night he marked where he
had seen the fire and he looked at the lay of the hills. The next day
he started off and headed right for where he had seen the fire. He
looked all over but could find no sign of any people or fire there, so
that evening he came back to his farm. That night he looked to the
west again and saw the fire in the same place. He thought, "I must
have gone to the wrong place and missed it." Now he watched
closely so he could be sure and locate the fire before he started
again. He figured out just where the fire was and when he was sure,
he went to bed. Next morning he sat in the same place he was last
night and looked towards where he had seen the fire. He thought
he knew just where it was. Then he told Turkey again, "Stay here
and look after the corn for me and cultivate it. I may be gone a long
time, if I find any people," and he started off to where he had seen
the fire. He looked all over, but could not find sign of anything.
All day he searched, and that evening went back to Turkey. That
night he sat in the same place and again saw the fire in the same
spot to the west. "I can't see how I missed it every time. I must
have passed near it. Now I will find it for sure." Next morning he
told Turkey, "Stay and look out for the corn. I'm going to look for
that fire today and if I find people I may not be back for some
time," and he started off. He looked all over but could not find any
fire or any people. All day he looked and at sundown went home.
That night he looked to the west again and saw the fire in the same
place as before. He thought to himself, "I must have gone right by
that camp." Then he set a crotched stick in the ground, so that
when he sighted through it he looked right at the fire. "This is the
only way I will find it, I think," he said. In the morning he went to
the stick and looked through it, right to where he had seen the fire.
Now he knew for sure where the fire was. He turned to Turkey and
said, "My bird, take care of the corn for me. I'm going now and I
may find some people over there. If I do, I won't be back for a
good while."

The man started off. He knew for certain where that camp was
now, and after a while he got to it. Sure enough there were some
people living there. These people were all different kinds of snakes.
Big Snake was the chief. He had four daughters. The youngest
one saw the man coming before he got there. She went and told her
father, "A man is approaching." Her father told her, "Tell him to
come over here." This man had no clothes on at all, not even a gee
string, and that was why he was ashamed to go to that place. The
girl called to him anyway and told him what her father had said,
but the man would not go to her. Then she went back and told
her father, "I tried to call him over but he won't come." So her
father said, "You had better go and see what's the matter with
him." So the girl went to the man, where he was standing in the

middle of a clump of tⁱo'tco' (a grass) because he was ashamed. "My father wants you to come over there. Why don't you come?" the girl said. "My clothes are all gone and I have nothing to cover me. That's why I don't come over there,"[1] he answered. The girl went back and told her father what the man said. "His moccasins are gone, also his shirt, gee string, and his hair even," she said. Then her father said, "Take these clothes to him and tell him to dress up in them and come here to me. I want to know why he is traveling here and why he has come." So the girl took the clothes to him and he dressed in them. Then he went over to the camp of Big Snake. There he stopped by the door, but the chief told him to come inside. "I want to feed you first, and then I want you to tell me all about why you have come here,"[2] the chief said. The man sat down and ate. When he was through the chief said, "How did you get here and why did you come? No people ever come here. Why have you come?" The man said, "I will tell you all about things since I left my home. Where I was living there was a lot of gambling with hoop and poles and other games. There at the hoop and poles game one man said to me, "Let's play!" I said, "all right and told him that I'd bet my moccasins. That's how I lost them. Then he wanted to bet me for my shirt, so I bet it. This I lost also. Then I was just wearing my gee string and belt. He wanted to bet me for this, so I bet. I lost them also. Then he wanted to bet me for my hair, cut close to my head. I bet this and lost it and had to cut my hair all off. This is the way I lost everying I had, my clothes and my hair. Then I went home. (He recites the rest of the story.) Then I came out from the log and that's the way I got on the ground again. I don't know how I came there and don't know which way I came through. I went over the country and started a farm. From that place I saw your fire four times. That's how I came here. After four nights I came here. I didn't know you were living here. That's all there is."

The youngest daughter of Big Snake was the one who looked after him while he was there. So after a while he got married to her. He had been living there quite a while now. It was about one year since he had left his family. Then Big Snake said, "This is the day you left your home so I want you to go back to your home this same day."[3] The man answered him, "I don't know where I was living

---

[1] A man would never expose his privates before women by omition of a gee string, and even among other men he is usually cautious about this. Men do not like to see each other entirely naked.

[2] It is customary to feed a visitor before discussing the mission on which he may have come.

[3] This concept is also found in other aspects of the culture. Thus a war party in revenge for the killing of a relative was often arranged to take place one year after the killing, though not exactly on the same date. Recently a custom of celebrating the first anniversary of the death of an important relative has come into use among certain White Mountain Apache. Again,

and which way I came here. I have forgotten all about this." Big
Snake said, "We know where you were living, not far from this
place." "Which way will I go to get there?" the man asked. The
chief said to him, "We know where you live and as soon as you
leave here you will get to your home in the same instant." That
man thought to himself, "I am living here well now. Why does he
want me to go back? If I do go, I might get lost. Also all my relatives are mad at me. What's the use of going home?" When he left,
all his people had trailed him as far as they could, which was to the
edge of the river. Here they thought he had drowned himself, so
they all cut their hair short and mourned for him because they
thought he was dead.[1] But in a year's time their hair was long again.
All his people thought he was no longer alive. Then Big Snake told
the man, "You go to your home today. Whoever that man was
whom you lost all your belongings to playing hoop and poles, ask
him to play again and show him well how to do it." Now they gave
him t'ạ·ji'isis (belt tied or buckled in back) and told him when he
got home to bet this against the other man. "If he sees this, he
will surely ask you to bet it," the chief said.

Then that man left there. His wife and her relatives cried for
him because he left.[2] He only thought once about starting and he
was there near his old home, close to where his people were. He
started toward them. They had forgotten all about him by this
time. As he was coming, only one, his younger sister, saw him.
"There is my brother coming here," she said. Her father said to
her, "Girl, he is dead almost a year now, so don't think he is alive.
Don't talk about him." Then the girl said, "I am telling the truth,
my brother is coming close now." "Don't say that. He's been dead
a long time. We don't know what happened to him,"[3] her father
said. The man was getting close now, and his sister said again,
"I say true. Step outside and look at him." So the father said,
"Let's see," and he sent another child outside to see if this was so.
This one said, "She is right. She told the truth. My brother is
coming back here." Now the father and mother stepped outside in
front of their doorway. When he got there, all his family grabbed
him and cried over him because he was home again. That belt he

---

it does not have to be on the exact date of the death, but it comes in the
same month. It is interesting to note that another late innovation in certain
families is the observation of children's birthdays, which it is frankly
admitted is borrowed from the Whites. However the reason why the two
above traits appeal to the Apache may quite readily be explainable in
similar "one year later" practices in the old culture.

[1] Adult close relatives cut the hair off in mourning.

[2] Crying is the common way of expressing sincere grief or other emotion.

[3] The names of the dead or they themselves are never mentioned. For an
unrelated adult to talk of one's deceased relative is a direct affront, ordinarily causing anger. For a child, "who naturally does not know any better,"
to do so may draw forth an admonition from elders, but never abuse.

had brought with him he hid, so no one would see it. His father and
mother and all his relatives asked where he had been, and he told
them the same story as he had told Big Snake. "That's how I got
there and lived among those people. I just left them now and right
away I got here," he told them.

That man lived there quite a while with his people, and then he
thought he would go to where they were playing hoop and poles.
When he got to the hoop and poles ground, the man who had won
everything from him before, sat there. As soon as he saw him, he
said, "ce"ile· (my gaming opponent), I want to play with you now."
But that man said, "I have nothing to bet." So the one who
had been far off let the end of his belt show, just the end of it hanging down. Then the other said, "I want you to bet that belt against
me," so they bet the belt and started to play. This way the one
with the belt won what the other had bet. They kept on till he had
won all the other man's things. "Everything I have, you have
won," he said, "But I want to bet my moccasins against you now."
"All right," the one with the belt said. They played and he won
the moccasins. "Now play for your shirt," he said. He won that
too. "Now bet your hat against me. I want it," he said. They
played, and he won it. "Now that gee string and belt." This was
bet and he won it also. Now he had won all the other man's clothes
and he said, "I want to bet all these against your hair." The other
agreed. They played and he won the hair. So the man who lost took
off all his clothes and also cut his hair short to his head and gave all
this to that man who had come back. The other had to go with no
clothes now. "This is the way they did with me some time ago,"
said the one who came back.

My yucca fruits lie piled up.[1]

---

[1] Francis Drake says that this tale explains the origin of the Lightning songs
which form a part of the Snake ceremony songs. The myth, "He Who
Became A Snake" is the origin of the present Snake ceremony, but Drake
believes that the Lightning songs in the ceremony were known and used
before the part of the ceremony based on "He Who Became a Snake."

Drake's version of Lost with Turkey is as follows: The young man goes
to the place he has seen the fire and finds a dirt-covered dwelling in which
Gray Snake Old Man lives. Gray Snake Old Man puts him through severe
tests (akin to those na·ye'nezγane experienced at the Sun's house), but he
survives them. He then marries Gray Snake Old Man's daughter and takes
her to his farm. She tells him many people (snakes) are in the corn, but
he cannot see them. She enters the field with a basket, turning to a snake
while in there and emerges with a basket full of corn. Gray Snake Old Man
gives his son-in-law a quiver and bow to hunt with. The young man has
a power behind his ear which guides him and instructs him not to eat from
the center of a basket of food brought to him by his wife, for Gray Snake
Old Man has put poison there. He eats from the edge only. While he is in
his wickiup, the power behind his ear tells him to go on top of the dwelling.
He does and just then two snakes come together where he has been below.
He descends and lies on his bed and from there sees the two snakes come
together again on top, where he has just been. They had come to kill him,

10. TURKEY TEACHES FARMING[1]

na·ye'nezɣane was the first one who started to farm. He had two grandsons and two grandaughters who stayed there with him (he was their maternal grandparent). Then he went out and found good ground, where it was soft and damp. He said to himself, "I think I will make a little ditch here." So he sharpened up a digging stick to dig the ditch. He dug along about so far (six feet), loosening the dirt. Then he scooped it out with his hands. Then his four grandchildren came down there to see what he was doing. "What are you trying to do, grandfather? You have nothing you can plant there," they said. "That's all right. Let me do what I want," he said. He dug the ditch toward a spring not far off. He dug it right up to the spring. In the other direction he dug the ditch to the plot of ground below, where he could put in his farm. When the ditch was all done, he used the digging stick to dig out the bushes growing in the field and to prepare the earth. "What are you going to do, grandfather? You have nothing to plant," said his grandchildren. But the old man never answered them at all. He had the field entirely cleaned now. Then he went to the spring and cut the water into the ditch, in this way irrigating his field all over.

In two days he came down to his field again. He just sat there. He had nothing with him at all. In some way he knew that someone would give him some corn. While he sat there, Turkey came to him. "Well, my cross-cousin, what are you going to plant?" said Turkey. "Well, I was just thinking about you giving me something to plant," said na·ye'nezɣane. "I have nothing. You know that I have no farm. But what do you want?" "I want corn. I want 'big corn' (dark red corn)," na·ye'nezɣane answered. "All right," Turkey said and shook himself. Lots of corn of that kind dropped out of him. "Where is your water and where is your basket tray?" Turkey asked him. "It is up at the camp. I will go and get it." While he was gone Turkey shook himself in four different places, so that there were four piles of corn. When na·ye'nezɣane got back, there was lots of corn. Turkey told him to put the corn in the basket with water. "Dont plant too close together, but put the seeds a little way apart. If you put them too close together the corn will not get large, but if placed a little way apart it will," Turkey said.

---

but missed. From there on Gray Snake Old Man gives up trying to kill his son-in-law, and teaches him holy power while he is there: the Lightning songs. Then the young man's wife begs him to take her to his people. They go to the river and she obtains two horses for them to ride to his home. When they come close to his home she warns him not to let his relatives cry over him, also never to maltreat her. If he abuses her, then it will thunder on the top of the hill and that will be she. The two horses sink into the water. They were snakes. They live there and have one child. He later abuses his wife, so she climbs a hill. He hears the thunder and knows she has gone with their child. They never return. They turned to clouds.

[1] Told by Anna Price.

He wished to plant 'big corn' first and the other four kinds of corn
he wrapped up, each separately, and put away. Turkey told him,
"Dont water it when it first comes up small. Wait till it gets about
so high (one foot). You can tell when to water it by digging about
the plant. If the ground is wet underneath a little, dont water it."
Turkey was watching him plant there.

An old woman came to them while they were there. This was
'isdzana·dlę·he (Changing Woman). She said, "I heard that corn
was being given away down here. That's what I came for." But
na·ye'nezɣane said, "I have had this corn a long time." Turkey
spoke, "He must have visited some places where there were farms
and got the corn there. I dont know where he got it. I was just here
watching him plant." But 'isdzana·dlę·he knew all about it. That
was why she had come there. Turkey thought he could fool her, but
he did not fool her. Turkey said to himself, "Well, this woman may
ask me for some corn, so I think I will get away from here," and he
left. But while he had been there watching the planting, he had
said for 'isdzana·dlę·he's benefit, "What is that you are planting
there?" and na·ye'nezɣane had answered him, "It is 'big corn'".
'When will it get ripe?" Turkey asked. Then he left, saying, "I will
come back when it is ripe. You can give me some then."[1]

na·ye'nezɣane had changed himself to a woman. That is the
way he could do. Since he first started working on the farm he
had been in this form. 'isdzana·dlę·he had the power to transform
herself also. 'isdzana·dlę·he asked him for corn, but he said, "I
have none left. I have used it all up." He had some more, but he
did not want to give it up. "Just one handful," she said, but he
refused her any. Finally he gave her half of what he had in the
basket. The same day she planted this seed in a farm she made
across from his farm.

In two more days the grandchildren went over to their grandfather's farm to see what was happening there. "Let's see what
grandfather did over there," they said. When they arrived at the
farm, the corn was all sprouting up. They came back to their
grandfather. "What is that coming up over there, grandfather?
Every hole has something sticking up out of it. What is it? There
are two places like this; one on this side and one on the other side,"
they said. "Don't go in there!" their grandfather told them. The
old man had some corn left still, but he would not let the girls see it.
Somehow they found it and stole it, taking it down to where the old
man had planted. They found the digging stick he had used and
planted some with it. They planted some on the other side of the
river also.

Then 'isdzana·dlę·he moved all her children down to be near the
farms. That is how they became well off and flourished. I am

---

[1] The professed ignorance of Turkey, from whom corn came, is considered a
great joke.

thankful to that old woman for the corn. I wonder where she got it. I think she must have got it from Turkey.

When Turkey had been there, he had told him (na·ye'nezγane), "When it begins to ripen, a small ear will appear on each side of the plant. Then after a while the corn silk will come. When the corn silk dries out, then the corn will be ripe. When the ears get large but are still green, roast them in the fire and eat them. Another way is to grind the corn and make gruel. Still another way is to make corn pudding. As well as this, you can tie up the ripe ears in bunches. You can cook corn in the ground, making corn pudding also. That is the way it will be good. Whenever the ears start to get a little white, dont let anyone get in the field for four days. There is lots of pollen at that time and there will be much danger in the field. Be religiously respectful and don't go in the field then.[1] But after those four days anyone can go in there. When the corn is almost ripe, go after yucca leaves so you can use them in tying the corn into bunches. Make it so there will be five ears on each side when you tie them up. This will make ten ears. Before you pile corn ears up, place four ears of corn on the ground, each one placed so that it points to one of the four directions and all butts pointing to a common center. Now pile your corn on top of these four ears. When you start husking, the first ear that you husk, throw it up so high (about four feet and a half), saying, "Let our pile of corn be so high." When you have done it all, pile your corn up to see how much you have. It will be as high sometimes as you have thrown the first ear. Then after you have tied your corn up in bundles, all that you had in the pile, pull out the four bottom ears that you put there, and tie them together by their husks." Turkey told him all this. Now here is the end of the story.[2]

11. HOW THE SQUASH PLANT WAS OBTAINED[3]

Squash seeds come from frog. A man was running, trying to escape from his wife, who was chasing him. She was djuc'isdza·hn (Vulva Woman, the one who killed men by getting them to

---

[1] Snakes are believed to be gathering the pollen at this time.

[2] This tale is a faithful account of White Mountain Apache farming and the use of corn as a food. All the practices mentioned are duplicated in the culture. Note the mention of getting corn seed from some place where people had farms. When people ran out of seed or wanted some to start a farm with, they visited a relative who had a farm. na·ye' nezγane changing himself into a woman as soon as he started to do the farm work and the fact that the two granddaughters and not the grandsons, stole seed and planted it, is significant of the division of labor between sexes in farming, where women worked in every agricultural process and men only helped in preparation of fields, planting and at times irrigation. The four corn ears placed at the bottom of the pile are always the finest and largest ears, put there to stand for all the corn, that it may be just as perfect as they.

[3] Told by Anna Price.

cohabit with her.) Frog Old Woman was sitting beside a little stream.
The man came to her there. A lot of squash plants were growing at
that place. Frog Old Woman said to the man, "What did you come
over here for ? Dont go in that squash patch, newly married man.
If you go in there the plants might all dry up. Nor may a woman who
is pregnant or menstruating go in a squash patch, for if she does the
plants will all dry up."[1] "But there is a woman running after me.
I want you to put me among the squash leaves and hide me there,
grandmother (maternal grandparent)," the man said. So Frog Old
Woman hid him among the leaves. A little later the woman got
there and asked Frog Old Woman, "Where did that man go ?"
"I have not seen anyone about here. I don't want any woman to
get in my squash plants. Get out of here," Frog Old Woman said
and she pushed her out, "If you go in there my squash plants might
dry up." "I can see the tracks going right into the squash patch
there," the woman said and she circled about the patch looking for
more tracks. But Frog Old Woman said, "You cant find any person
about here. I am going to stay here till dark and watch these
squash plants." But still that woman hung about, looking for the
man's tracks. Finally she went off, following the edge of the creek
to the north, looking for signs of the man.

"Well, that woman has gone quite a way along the creek from
here, so you can come out. On the point below here is where Rock
Squirrel Old Man lives. You see that hole in the rock there, well
that is where he lives. You better go there," said Frog Old Woman.
So the man ran over to the hole. But before he left Frog Old Woman, she gave him squash seeds to plant. She also showed him how
he should plant them. "Dont dig a hole to plant them near a gopher
hole.[2] Plant the seeds about so deep (from wrist joint to outstretched
finger tips). When they are green dont let any pregnant or menstruating women go among them."

When the man got to the hole in which Rock Squirrel Old Man
lived, he entered it. He spoke to Rock Squirrel Old Man as his
maternal grandparent. Rock Squirrel Old Man plastered up the
outside of the hole so no one could see where he had gone in. Then
Rock Squirrel Old Man spoke to him, saying, "My grandson, I am
going to take you home tomorrow. You live to the east, where crops
and ripe fruits are continual."[3] "All right, I wish you would take me
right now," the man said. It was a long way to this man's home,
but Rock Squirrel Old Man said that he was able to have them
arrive there immediately. Next morning they started and arrived

---

[1] A newly married person is not supposed to enter a squash patch lest the
plants wilt and dry.

[2] Gopher would eat them.

[3] This is a figure of speech used, particularly in ritual, to describe a beautiful
land. It is illustrative of the Apache feeling and dependence on farm crops
and wild plant foods.

at the man's home in the early part of the morning. There were some girls gathering walnuts. They had piled them up and were busy pounding off the hulls. One of the girls there was the man's relative. She said, "Oh, my maternal uncle, you have been gone a long time." "How do you know that I am your uncle," asked the man. "My mother told me about you." Rock Squirrel Old Man looked different from these people. The girls looked at him and laughed. "Where did you get that funny man. His eyes stick out," they said. "Don't make fun of him! He saved my life. He is like a chief,"[1] the man told them. Then Rock Squirrel Old Man left and went to his home.

The man's relative showed him where his family was living, "There where the three big ramadas are standing, right at the end," she said. "Well, I will go there, approaching from the other side," the man said. Lots of corn was planted there and he pulled down and broke off one of the stalks. He chewed it as you do sugar cane. Then he came to the place where his mother and sister were. "My younger brother, I have not seen you for a long time," his sister said, and his mother told him, "My child, I have not seen you for a long time." They both wept and cried over him. The mother told his sister, "Cook some corn pudding for him." When it was done he ate till he said, "Take it away, I have had enough. I cannot eat because I have gone so long without food I have no appetite."

This man's mother had told him to marry Vulva Woman, the one who had pursued him. "You should not have done that, mother. I had lots of nice girls, but by marrying her I had a hard time. Rock Squirrel Old Man was the one who saved my life. One girl working below here called me her maternal uncle. Is that the one who used to be just a little girl when I left here?" "Yes, she has moved down that way. It must be she," the mother answered. Then the man told his mother, "My mother, the sweetheart that I used to have here, I could talk well with her. Go and bring her here. I want to marry her. But I will not stay here. I am going to move away." "Wait, my son, not today. In two or three days I will go for her," his mother told him. But never-the-less the next day she went after the girl who was staying with her mother. When she got there, she said, "I came after this girl. I want her for my boy." "Throw my moccasins to me," the girl said to her mother. The girl put on her moccasins saying, "All right, lets go!" for she had loved that man before. The mother brought the girl home with her, and she stayed there all day and that night. The next day the girl returned to her mother and told her what the man had talked of, "This man has a maternal uncle living far off and he wants to move over there with me, his mother and his sister. Their farm down here, with squash planted on it, is to be given to you." The

---

[1] Bounteous and with power, like a chief, is signified here, as well as the importance of Squirrel. "No one laughs at a chief!"

girl went back to the man again. The next day they left, but before
going they sent two horses up to the girl's mother by an old woman.
The old woman told the girl's mother, "Whenever you want to see
your daughter, come up there to where she will be living. There
is a farm down here with corn and squash on it. You can have all
that."

"This is a long way we have to go, but we will make it in one
day," said the father of the man who had just been married. "Carry
some water on the journey, we might need it. My daughter-in-law,
put some water on the horse. We might need it to drink with our
food. We might stop to eat at some place on the way." The man's
uncle, with whom they were going to stay, was a chief. He was a
chief in the tseyi·'dn (in the rocks people) clan.[1] They arrived at his
place the same day that they started.

After they had been there for some time, persons who were not
relatives or of the same clan, started to gossip.[2] "What is the
matter with that chief. He ought to go and kill some deer for his
nephew who has just been married and has brought his wife here to
live. He ought to kill some deer and take the meat down to the girl's
mother."[3] But the tseyi·'dn chief had already sent word about
among members of his clan. The people not related to him did not
know this. The next day one of the chief's nephews (sister's son)
went hunting and killed a deer. This was to be for the people who
had come to live with them. "Go get some corn and squash and
cook them up. Dont let that girl be hungry. Give her plenty to
eat," the chief said. He sent word among his relatives and they
all went out hunting, but the people who were not their relatives
did not know this. Then the chief said to his sister, the mother of
the man, "How did you get your son back? I thought he had
married another woman." "Well, I gave my son to the other girl,
but she was not good, so he is back. He was saved by Frog Old
Woman and Rock Squirrel Old Man, and by his own endurance.
She (Vulva Woman) never caught him."

The chief had told the men who did not go hunting, to gather
together at his camp. When they got there he said, "I made you
all come together because you are all relatives to me. I want you
to help out and do something for this man who is our relative and
who has come here to live with us. If any of you want to throw in a
horse, just send it over. I have a horse, but it is the only one I own,
so I cannot put him in. Bring your horses in if you want, at the end

---

[1] This is not a White Mountain clan, but two clans in the group are said to
have originated from it.

[2] This tale contains an excellent example of the customary procedure
accompanying marriage of well-to-do people. Poorer people could not
afford such displays, both from lack of property and lack of kin to help
them.

[3] Petty gossip such as this is very common camp talk, especially among
women. It serves to delineate cultural opinion, though it is not condoned.

of two days, when the men out hunting will be back." In this way three horses were put up and in two days the meat that the hunters brought in was to be sent with these horses to the old woman at the farm, the mother of the girl who had married the young man. It was the father of the young man who would send this all down to her. In two days time the hunters returned with a big load of deer meat. They unpacked all this at the camp of the man's father. Then the chief said to this old man, "These horses are too tired to go on, so in the morning we will pack up the three horses that are going to be given away and take the meat down on them." "All right, thank you, my brother-in-law," the old man said.

So they packed up the three horses and there was lots of meat on them. The two horses ridden by the persons taking the meat down were also packed with meat. This made five loads of meat. When the two men arrived at the girl's mother's camp, they unpacked the loads. The old woman sent word about among the camps for people to come and get some of the meat. When all the people had come together at her camp, she spread a deer hide on the ground and put meat on it, giving this to a man. But she gave only to the men who were good hunters.[1] With each gift of meat to a man, went one deer hide. The two men who had brought the horses down, stayed there all night and next morning returned home.

In about three days the old woman, mother of the girl, started to call from her camp, "Come on, come on, come on. I am asking you to go for a walk (she meant hunting)," she said. "All right, all right, all right," the men said, "Let's go!" "I have stayed here a long time among you and am your relative," the old woman told them. So the men went out hunting for her. In about four or five days they came back bringing a lot of meat. All this was given to the old woman. "There is meat, lots of meat for you," they said. But there were no horses. She had given away the three horses sent to her and had not received any in return yet. One of her brothers was living close by. He came to her and asked, "How many horses have you got?" "I have no horses. I gave three away, but have received none back." So her brother told her, "Why didn't you tell me? I will go about and get horses." So he went about among the people and got three horses. Packing the three horses with meat and riding two more also loaded with meat, the old woman's husband and one boy took all to where their daughter was now living. They spent the night there and next morning the people did exactly the same as the girl's mother had done. It was as if the men who had gone hunting in the beginning, received their meat back. The girl said to her father, "Father, I wish you would come over here. I am lonesome for my relatives." · "Well, I don't know. I have to tend the corn over there. But I can give half of the corn to your

---

[1] Because she would rely on them to go hunting and get deer for her.

brother and half to your uncle and then come back here," he told
her. "All right," the girl said.

He went back to his home that day. The next day he spoke to
the people there, "Well, people, I have been a long time with you.
Now I'm going to move over to where my daughter is. This is why
I have to go. There is a good patch of corn and squash here, so I'm
going to give it to my daughter's distant maternal uncle and one of
her distant brothers. The ditches and land are in good condition.
I am going up there to live with my daughter." "All right. That is
up to you. She is your daughter," they said. So the old man and
his family moved to where his daughter was living. The day after
they arrived there, their son-in-law's mother came to them and
said, "There is a lot of corn and squash down below here. It has
all been given to my daughter-in-law. So you can help yourselves
to it all you want." The tseyi·'dn chief had given it all to this
woman's new daughter-in-law.[1]

Then they gathered up the squash lying on the ground. They set
them down a little way apart from each other. If you place squash
too close to each other they will get rotten. For this reason they
packed dry grass between them where they stored them away,
putting the same over them to shelter them. That man who had
been saved by Frog Old Woman, had shown the people how to plant
the squash seeds he had brought home with him. From that time
on our people had squash and that was how we first got them.

---

[1] Notice how the functioning relatives in this marriage are stressed. The
man's mother makes the request to the girl's mother for the girl. The man
chooses to take his wife and parents to live with a maternal uncle who is a
chief, because of the kinship involved as well as the desire to ally himself
with the local group of a rich and influential man. He depends to great
extent on this chief, his maternal uncle, in Apache thought the closest
(excepting his father) of all male blood relatives because of obligations
involved. The chief's sister's son (again a maternal nephew) is sent out to
hunt deer by his uncle, typical of existing practices where a man will send
his sister's son on a mission almost as quickly as his son, and where the
obligations are strong. Important is the fact that though the greater part
of the gifts are from the man's mother's close kin, when the gift is made to
the girl's parents it is nominally from the man's father, though everyone
knows others are involved. When the girl's mother lacks horses for the
return gift to the man's family, her brother is the one who quite typically
helps her out. When the girl becomes lonely away from her parents, she
requests that they come to live near her. Though matrilocal residence was
the more common, patrilocal residence and the presence of the wife's
parents at the same time was not uncommon, especially when the daughter
was an only child. When the girl's parents move to be near her, they give
the farm they had to a parallel cousin and a distant maternal uncle of the
girl, just such relatives as might receive it in real life. On reaching their
daughter's new home, they are graciously approached by the man's mother,
who puts at their disposal many farm products.

12. *HE WHO BECAME AN ANTELOPE[1]

Long ago a man went off hunting somewhere. He did not return for a whole year and no one knew where he was. He had a wife and two sons and one daughter, still children. When he did not come back, his brother married his wife and lived with her and the three children.[2]

Now all the people went off to hunt deer and make jerkey. Where this jerkey camp was the people killed lots of deer and had lots of meat to dry, but the man who had married his brother's wife could kill no deer at all. All the other people got enough meat and moved home again. This man had killed no deer and so he stayed on with his family. He tried hunting, but he could see no deer at all. One day, up in a flat park, he saw an antelope and started to crawl toward it. But the antelope would not let him get close, so he came on back to his camp. His wife was out gathering nadji·djitsige (an edible seed) and only the three children were in camp.

When the man got back, he found the children with grease rubbed all over them. He asked the children who had put grease on them that way. "Our father brought this hind quarter to us and cooked it for us. That's the way he told us to put grease on ourselves," the children said. That antelope the man had tried to get close to was the father of these children. He told the children that it was he whom their stepfather had tried to crawl to and said to them, "I want you to tell your stepfather to go back to the same place where he saw that antelope, tomorrow. If he does this, I am going to show him what he is looking for. If he kills a deer tell him he must not butcher it there, but must put it on his shoulder and go back to camp with it." The children told all this to their stepfather, but he could not understand how it could be, so he went back to the same place the next day to see what would happen. When he got there he saw the same antelope and at the same time the antelope saw him and started to come towards him. He had to come up over a little grassy ridge and when he got there, there was a big blacktailed deer following him. The man killed the deer right there and carried it back to camp on his shoulder without butchering it, as he had been told to do.

The father of the children had told them to tell their stepfather to go back to the same place four times. So the next day he went back again. There he saw the same antelope and as soon as the antelope saw him, he started to come towards him. Two big blacktailed deer were following behind the antelope. When they got close, the man killed them. Then he put one on each shoulder, whole,

---

[1] Told by Palmer Valor. "This story was told me by my uncle, na·γinłt'a' of the na·dohots'usn clan (a chief). He was a shaman. One time he wanted to bet a rifle that he could take the leg bone of a horse, lay it on a rock and smash it with his fist. But no one would take him up on it."

[2] The common practice of keeping a widow in her first husband's family.

and went back to camp. The third day he went to the same place again, and the antelope was there. It turned and came towards him. It went by a patch of thick brush and out of this came three big black-tailed deer and followed behind. When they got close, the man shot and killed the three deer. He packed all three back to camp whole. As soon as he skinned the deer there, their hides turned to buckskin. There was only one day left. He went back the fourth time, up on the hill to the same place, and there was the same antelope. When the antelope saw him, he turned and came over towards him. Behind the antelope there came four big black-tailed deer. The man killed all four of the deer and put two on each shoulder and carried them back to camp.

Now he told his wife, "I want you to fix that meat up well and cut it thin." Then the man worked on the hides.

Pretty soon the father of the children came to them and told his children, "I want your stepfather to go home and trade with his buckskins. When you get home, tell all the people about this. I want you to tell them also to make bị·bina·dn'a‘ (deer his stick)[1] so that it stands up as tall as you are when you stand, a little taller than you. Then, while you are there, I want you to put in four parts black jet, turquoise, red stone[2] and white shell beads. Fill a łe·ts'a· (kind of basket) with them. Then tell them to start making beads. Make enough so that when they are strung the black jet, turquoise, red stone and white shell beads will be as tall as the bị·bina·dn'a‘. Then I want all the people to go there. This is the way you must do it," he told them.

Then that family started home and came to where the other people were living. When the man had traded his buckskins, they started to do what they had been told to do. The wife and children turned to antelope. The children said, "We are going to travel in other places with the antelope. When you see antelope traveling and one of them whistles, then that one will be I." It was the same way with the female deer. The youngest always goes with its mother. "Now, I want the children to go by the bị·bina·dn'a‘ and when they are standing by it, they must keep their arms straight at their sides and down," said the children's father. The children went under bị·bina·dn'a‘ and went round it. Around them were running big black-tailed buck deer, and female black-tailed deer in a circle on each side. That's the way they were to do.

"Now I want all the people to make a corral for the deer, a big circle of brush. Make the gate of it from young juniper so you can close it. When it is all finished, go to the east side of it and touch your foot to the ground there (scrape the earth a little with ball of foot)," he told them (the father of the children). There was a little white mound on the east side of the corral, and he touched his foot

---

[1] A ceremonialy decorated pole for deer. It is mythical only.
[2] A material similar in appearance to catlinite.

to the ground there as told. Then when he did this, the earth rumbled, di+, gą+, like that, and lots of dust came up out of it as if blown by the wind. After that lots of antelope came out from that place. In the front, leading them, was big deer. He was hollering as he went. Now all came to the corral and when they got in, they closed the gate of young juniper. Where the bį·bina·dn'a' was, the three youngest deer were under it, because before they started this that's the way they had said they would do. The man and his wife were going around that place. "I don't want you to kill them, they are the ones who are doing this," they said. Then they started to kill all the deer in the corral. Then he told them, "I want you to butcher all the deer on their right side and take out the sinew there from their backs." They did this way and took the sinew out on the right side of all of the deer. Then when all the deer had been killed, those other four deer had run off somewhere and were not there.

"Now take that sinew and lay it on the ground in four places to the east, four parts of sinew. Then touch this on the ground with your foot in four places," he told them. He did like this and laid the sinews in four places to the east. Then he went and touched them with his foot one time, and lots of antelope came out there and ran off toward the north. The second time he touched his foot, lots of antelope came out. It was the same the third time also. The fourth time he touched with his foot lots of antelope came out and went off toward the northwest.

This is the old White Mountain Apache story[1] about the time when those people were turned to antelope, and I guess they are still living with the antelope to this day. These people who were turned to antelope were that man who married his brother's wife, the wife, and the children. This family were ba·tci· Indians (Apache Mansos), the ones that are living over by Tucson now. They are Indians as we are and are like us.

No one knows how to make bį·bina·dn'a' now. It was a pole set in the ground, straight up, and a little higher than I am, I guess, and that's all I know.

13. *HE FELL DOWN ON BEAR[2]

Long ago they say. There were some people living in a place. One time they went out hunting in the winter. There was snow on the ground, lots of it, about three feet deep. There was a big rock and one of the hunters saw it and climbed up on top of it. Under this rock there was a bear den. The rock was very slippery all over and the man fell off it and into the bear den. When he fell down he landed right on the bear who was living in the den. So the bear got up and

---

[1] It is closely connected with Antelope power and ritual.
[2] Told by Bane Tithla. This is the origin myth of the Bear ceremony. Compare Goddard, ibid pp. 136—137.

sat with the man. This did not happen long ago. It happened to a
man who used to live here.

Then the bear asked the man, "How did you get here ?" The man
answered, "I started out to hunt and got up on this rock to look
around. Then I slipped and fell down here in this hole." Then the
bear said that he had never seen a man at this place before, that no
one had ever come here. So he told the man that he should stay with
him. When it came evening, the bear asked him if he wanted to eat.
The man said, " I would like to eat, but there is nothing." "Well,
what do you want to eat," the bear said. "I eat xuctcoꞌ (a cactus
fruit)," he said. Then the bear shook himself, and out of his coat
fell lots of xuctcoꞌ. The man ate these, and then it was evening.
Now the bear said it was time to go to bed and so they did. About
midnight the bear asked the man if he was cold and the man said
that he was. Then the bear told him to lie down close against him.
This way the man kept warm and slept all the rest of the night.

When they got up in the morning, the bear asked him if he wanted
to eat. He said yes, but that there was nothing. So the bear shook
himself and lots of juniper berries fell out of his coat. They ate
these together. The two stayed in the den all day. When it came
sunset, the bear said, "Do you want to eat ?" The man answered
that he would like to eat, but there was nothing there. Then the
bear shook himself and out from his coat fell lots of xucnk'u·je (a
cactus fruit). They ate these together. After this they went to bed.
The bear thought that the man would be cold during the night, so
he put him right between his legs where he would keep warm. In
the morning they got up and the bear asked the man if he wanted
to eat. "I would like to eat, but there is nothing," he said. Then
the bear shook himself and out of his coat fell lots of piñon nuts.
They ate these together.

This way the bear and the man lived there in the den together
for about a year,[1] till it came to the month of small leaves (cor-
responds to March) and then the bear went out and stayed in a
warm sunny place. Then he came back to the man and said that he
smelt xa"itc'i·gełba·ye (a plant said to be first to come up in spring),
and that was a sign that spring was come. Then the bear made
a hat, and put in his time working on it. It was getting warmer.
Then the bear had his hat finished and he said to the man, "You
will know me by this one, wherever I go." The two started off together. The bear went up on a mountain and the man followed him.
He told the man that there was another bear living on the other side
of the mountain and that they were going to visit him. He said to
the man, "When we see this bear, don't get scared." Then the two
came close to where the other bear was living. That other bear
knew that they were coming. When they were near, he ran out at

---

[1] Probably an error and should read "a month or more".

them and went for the man. When he did this, the first bear told the man to get close to him and he would be safe. So when the second bear ran after the man, he got behind the first bear. When he was just about to be caught, he ran around on the other side of the first bear. The second bear stopped and started to laugh at the man.

Now they all sat there and talked with each other. "It is springtime," they said. Then the first bear told the man that they were going around to where other bears were living and about to make a dance. So the second bear told them to follow him, and they started off. The first bear told the man that there was another bear living behind the mountain and that they were going to visit him. This way they traveled together, sometimes trotting and sometimes walking. The bear who had the hat wore it so that the man would know him. He had told the man not to get scared when they came to the third bear, but to just get behind him. Now they were close to where that third bear lived. He knew that they were coming. Then the third bear saw them and ran out at them. He was just about to catch the man, when he ran back of his friend and got away. The third bear sat down and started to laugh at the man. That bear had just run after the man for fun and would not have hurt him at all. Then they stopped and talked together. They said that they were going to where there were lots of bears living.

Then they set out together. On their way, whenever they got hungry, they shook themselves and food fell out. This way they had lots to eat. After they had been traveling a while, the man gave out, so the first bear told him to get on his back. Then they were heading for another mountain. The bears told the man that there was another bear living behind this mountain, and for him not to get scared and run off when they came there. This fourth bear knew that they were coming, so he came out on a level place. When they got near to him, he ran out at the man. The bear chased the man and he ran behind the first bear. This fourth bear sat down and started to laugh at the man. Then the fourth bear said, "He thought that I was going to catch him and he got scared. That is why I am laughing at him."

Then they stopped and talked together. That man had made up a song as they traveled along, and it went this way, "I go on your back, you run with me wherever I go," and he sung this song when he rode on the bear's back. He had made up another song when they had first started out. It went this way, "We are going some place wherever we go." From that place they all started out again. The bears said that they were going to another mountain where another bear stayed. On there way the man gave out again, so he got on the back of the bear. Then he started to sing, "You go with me wherever I go." This fifth bear knew that they were coming before they got there and so he came out of his home. Then they were all coming

7*

together when the fifth bear ran out at the man. The man knew the first bear by the hat that he wore, so he ran behind him. The fifth bear chased him around and pretty nearly caught him. Then he sat down and started to laugh at the man. He said, "He got a bad scare because he thought that I was going to catch him. That is why I am laughing at him."

Then the bears told the man that they were going on to another mountain where lots of bears were living. So they all traveled on together. The bears to whom they were going knew that they were coming, and so they all met together at that place. Then all the bears were at that one place. They started to dance. The first bear talked to the man, and told him that he would always know him by the hat that he wore. This way the man was able to tell his friend. He kept close to him all the time. They danced all night, and the man stayed close to his friend. While the bears danced they made lots of songs. The man heard these song and learned them. The next night the bears held their dance again. The man was there and watched them. On the third night they had the dance again. When the fourth night came they held the dance also. The man was there all the time and he learned all the songs that they sung. The bears made lots of songs for that man.

After the dance was over, the bear who was the man's friend said that they would go home now. They started off. When they had traveled some way the man gave out. He got up on the bear's back and they went along thus. They came back to the den the man had fallen into from above. Then the bear said to the man; "This is the same day, just one year ago, that you came here to me. So I want you to go back to your people this day." The bear started off with him and showed him where his old home was. There he left him. This man had been gone for one year. None of his people knew where he was. They had looked for him for one year. Then he came back to his family. When his people saw him coming they were glad, because he had been off for a long time. When he got back, his father and mother and his relatives cried over him, because they were glad to see him back again.

That man was living with his people once more. Then he told them what had happened to him. "I was out hunting and there was lots of snow. A bear hole was there, but I didn't see it, I fell into it. I fell right into where a bear was living. Then I lived with that bear a long time." The man told the story to all the people. He went on and told how the bear had shaken himself and four kinds of foods had fallen out; how they had lived on these fruits. "In the night I slept between his legs. That way I kept warm. Then one day the bear went outside. When he came back he said that he had smelt xaⁿitc'i·gełba·ye and that it was spring time. When it got a little warmer I went with him to where there were other bears," and he told about meeting the five bears. "All the bears had a dance that lasted four nights." Now the man sang all the songs that he had learned from the bears. "After the fourth night of the dance, I came away with the bear. Then this day the bear told me that I was to go back to my home. This is how we came back here. When we got close the bear went back and left me. This is the way I got back here." Then that man had told all about what had happened to him. He got used to being with his people once more.

My yucca fruits lie piled up.

14. *THE TALKING HORSE[1]

Up north our people were living. Some 'inda· (enemies, apparently Mexican or Spanish) came over to our country and fought us. When they started to fight us, all our people ran away and escaped. Just one youth was left. He thought he could save himself by hiding in a thick growth of wild canes. But the enemy set fire to the cane patch and burnt him out. When he ran out, they caught him. They started home with him, to the south. They traveled for about ten days before they reached their home. When they arrived there they locked the youth up. He stayed there for six months or so. Then on a Sunday morning one of the enemy soldiers took him out. He gave him a horse and the soldier rode a horse also. They just played about with the horses. The soldier had a pistol. They used to do this every Sunday, because the soldier liked the Apache. In this way they became good friends. The horses they rode could talk.

Then this soldier came there on a Saturday and told the Apache that they would play again the next day. He also told him that he was going to cache a sack full of food and plates to eat off, up on the hill in a place where he could get it. "The horse also knows where it is. You have had a hard time here, locked up for about six months, so I am going to help you. This is why I am telling you," the soldier said. Then on Sunday morning the soldier took him out. He told the Apache, "When I take you out and you start to run your horse, I am going to fire my pistol." When they went out together, the Apache got his horse quite a distance from the soldier and then started to make a run for it. The soldier followed him, pretending to pursue and fired his pistol off over his head in order not to hit him. Both horses were equally fast and kept an even distance apart. When they had gone about as far as from here to the foot of Turnbull Mt. (eight miles), the soldier gave it up and returned.

Then the horse told the Apache, "Here is the sack of food. Put it on me and we will go on, but don't go fast. Just go at a good steady pace. Dont cinch me up too tight." The horse ate out of the man's dishes. Man and horse traveled along all that night. The

---

[1] Told by Francis Drake.

next day the horse told him, "There are people following us, so we must go on." They traveled on all the next night. The next day the horse told him, "Go to sleep for a while here and get some rest." After a while the horse woke him and told him that people were still following them, so they must go on. The reason that the people had followed them all this distance, was in order to get their horse back. He was a good horse. They traveled on all that night again. The following day the horse told the man, "Go to sleep for a spell." Then he woke him up after a while and said, "There are people following us still." So they traveled on. In this way they had traveled four nights and days. Then the horse told him to go to sleep again.[1]

In a while the horse woke the man up and told him, "There are still hard times ahead of us." He meant that they were to meet a lot of bears on their way. These bears were the soldiers of the enemies who were following them. They were all black bears, but when the man came to them, he passed through them without harm, because they had not yet heard about him and that he was being pursued. They traveled all that night and next day they came to a place where there were many blue bears, walking back and forth across the trail. But they passed through them safely. They traveled on all the following night and again they came the next day to many yellow bears walking back and forth across the trail. But they got by them without harm. They traveled on all that night and again on the following day they came to many white bears walking back and forth across the trail. They passed through them without mishap. In this way the enemies had pursued him for four days and it was as if the bears had been after him for four more days.

Then the horse told him, "We are out of dangerous places now, so we can go slowly." They came to the place where the enemy had captured the man and he pointed it out to the horse, telling him how he was taken prisoner. There was lots of cane growing at that place. The horse did not eat any grass or plants. He only ate of the food from the enemy, in the sack. He asked the man, "Are you married?" "No, I am not married," the man replied. "Well, don't get married. If you do it will be the end of things between you and me," the horse told him.

Then they arrived home. As the man rode towards camp, one of his sisters saw him and said; "There is my brother coming." But her mother said, "No, he will never come. He has been killed long ago." The little girl told her, "No, that is he coming for sure." All his family had cut their hair off short, in mourning for him, but it had grown to their shoulders again. It was a year since the man had been taken by the enemy. The man unsaddled the horse and

---

[1] This description is the normal return from a raid into Mexico.

tied him to a tree. After a while he told one of his sisters to water the horse, so the little girl led the horse down to the river and said "tch, tch, tch," to him. That is the way to urge a horse to drink. The horse would not drink. Then the horse said, "I never drink that way. I always drink out of a pan." The little girl was frightened. She had never heard a horse talk before. She ran home crying. When she got there, they asked her what was the matter and she told them what the horse had said to her. "Oh, I forgot to tell you that the horse talks," said the man. Now the girl took a pan down to the horse to drink out of. He drank and she brought him back and tied him up again.

In a short while the man's family came to dislike the horse, because he ate too much food. They said, "This horse should not eat food. He should eat grass." In about one month a girl came to see the man. He sat up with this girl all night. The next morning the girl was gone and he went out to see his horse. He wanted to water him, but the horse would not come to him. "You stink too much," the horse said. He did not like the girl. Because of this the horse would not drink with the man for three days. All this time his sister had to look after the horse, water and feed him. The man felt badly about his horse. The following day he went to where his horse had been tied, but he found only the rope there. The horse was gone, leaving no tracks by which he could follow him.

This man had a turquoise flute. He blew on it and in this way traveled with it over to the top of a big blue mountain. On this mountain top he found the tracks of his horse. From there he could see another mountain, far off. He blew on his flute and traveled to the top of the second mountain. There he found the tracks of his horse again. A third great mountain lay far off beyond. He blew on his flute and arrived on top of the mountain. Here were the tracks of his horse as before. Far off was a fourth great mountain. He did the same as before and traveled to its top. At this last place he found the tracks of his horse leading off. He was able to follow them. In a little way his horse came to him and talked with him: "Well, there is nothing to be done now. You can't take me back. I have been to my old home and eaten food there already. For this reason I can't go back with you. I told you not to have anything to do with a girl, but you stayed with a girl all night. When you get home, go and look for a place where there are four ridges coming together from the four directions. If you find such a place, put a halter on the east one and put a rope on the south side; put a saddle on the west side and on the north side put a saddle blanket. Then leave these things there for four days. Don't go back during that time." The man cried over his horse, because he could not have him back.

The man returned home and found the place where four hills ran together, as he had been told. He placed the things on the four sides. Then at the end of four days he went to them to see what had happened. He arrived there.

> Big black cockle burr beside dark sand had thus become.
> Big blue cockle burr beside blue sand had thus become.
> Big yellow cockle burr beside yellow sand had thus become.
> Big white cockle burr beside white sand had thus become.
> Exactly in the center cottonwood tree towering up had thus become.

He went back home. In another four days he returned. This time he found the tracks of colts on all four sides. He went back home. In four days more he came to that place again. Then he heard the neighing of stallions, stallions on all four sides, but he saw nothing. He returned home. On his next visit he found lots of horse dung under the cottonwood tree. Then in four more days he came back to that place. This time, on the east there was a black stallion, on the south a blue stallion, on the west a yellow stallion and on the north a white stallion. Then on all four sides there arose dust from running horses. This is the end of the story. It was this man who first acquired the horse power and ceremony and this was how he got it.[1]

15. *HE RELEASES THE DEER[2]

In the old times all the animals acted like men. They all started out to hunt one time. Raven was along with them also. After a while they killed a deer and made a fire to cook some of the meat. But they did not give any meat to Raven; they just ate it themselves. Raven was sore about it. Then they told him, "Go over there where the deer blood has run on the ground. That is good for you to eat. We are not hunting for you." Then Raven got mad because they gave him no meat, and so he went off home.

When Old Man Raven got home, his children asked him where the deer meat was. He told them, "When those people killed a deer, they told me to go away and that is why I came home." Old Man Raven started to think about what they had done to him. "I am smart, I can do smart things as well as the rest," he said. Then he herded all the black-tailed deer together, all over, and drove them down to a place under the earth. There he had made a hole for them. When they were all in, he closed the entrance with a door of jet. Then he herded together all the white-tailed deer and drove them under the earth into another hole. When they were all in, he closed the entrance with a door of turquoise. Next he herded to-

---

[1] The episode "na·ye'nezɣane Obtains Horses" is also referred to as the origin of horse power.

[2] Told by Palmer Valor. Also called "Concerning Raven Old Man and Deer." Compare Goddard, ibid pp. 126—127.

gether all the mountain sheep and drove them under the earth. He closed the entrance with red stone. Then he went out and herded all the antelope together and drove them to that place under the earth. He closed the entrance with a door of white shell beads. This was what Old Man Raven did.

Then the other people could not find deer anywhere over the earth. na·ye'nezγane turned himself into a fly, as he could change himself to anything and this way he could go any place. He flew to where Old Man Raven was sitting and lit right on his beak. Pretty soon he came back and told the others, "My friends, Old Man Raven's lips smell of deer tallow." Then na·ye'nexγane talked about all this. He said, "I want you all to move this camp to a different place. I will change myself to a little puppy and I think the Raven children will come here after you leave, and pick me up."

Then all the people moved away, and na·ye'nezγane changed himself to a little puppy. Pretty soon the Ravens came to this old camp as they always do come to any camp that has just been abandoned. The Raven children saw the puppy and picked him up and took him home to Old Man Raven's camp. The Raven children said, "My father, we have found a puppy and we want to take it to tse·dadet'aha (rock plugged up)."[1] Then Old Man Raven got angry at his children and wanted to know where tse·dadet'aha was anyway. About evening their father wanted to see the puppy. They brought him to their father. Old Man Raven took a burning stick and stuck it in the puppy's eyes. Then the puppy ran around yelping. They left for tse·dadet'aha within four days.

When they got there, they all went down into the earth. On one side Old Man Raven took down the jet door and grabbed out the biggest black-tailed deer. On the other side he took down the turquoise door and grabbed out a white-tailed deer. The puppy was right there. Then on the other side Old Man Raven took down the red stone door and grabbed out a mountain sheep and then the white shell door and grabbed out an antelope. These four they killed. They gave the puppy lots of meat to eat. They all had lots of meat.

In four days they were back in Raven's camp again. The puppy lay down close to Old Man Raven's face, as he was resting. In a little he reached over and licked Old Man Raven's mouth. "Phew, you just ate a lot of meat!" Old Man Raven said, and he took the puppy and threw him outside. As soon as he was outside, the puppy started back to the other people.

When na·ye'nezγane got to them, he told how Raven had all the deer hidden under the earth; on one side a door of jet, on another side a door of red stone, on another side a door of white shell, and on another, a door of turquoise. Then he said to them, "We had better look for canes to make arrows with." They made their arrows, but

---

[1] Where the animals were confined. A hole in the rock there was plugged with another rock.

put no feathers on them, only the hardwood for-shafts. "Now we will go to that place," na·ye'nez·γane said. When they got there, he told four men to stand by the jet door, four men to stand by the turquoise door, four men to stand by the red stone door, and four men to stand by the white shell door. When they were all ready, they took down the four doors and all the deer, antelope, and mountain sheep started to run out. Then it rumbled on the earth like thunder. As the deer ran out the men stood there and shot them. It did not matter what part of the body they hit them in, ears, legs, tail, anywhere, it killed them. Then Slim Coyote called out, "'iti·naɫnda (wounded, one got away), I will trail it tomorrow."[1] Right then the deer did not die when you hit them any place. You had to shoot them in the heart to kill them. That was the only vital place.

Then Old Man Raven woke up and said to his wife, "I want you to make the deer so they can scent things a long way off." His wife took a part of her clothing from between her legs, and touched the deer's noses with it.[2] "This way I will help you so you can smell danger a long way off and run away," she said. That is why deer can scent things so far off.

16. *SHE WHO BECAME A DEER[3]

Long ago they say. There to the north lots of people were living. At that place there were boys and girls going together. One couple got married. After they were married, the husband set out to hunt deer. That man had a deer head, and also a shirt to go with it. If he saw a deer he would put this deer head on and the deer shirt. Then he put his bow and arrows inside his shirt, against his breast.[4] He also had made some big deer tracks, just like a deer's foot. Of female deer he had feet like this also. When this man went out to hunt deer, he left the deer tracks at home, but he took the shirt and stalking head with him. If he saw a deer and put on his shirt and head, he could go to it. He would go around with the big deer and the deer would just look at him. He went on the side where the wind was not blowing, so the deer would not smell him. There he would go around, working closer and closer all the time while the deer just looked at him. The deer would think he was only a real deer and would not run off. Then the man would go straight to the deer and as he went he moved his head from side to side, this way.

---

[1] At this point men listening to the tale not uncommonly comment in disgust and anger on Coyote's misdeed.

[2] This also causes the listeners disgust.

[3] Told by Bane Tithla. This sacred tale connected with the deer ceremony, is also called "The Maiden who Became a Deer". compare Goddard, ibid pp. 127—128.

[4] Stalking deer and antelope in this manner was fairly common.

He put his hands down in front, straight, and as he went he never turned but kept facing the deer all the time. Then when he was close, about forty feet, he stopped, took out his arrow and bow and when the deer was looking down, shot him. After he had killed the deer he brought him home and gave him to his father-in-law.[1] This same man, if he saw a doe, put on a doe head and shirt. Then he would go to the doe, always walking with his head down so that the doe would think he was eating. When he got close, he bent down, and when the doe did the same he took out his bow and arrow and shot her. When he had killed her, he took her home to his father-in-law. Now this man and his relatives were eating lots of deer meat. The man's father-in-law liked this and also all the relatives were glad, because they had lots of meat. If this man hunted antelope out on the level plains, he would put on his head and shirt when he saw an antelope and go straight to it. Even if the antelope saw him they would not run away. The man would go slowly toward the antelope and when he got close he would pull out his arrow and bow and shoot the antelope. After he had killed him he took him from that place to his father-in-law's camp, first butchering him. This man had brought meat to all these people, and because of this they all liked him.[2] That is the way these people were living.

Then that man saw many deer in another country, so he told his wife to get ready and go with him. He went to that country and made camp there. In the morning he talked to his wife this way, "There are no people living here, and I am going to hunt where there are lots of deer. I will come back here in the afternoon. You stay here and don't be afraid." Then the man started off to hunt. About mid-morning someone came to his wife in the camp. This was Dark ga·n.[3] The woman sat on her bed and Dark ga·n sat by her. Then that woman started to cook. There was lots of deer meat and she was cooking this together with some ground corn. When the cooking was done, the woman took it off the fire for Dark ga·n to eat it, but Dark ga·n said that he had never eaten this kind of food and so he would not eat it. So the woman picked the food up and put it back. Then Dark ga·n said, "Get some mountain mahogany and k'į·ntc'i'[4] (a shrub) and put them in a basket here by me. That is my food." This man (Dark ga·n) had on a deer head and a deer shirt. Now he took off the deer head and put it by the basket, and the deer head started eating the mountain mahogany and k'i·ntc'i'. Just that deer head ate it all.

---

[1] A man, especially when recently married, was expected to give the greater part of the game he killed to his parents-in-law. Until his wife bore her first or second child, he actually worked for his parents-in-law in the sense that continual gifts were expected from him.

[2] It is often remarked of a generous man, "That man gives meat to everyone. That's the kind of man people like."

[3] Or Black ga·n, a supernatural always associated with deer ceremonies. ga·n are a class of supernatural beings, comparable to the Pueblo kachina.

[4] Deer brouse on these plants.

It was about afternoon now and that man started to talk to the woman. He had a doe shirt and head with him there also. He told the woman, "All the deer get wild when I go close. Even if I put on my deer shirt they always run from me." Then he said, "Let me see you put on that shirt. Maybe it is crooked, so put it on and I will see if it looks straight on you." But the woman said no. Then he told her just to put on the hat for a little while, so he could see how it looked. "No," said the woman. "But just do it for a little while," he said, "it won't hurt you."[1] The woman would not do it and so the man told her to just stand there and hold the deer hat, facing him, so he could see if there was anything wrong with it. But the woman would not. "It won't harm you, so just hold it there for a little while and it will be all right." The woman thought to herself, "There can be no harm in holding it for just a little while, so I will do it." She took it up as he said and when she did so that man threw a deer foot at her. The foot hit the woman in the side and as it did that the deer head that she was holding covered her head and the deer shirt went over her body. She started to jump around like a deer and she whistled just like a deer, as she looked at the man there. Then the man put on his own deer head and deer shirt and became a real deer. He went to the woman's side. Then they both ran off.

In the morning they went together to Black Jet Mountain. At that place those two played together. There were lots of deer there and those two went right among them. Further on was another mountain, Turquoise Mountain, and those two went there and played together. They went right in the midst of many deer there. From that place the two went to Red Stone Mountain, and played together there. They went right among many deer that were there. They went straight to them. Then to the north was White Shell Bead Mountain and to that place they went next. They started to play there. There were four places on the other side then, and there these two lived together.

Back at the camp that the woman left, her husband returned. It was late afternoon. He looked all around but he could not find his wife anywhere. The woman was not there at all. He went all around the camp but he could not find her tracks anywhere. So he just left there and went back to his own people at home. There he told the people that when he left his wife to go off hunting, he had come back in the afternoon and could not find her anywhere. He could find no tracks of hers going off anywhere, though he had looked all afternoon. The only sign of anything were lots of deer tracks around the camp, all going off to the east. Then the people said, "Let's go back to that place and look again for that woman."

[1] It is said that for one who does not have the power and ritual knowledge for stalking heads to put on or handle one, may result in insanity or other misfortune. Consequently laymen used discretion.

The ga·n people were there and to them the people gave jet, turquoise, red stone, and white shell[1] in order that they would get help from them. They all started out. Wolf was there and Mountain Lion also, both going along with the people. That woman's mother and father went along too. This way they came to the camp. Then the man said, "Here is the place that we stayed all night, and from here I started out to hunt in the morning." They looked all around the camp, but could not find the woman's tracks. The only place where her tracks showed at all was right in the camp. Outside the camp there were only deer tracks, lots of them all around. The deer had been playing about there and the people could see the tracks leading off to the east.

All the people set off to the east now, following the deer tracks. The deer had been playing on their way, and it was not hard to follow them. Then to the east was Jet Hill Running Across, and the people went to it. From that place they sent the woman's father and mother back home. Only Wolf and Mountain Lion and the ga·n people and the woman's husband stayed to follow the tracks.[2] This way there were only four parties now. There were many tracks and Mountain Lion was the only one who knew which were the woman's. This way he could follow that woman. There were many deer in those four places where the woman had gone, but the ones who were following kept on and went to each of those four mountains. There where they were following the tracks Mountain Lion was the only one who could tell the right ones. On the other side of Jet Mountain was Turquoise Mountain. There were lots of deer tracks and they all went straight ahead. The people kept on past all the other deer tracks, still following the woman. They came to Red Stone Mountain and there were lots of deer there. But still the deer had kept on playing from that place toward White Shell Mountain where they followed them. Then in one place there were lots of deer, in four parts in the shape of a cross.[3] To this place the people followed that woman's tracks. Here on the south side there were lots of deer and they looked for that woman among them, but could not find her. Then among the deer on the west side they looked for her, but she was not there. Then on the north side they searched among the deer, but could not find that woman. Now they went to the east side and looked for her among the deer, but still they could not find her. They looked all around for her in that place, but she was not there. Then right on the other side of the last place there were deer standing, and the last one of them was that woman. These deer would not let anyone get close and instead

---

[1] It is customary to make offerings of one or more of the four sacred stones to beings and shamans with holy power, when their help is needed.

[2] ga·n, Wolf, and Mountain Lion are all possessed of power over deer.

[3] The Greek cross is often used in design. It is very common in ritual paintings and may symbolize the four directions among other things.

they jumped around and whistled at the people. So Wolf and Mountain Lion and that woman's husband stayed back and only the ga·n people went toward the woman who was a deer. Before that the deer were all jumping around, but now they all stood still. Then ga·n was close to that woman and he knew just what to do because someone had told him. He took black jet hoop and threw it at her and it went over her head. She became human to her chest. He took turquoise hoop and threw it at her, and it went over her and she became human to her middle. Then ga·n threw red stone hoop at her. It went over her and she was a woman to her knees. Last he threw white shell bead hoop at her, and when it went over her she became all woman once more. Then ga·n said to her, "Come here," and she came to them. This way they took that woman back home with them, and she and her husband lived together again.[1]

This man and his wife had been living for quite a while together, several years, when the woman became pregnant. She had become pregnant from the deer and she was going to have two baby boys. After some time that woman had her babies. She went off to the ridges where the brush was thick and there she had two babies, black tail fawns, below on the ridges. Then she came back home by herself. That woman had two brothers also. Soon after this the people went hunting and brought in deer that they had killed. That woman's two brothers went out hunting. The two brothers brought back with them black-tailed deer fawns, two, and the woman was afraid that these might be hers. When everyone had gone off hunting again, the woman went to her mother's camp to look at the two fawns that her brothers had killed, but these were not her babies, she knew. Later on again that woman's two brothers went hunting and brought in two black-tailed deer fawns. Again she was afraid these were her own children and so she went to look at them. But they were not hers. Now she told her two brothers not to hunt on the other side of the ridges over there (where she had had her babies). Her brothers wondered why she had told them not to hunt over beyond the ridges, and so for this reason they went hunting that way. When they got over beyond, where the woman had her babies, they found two black-tailed deer fawns lying there. The two babies had yellow spots over their eyes. The brothers killed them both and then took them back to the camp. As soon as they laid them down and the woman saw them, she started to cry. "I told you not to kill these fawns. Why did you do it?" she said. Then that woman was crying and fondling her dead babies, all over their faces, legs, and bodies, and between their feet. Then, "From now on I will not be your relative any more, because you have

---

[1] In several tales this same method of bringing a person back to human form is used. Hoops of wood ceremonially made and endowed with power are used in sets of four in various curing ceremonies, being passed over the body of the patient to remove the sickness.

killed my two babies," she said to them. When she said that, she
went over to a mountain mahogany and stood beneath it. She
broke some of its leaves off. Right then a big female deer jumped
out from that place and ran off. This way she went away.

My yucca fruits lie piled up.

There is a song that goes in this story but I have left it out. It
comes in when the woman's husband is about to start out to hunt
deer and leaves her alone.

17. *A GA·N BECOMES RAVEN OLD MAN'S SON-IN-LAW[1]

One time, long ago in a certain country Raven People were living.
Among them was Old Raven who had four daughters. Only the
youngest daughter was good looking. She smiled nicely. Some time
ago I told you a story about how the ga·n people disappeared under
the water ("The Maiden from whom They Disappeared into the
Water"). Now after that, at the time of this story the ga·n people
were living in the mountains. With the ga·n was living a good boy.
This boy came out from the ga·n home on to this earth and started
traveling around. While he was traveling, he came to where the
Raven people were living and met the youngest daughter of Old
Raven. This boy killed rabbits and gave them to the girl. Also he
gave her deer that he had killed, for a present. The boy was thinking
that only in this way would he get married.

About sunrise one day he stopped in front of the door of Old
Raven's wickiup and dropped a bunch of wild rats he had caught.
Old Raven was in the wickiup and he told his daughter to look
outside. "I heard something drop. It must be tsigizis (a small
buckskin pouch worn on belt at side) has been dropped there."
The girl went outside and looked and then came back and told her
father that there were a lot of pack rats lying there. "That's what
you heard drop." she said. So Old Raven told her to bring them in
and they would eat them. They cooked and ate the rats.

The next day at the same time they heard something drop in
front of the wickiup again. Now Old Raven said, "Look, I hear
something drop, I think it is tsigizis." The girl went out and looked
and saw a bunch of cottontail rabbits lying there. She went back
and told her father about it. Then Old Raven said, "Go get them
and bring them here. We will cook and eat them."

The next day at the same time, they heard something drop again
in front of the wickiup. Old Raven told the girl to go look. "It
must be tsigizis," he said. So the girl went out and found lots of
jack rabbits lying there. She came back and told her father about
it. Then Old Raven said, "Go bring them in and we will eat them."

Next day at the same time they heard something drop outside
the wickiup again. "That's my tsigizis dropped down now, surely.

---

[1] Told by Bane Tithla.

Go see what it is, my daughter," Old Raven said. The girl went out and looked and saw a baby deer lying there. She told her father about it. He said to go get it and bring it in and they would cook and eat it.

The next day at the same time, Old Raven heard something drop again in front of the wickiup. "That's my tsigizis dropped down. Go and see about it," he said. So his daughter went out and found a female black-tailed deer lying there. She told her father. "Bring it in here and we will eat it," Old Raven said.

Next day at the same time they heard something drop again. Old Raven said, "That must be my tsigizis, go see about it." So the girl went out and found buck black-tailed deer lying there. She told her father and he said to bring it in and they would cook and eat it, put it in a pot and boil it and make a stew.

Then Old Raven started to think. "Why does this happen every morning? Why is it?" he said to his wife. "I think this is about my daughter here and soon I will find out.[1] Why don't you build a wickiup for this girl, away from camp here and make a doorway to the east. That would be best." So his wife set to work and they made a new wickiup way off, with the doorway to the east. When it was all built, at night the girl went to lie down inside it and sleep. She lay there that night. About midnight she heard the rattling sound from the dangles on ga·n clothing. She could hear them dancing toward her. In the morning she went back to her father's camp and told him, "When I stayed in that wickiup last night, I heard the ga·n hooting as if they were talking together[2] and also the jingle of their clothes. Only once I heard it." Old Raven said, "Do some cooking and when you finish it, take it to that wickiup and leave it there. Then come back here." So the girl cooked some corn gruel and carried it in a basket and left it there in the wickiup. Then she came away. Later on that day she went back there. She saw that whoever it was who had come there had stuck only one finger in the food and had not eaten any. She came back and told her father about this.

That night she went to the wickiup again and slept there. Late that night she heard a sound again of ga·n and the rattle of their clothes coming close. But she only heard it one time. In the morning she went back to her father and told him about it. He told her to cook some more food and leave it in the wickiup again and then come back. So the girl did this. After a while Old Raven told her to go and look at the food. The girl went over and found where the person had stuck two of his fingers into the t'a'diḷ (gruel), but had eaten none. So she took the food back and told her father, "There are two finger marks in the gruel but I never saw anyone there."

---

[1] Young men in courting frequently hunted small game which they brought as gifts to their sweethearts.

[2] In the ga·n dance the dancers make a hooting sound.

That night Old Raven told the girl to go back and lie down in the new wickiup again. She did this and late that night she heard the ga·n hooting and the rattle of their clothing. She could hear them dancing in front of the wickiup. But that one never came inside to her and she saw no one. In the morning the girl went back to her father's camp and told them about it. "I heard the hooting and jingling of the ga·n close by, but I never saw anyone." Old Raven told her to cook some food and take it back to the wickiup and leave it there. "Then come back here," he said. The girl did this. After a while she went back to see the food. The one who had been there had eaten just a little bit of it. She brought the basket back and showed it to her father. "He ate some of it," she said. Now Old Raven talked with his wife. "He has eaten some now. I don't know who he is, though."

That night before the girl went to the wickiup, her parents told her, "Go to the wickiup and lie there perfectly still. Don't move at all. Whoever it is who has been around here is coming to you this night. Don't get scared and try to get away from him." So the girl went over to the wickiup and lay there as she had been told. Very late that night she heard the ga·n coming. It sounded as if lots of them were coming. She could hear their hooting and the rattle of their clothes and also the bull roarer that Clown was swinging, as if they were all having a good time. When they got to the door of the wickiup they stopped and there was a lot of noise from outside. After a while a ga·n came in and sat down close by the girl's pillow. She was badly scared and wanted to run, but she remembered what her father had told her and lay there perfectly still. When this one came in, he had no ga·n clothes on.[1] He was like an ordinary man. While he sat there he talked with the girl and she talked with him. They got along well and held hands. He stayed all that night and in the morning they made him lots of food to eat and took it to him at the new camp. He ate it all.

Now this man lived there at the new wickiup. He used to go out hunting. First he killed a baby deer and brought it to Old Raven's camp. The meat was cooked there, and some of it was taken to the man at the new camp. There the girl ate with him. After that he killed a female black tail and took it to Old Raven's camp. When they cooked this they gave some back to the man to eat. Then he killed a male black tail and took it to his father-in-law's camp. They cooked and ate it and he ate some also.

This man had lived with the girl for quite a while and they were married to each other. One night the girl spoke to him and said, "Where do you live? We had better go back there where you came from." "I live where it is dangerous. Don't ask to go there," he

---

[1] Actual ga·n are sometimes said to appear just as ga·n dancers do in ceremonies, with decorated kilt, moccasins, mask and headdress, painted bodies, and wooden wands.

answered her. So they lived on a while longer with her people.
Then again she asked him, "Where do you come from? Let's go
there." "No, I told you about where I live, that it is dangerous.
Don't talk about going there," he said. The two lived on a long time
and then the wife said again to her husband, "Where do you live?
Let's go to your people." "No, I told you, no. I live far off and in a
dangerous place. You can't go there," he said. For quite a while
longer they stayed on. Then one night his wife said again, "Let's go
to your home. Even if it is dangerous there, let's go all the same."
So the man thought about it, whether she would be able to get
there or not. The girl said, "I mean just what I say. I want to go
back to your home. I think you have lots of relatives. That's why
I want to go there and see some of them." "All right, I told you we
ought not to go, but we will go anyway tomorrow," he said. About
sunrise they started off to the east. After they had gone a way
they went up on top of a butte, then over it and down and when
they got to the foot of the slope they came to a sulphur wheat shrub.
The man told his wife to pull this up. When she did so the bush
came out and there was a hole down below. It was blue like the sky
inside there. They looked down in and could see the branches and
needles of a spruce swaying back and forth below them. It was as if
they were looking down into another world. That man told his
wife, "I don't want you to hesitate when you go in this hole." They
started into the hole. Black Wind blew her back. Then the woman
tried to go in the hole again, and Blue Wind blew her back. She
tried to go in a third time, but Yellow Wind blew her back. Then
there was only one chance left and her husband said, "If you hesitate
this time again, you will have to stay on this earth always and
cannot go to my home." They went to the hole, and this time both
jumped into it and went down and lit on Black Spruce. Then on the
other side they went to the top of Blue Spruce. Then they went to
the top of Yellow Spruce, and then on to the north to the top of
White Spruce. From here they went down onto the ground. On
the ground were growing all kinds of grasses. This was a good
country and they started along through it. Soon they came to a river
with cottonwoods and sycamores growing along its banks. Further
on they found tracks of peoples on the ground. They followed these
and came to a trail which they took. After a way, at the side of the
trail, they found where some corn leaves had fallen from a load.
They kept on and in a while came to where a lot of corn was planted.
Beyond the corn were growing squash. Yet further on they saw all
kinds of plants that grow on this earth and all kinds of fruits. They
went by these.

   This man and his wife were going to his people. His people already knew that he was coming. "This day he will come back home,"
they said. Just before they got to where his people were living, the
man said to his wife, "I told you I lived where it was dangerous.

Don't get scared and try to run off, though. We are getting close now." They kept on, but before they got to the camp Black Bear ran out at them. The man told his wife, "Go behind me and hide there." She did and Black Bear ran out around them. After a while he sat down at one side and looked at them. So they started on, but soon Blue Bear ran out at them. The woman hid behind her husband while Blue Bear ran all around them. Then he sat down, off to one side and they went on. These Bears did not really want to catch the woman; they just wanted to scare her, but she thought they were trying to catch her. They started on again. Then Yellow Bear ran out at them. The woman hid behind her husband and Yellow Bear ran all around them. Then he went to one side and sat down. They started on. After a way White Bear ran at them. The Woman hid behind her husband and White Bear ran all around them. Then he went to one side and sat down. They went on. That man had lots of sisters and brothers, and these bears were their pets. They also belonged to his father and mother. They went on to the camp. When they got there, his sisters, brothers and father and mother stepped outside the camp. That man left his wife standing there and went among his people to see them.

Then he was home again with his wife, living among his people once more. There were lots of plants that had fruit and seeds good to eat at this place. So the man told his relatives to gather some for him and his wife to use. While they were living there Clown came to his camp. He wanted to see this woman's face, to see if his sister-in-law was good looking. If she was, he said he was going to hunt deer for her.[1] When he saw the woman's face, he said, "My sister-in-law is goodlooking all right. I'm going to hunt deer now," so he started off. But when Clown came back, he brought only the sinew from the deer's back to that man's camp. This meant that it would turn to lots of meat when it was taken back to his father-in-law, Old Raven. Next Black ga·n came there. He said that he wanted to see his sister-in-law's face. "If she looks good I'm going to hunt for her," he said. After he saw her he said, "My sister-in-law looks good, so I'm going to hunt now," and he started off. When he came back he brought only the sinew from the deer's back to that man's camp. Red ga·n came and did the same way. Then Talking ga·n came there and said, "I want to see my sister-in-law. If she looks good I'm going to hunt for her." When he saw her he said, "She looks good, so I'm going to hunt now," and he started off. But when he came back he just brought sinew.

After that, these people wanted a horse in and told the woman to go out in the pasture and bring in a horse, so they could go to the fields to get some corn. The woman took a rope and started off to catch a horse. When she got to the horses, she saw that they were

---

[1] To hunt deer for a new sister-in-law, that the meat might be taken to her family, was quite regular.

really bears. She was afraid and ran back to camp. When she did
this her husband's people laughed at her. "Those bears you saw
are our horses. They are gentle and not mean at all. We use them
for horses all the time. Why did you get scared," they said. Then
the woman's mother-in-law went out and got one of these horses
herself and brought it in. Then she put a saddle on it and a bridle
and told the woman, "Let's go to the cornfield." But the woman
would not go; she said she was scared of the horse. "Anyway, come
on, you can walk apart from this horse," the mother-in-law said.
So they started out and went to the cornfield. There they packed a
load of corn on the bear and brought it back to camp. But when
they got back, the woman was still afraid of that horse. These
people gathered lots of squash, beans and other foods and brought
them in for that woman. She lived there quite a while, till everything was ripe. All the corn was ripe, but she was still there.

Then that woman's father-in-law talked to his people and said,
"This woman and my boy have come back from over there and have
lived with us for quite a while. Since they have been here we have
given nothing to the woman. We had better give her some deer meat
and all these foods we have gathered, so that when she goes back
they can take them to where Raven Chief is living." This is the
way they told that man also, "You came back from that woman's
home a while ago. When you go back to your father-in-law, you are
going to take all this corn and other food to him. When you get
there tell him to eat it. Then these corn seeds, show him how to
plant them and raise corn, so he can do it like we do." Then those
people gathered a little of each kind of seed and tied them up in a
bundle. Then they brought in a horse and packed the load on it.
When all was packed the man and his wife started off. This all
meant that when they got back to Old Raven's country, all these
seeds would become many. All was ready and that man told his
wife to ride on the horse, but she said, "No, I'm still scared of it."
She did not want to get on, so her sister-in-law got on and showed
her how to do it, "Look at me here! This horse is gentle and not
mean." Then they tried to put the woman on, but she said no,
she was afraid. "Well, lead it then!" they said. "All right," she
said and started to lead the horse off. The mother of the man told
her children to go a little way with the woman. "Maybe if you tell
her to ride later on she will do it and not be scared," she said. So
they all started off and after a while came to the foot of the trail
up out of this country. Now the woman got on the horse. This
trail was steep and went in switchbacks to the top. It made four
turns on the way up. When they left the man's people at the foot
of the trail, these relatives told her, "Don't look back towards
where your mother-in-law and father-in-law live. Just keep on to
the top." So they started on up the trail. When the two were almost
to the top, the woman looked back just as she was about to step into

her own world. She thought she would like to look back once more
to where she had been. When she turned back, right then the horse
fell down and rolled to the bottom of the trail. The pack fell off and
was scattered all over the trail. Then they got it into a big pile.
That man said to his wife, "Before you started up the trail they
told you not to look back to where they were living. Now see what
you have done!"

Where Old Raven was living, there were a great many people
living also. When that man and his wife got to where they were
living, these Raven People helped to carry all the things that they
had brought back. They went every day and kept on carrying it
back, but still there was more. All the Raven People helped and
after a few days they had it all brought to Old Raven's camp.
Now they used this to eat. Then later they were ready to plant
corn and other seeds. Old Raven was thinking about the corn.
He always liked it parched in a basket, so he said, "That corn you
parched, I am going to plant that way, and when it gets ripe I will
be able to eat it without having to cook it." So he went ahead and
planted it. All the other people planted their corn in the right way,
plain, and it grew up well. But where Old Raven planted his,
nothing came up at all.

Later on, when every bit of the corn was ripe, all the people who
were living there started in to harvest it. But there was still a lot
ungathered. Then that man who married Old Raven's daughter
thought to himself, "These people are doing a lot of work. I would
like to go and get my relatives to help them on this corn and finish
it." So he went off and later came back with all his sisters and
brothers to that place. This way the girls and boys who liked each
other worked together in the fields. Some of the corn that they
raised at that time, was short and had little ears on it. These little
ears of corn the boys and girls tied on each side so they hung over
their ears. This way they were flirting in the fields.[1]

Old Raven did not like it because so many people were working
in the fields, all his son-in-law's relatives as well. He thought with
so many people working, it would take all the corn to pay them and
only a little would be left for him.[2] The sisters and brothers of Old
Raven's son-in-law knew what Old Raven was thinking, even though
he had not told them. They knew everything this way. Then they
said, "Old Raven is thinking something bad about us. He thinks
that we will take all this corn back with us, but we just want to
help him, that's all. If he thinks this way, we had better all go
home." While they were working in the fields the Raven People
saw them there, but the next thing they had all disappeared and they

---

[1] Courting while working in the fields was common, as young people might
work side by side.
[2] Rich men with large farms hired labor to work their fields, especially at
harvest. Workers were payed in produce.

could not see them anywhere. At the same time all the corn and other crops were gone out of the field. They took them away. This is the way they took all the crops back with them and made it hard for the people to make a living.

My yucca fruits lie piled up.

18. *THE GA·N PEOPLE MOVE AWAY[1]

On the other side of the White Mountains there is a big mountain called ntca'na·sk'id (big ridge running along). Long ago there were ga·n people living there. They were living well at that place. There, all kinds of animal people were living also. Hawk people and Eagle people lived there. Their children intermarried and became close. On one side of the river the ga·n people lived, and on the other side of the river all the other kinds of people lived. The children of the ga·n people used to play with the children of the other peoples, and this way they made friends and went around together. This way the children of different kinds of people playing around touched each other, and from this they got all kinds of sicknesses. Then they touched their heads to each other and got well again.

Then ga·n people said, "We were all well before we lived together. We had no sickness, but since the Hawk people settled here near us, we have had sickness." Then Talking ga·n went up on top of the mountain and in the morning came back down again. Then he talked from the mountain. "This is not right," he said. After that a little ga·n child got sick and vomited some white stuff. "This is no good," Talking ga·n said, "Let some one of our men go to the Hawk people and carry 'turquoise with downy feather going through it'[2] to them and give it to one of the Hawk people in their camp." So they did this and gave this thing to Hawk shaman. Then the Hawk shaman came over to the ga·n camps and sang Hawk songs over the sick ga·n child. When he did this, the child got well. This is the way the child was cured. Then the children were all gathered up and taken back to their homes again.

Not long after this, when the Hawk children all came home, one of them got sick. The Hawk people talked it over and decided to carry "downy feather tied to turquoise" over to the ga·n people to a ga·n shaman. They did this and gave it to the ga·n shaman. Then the ga·n shaman said to make a sweat lodge and that they would talk about it in there. So they made a sweat lodge, and it started to rain. Then ga·n shaman said to find a good level place and pile wood there

---

[1] Told by Bane Tithla. This tale is the origin myth for an important curing ceremony in which masked dancers representing ga·n are the principal participants. Compare Goddard, ibid 124 ff.

[2] A conventional offering made to a shaman to gain his help. The feather is tied to the turquoise by a strand of buckskin. It is placed on the shaman's foot. There is a hawk sickness and curing ceremony.

in four places, east, south, west, north. So the Hawk people did this and put the wood in four places on level ground. Then the ga·n shaman said to put the sick Hawk child on the east side, and they did it. Then he said to the Hawk people that they must all stay together and not let anyone go off. He told them to fix up a drum also. When the drum was ready, the ga·n shaman said to them to all sit together with that drum, and they did so. Then the bullroarer sounded in four directions and the ga·n (dancers) came down upside down. Then Talking ga·n, Big ga·n, Dark ga·n, and ga·n'owaŋ came out and down. They were all upside down. Then all the ga·n put pitch on the palms of their hands and rubbed them together. Then Clown came in, carrying blacktail deer fawn on his back. Every ga·n had a knife in his hand. They put the sick child there and wrapped it up in yucca leaves from foot to head. Then the ga·n started to cut the yucca off the child. Then with their wands they carried the sick child to the east, then to the south, then to the west, then to the north. Then they put it down again, and the ga·n went away. Now the Hawk child got well. Then ga·n people said to the Hawk people, "If this happens to you again, if one of you gets sick like this again, do the same way you have seen us do, and the sick person will get well." Hawk people also told ga·n people. "If one of you gets sick again, do the same way as you saw us do and you will cure the sick one all right. Use Hawk songs." From that day on both these people did this way, using these new ceremonies that they had learned from each other.

After that the ga·n people talked among themselves again: "This is not right, we ought to leave here," they said. Black ga·n had a bird, Hummingbird. He told Hummingbird to go down on the earth and find a place where there was never any sickness, or no one ever died. So the next morning Hummingbird set out. Later on Hummingbird came back. There was sickness everywhere he went, he said. Talking ga·n told Hummingbird to go up in the sky and look there for a place, then to go to yahit'ą·yu· (center of sky ?) and look there. Hummingbird set out, but when he got back he reported the same thing, "There was sickness and death up there also." After that Talking ga·n made a big hill out of mirage and took it to the sky above. But still they had all kinds of sicknesses up there, living on that hill, so they came back on the earth. Then Talking ga·n told Hummingbird to travel all over the earth again. Hummingbird set off once more. This time he found where Gopher had dug out a little pile of dirt, at the mouth of his hole in the ground.

At the place Gopher was living with the other people, he said he wanted to be chief. But they made fun of him and said, "You have big pouches in your cheeks." So Gopher got mad. Where the Gopher people were living, they had lots of rain and everything grew well. But now Gopher, who was mad, took all the rain and clouds and grass and plants and trees away with him inside the earth. After

that it never rained for a long time. No one knew where Gopher
had gone. But now Hummingbird, while he was searching, found
Gopher's hole, went in and traveled along it until he found Gopher
in a good country, where there was a lot of food and all the plants
grew well; lots of ripe fruits and lots of rain. Gopher was living here.
At that time, on the earth there was no wind, and even if you put a
downy feather on the ground it would not move. There Hummingbird ate lots. He spent all day eating. Then the next morning he
went back to the people on the earth. When he got home, all the
people came to his camp, but he told them nothing of what he had
found. All the people crowded into his wickiup and asked him to
talk, but he would say nothing and just went to bed. All the same
the people still sat in his wickiup. Pretty soon, Hummingbird broke
wind. When the people heard this they said, "If Hummingbird
didn't have plenty to eat, then he couldn't break wind." They
started to talk to him. "Where have you been eating all day?"
they asked him. "I have eaten nothing any place. I just naturally
broke wind, that's all," he said. But the people told him, "No, you
are fooling us. You broke wind all night and it was because you have
eaten a lot." Finally Hummingbird said, "I have been to Gopher's
place. There I found lots of food and I ate lots. The wind blows
there and there is a lot of rain," and Hummingbird told them all
about it. Then the people talked about it and decided to make
na·t'o°ke·ge° dį· bigant'i°go°¹ (na·t'o°ke·ge°, four sticking through
each other) and send it to Gopher. So they did this and took it to
Gopher and laid it on top of one of his moccasin toes where he was
standing. This meant that they wanted Gopher to come back to
them. So Gopher came back to them. "You have been having a
bad time," he said. Then the people said they would make him
chief. Now where they were living they had lots of rain again, and
all grew well.

After a while Talking ga·n began to talk again about the place
where they were living and how they were having a hard time.
"This is no good," he said. He talked all night long. Then he
found a mountain, a good place where there was no sickness or
death. He told the ga·n to leave one of their children behind here
where they were. But none of them wanted to leave one of their
children behind. Talking ga·n had a daughter there who was now
a young maiden. He finally thought about her. Then he went to
talk to the ga·n people and said, "Get all your belongings together
and be ready to move. I am going to leave my own girl behind."
So all the ga·n people got ready and packed to move. When they
all started off they left a grass hair brush behind on purpose that
belonged to the daughter of Talking ga·n. After all the people had

---

¹ na·t'o°ke·ge° is a section of cane filled with tobacco sent to a chief to ask
his aid and his people's aid in a ceremony. If the recipient accepts and
smokes it he cannot refuse the request. Only important men receive them.

gone a long way, they said to the girl, "You left you hair brush behind. You had better go back and get it." So the girl went back and looked all over to find the hair brush. When she got it she came back to where she had left her people, but they were all gone and she could not find their trail. All the ga·n people had gone in under the big water they came to, and after they had gone in, the water closed back over them and they disappeared. Finally the girl trailed them to the edge of the water where they had gone in, but she could not follow them beyond here into the water, so she started to cry. There were no other people left at that place, so the girl went off. For a long time she wandered about by herself. Finally she came to where an old woman was living with her son. When she got there, the old woman said, "Where do you come from? There are no other people in this country." So the girl told her how when her people got close to the water, they had sent her back for a hair brush. "When I got back to where I left them, they were all gone and I couldn't find them anywhere," the girl said.

Then that girl started to live with the old woman and her boy. Later on the boy was grown up and was able to kill lots of deer and bring them home. The girl was grown also, and she gathered all kinds of seeds.[1] They had lots to eat at that camp. Then the girl and boy got married to each other. The girl belonged to the ga·n people and the boy was Apache. This way they lived together. After a while, the girl became pregnant. Then the baby was born, well and smooth all over, as it should be. That midnight the ga·n started to where the woman had had her child. They said, "Let's all hurry and go see the baby." Soon the ga·n reached the camp of the woman's husband. They all went into the wickiup. The man's brother-in-law (ga·n) went to his sister. Then he told the man, his brother-in-law, "Don't get close to me!" There in the wickiup were all the different ga·n. Talking ga·n, Dark ga·n, Red ga·n, ga·n'o·waṇ, all of them. More of them kept coming in and coming in, and the wickiup kept spreading out so that all of them could get in. Then the ga·n who was the woman's father lay down and told a story. Then he said something: "Come here, give me the baby, bana·idnlaʻ (he takes two things from someone)." He called him by this name. Then he had the baby and sang for him and danced him up and down on his chest as he lay there. Then, "This is enough, bana·-idnlaʻ," he said, "Take him back to his mother," and they did. Then the ga·n told another story there and then all the ga·n went away, back to their home.

For a long time the woman and her husband lived there, and then she bore a daughter. Her ga·n father heard about it. "Let's all go

---

[1] Notice the mention of economic activities of boy and girl (or man and woman). To say that the boy hunts deer and the girl gathers seeds is to say that they are mature and performing two of the most important economic functions of adults.

to that place again," he said to the others. It was at midnight. So
they all set off again to go to the man's camp. The man's brother-
in-law came into his house and said, "Don't touch me!" (he meant
the wickiup not to touch him; for it to move out). All the different
kinds of ga·n entered the wickiup, Talking ga·n, Dark ga·n, Red
ga·n, ga·n'o·wan̦, all of them. As they entered, the wickiup spread
out. Then the woman's father lay down again by the door and told
a story. Then, "Give me the baby, tsehisba·ha," he called her.
They gave him the baby and he sang for her and danced her on his
chest again, as he lay there. "All right, take tsehisba·ha back to her
mother," he said. Then the ga·n told a story again and after that
they all went back to their home.

Then that man had good luck from the ga·n, and he was able to
kill deer every time he hunted.[1] They lived together that way well,
the man and his wife. Then after a while the woman bore another
child. When the ga·n found out about it, they all came again to
visit at the man's camp. When they got to the wickiup, the man's
brother-in-law came in and said, "Don't touch me!" and the
wickiup walls moved outwards. Then all the ga·n, Talking ga·n,
Dark ga·n, Red ga·n, ga·no·w'an̦, all the rest, entered. The man's
father-in-law lay down by the door, outside it again and told a
story. Then, he said, "Give me the baby, bana·idnla' bik'isn
(bana·idnla''s brother)"[2] he called him, and they gave him to him.
Then he sang for him and danced him up and down on his chest as
he had done before. Talking ga·n said, "We came to name my
grandson here. Now give it back to its mother." He called it by
its name. When the mother had the baby, Talking ga·n told a
story again and when it was all over they went home.

The man and his wife lived on as before. After a long time the
woman had another baby. This time it was a girl. Then the ga·n
knew it, and he said to the other ga·n, "Let's go and see the new
baby again!" So they all came to the door of that man's camp.
Then his brother-in-law said, "Move out," and all the ga·n came
inside as before. Then the one whose daughter had the baby, lay
down at the door and said something, "Come here, give me the baby,
naba·dzisnda·ha," he said, and they gave her to him. He sang over
her and danced her on his chest as before. "All right, naba·dzisnda·ha
(baby's name), give her to her mother," and they did. Then Talking
ga·n told a story, sitting there. When it was over all the ga·n went
back to their home. This way they made up four names on the
earth. Talking ga·n gave his four grandchildren names. Before that
time the people on the earth had no names.

---

[1] Deer are the cattle of ga·n, but the man's affinal connection to ga·n would
naturally benefit him because of their great holy power.
[2] The narrator could not remember the real name, so substituted the sibling
term with the name of the older brother. This is rather infrequently done
as a means of identification.

Those two boys, sons of the man and his wife, grew up. The two girls, their daughters, grew up also. Then the two boys learned how to hunt deer well, and they had good luck in this from their grandfather, a ga·n. Thus they were able to kill deer right away. Later on the two girls married some young men living there. Then those two girls bore many children. Afterwards the two boys started off to where the ga·n were living, but they came back at sunset. They had had something to eat where they had been, so when they got home and their people told them to eat, they would not. Those two boys had eaten at the home of the ga·n and that was why they would not eat at home. "Why don't you eat. You have not eaten for a long time," their people said. The boys said they were not hungry, that that was why they did not want to eat. But their people said, "You lie, you have been some place where people are. That's why you won't eat now." "No, we were only around home here," the boys said. Then after that the two boys went off up a mountain, on top of it. There the oldest one sat down and the youngest one went off some place. The oldest brother started to sing. Right then there were people who had songs. When it was sunset they came home. Their people told them to eat, but they did not want anything. The younger brother had heard his older brother singing on the mountain. He told about it. "My brother was singing up there on the mountain," he said. After he told this, all the people came to the boys. Some of them talked with the boys. "Why do you go up there in that place on the mountain and not tell anyone about it," they asked. The boys said, "We haven't been any place yet," but they were telling a lie for they had been to the place where the ga·n were living. But even that night the boys would not tell about it.

Later on one of the people there got sick and all twisted up,[1] so a shaman sang over him, but he did not get well. Then the younger brother who had heard his older brother singing on the mountain, spoke with a friend of the sick man. He told about his brother and said, "Make na·t'o'ke·ge' and put black jet, turquoise, white shell beads on it, on each point of the cross.[2] Then tie the best downy eagle feather on it. When you have made it, go and lay it on his foot." The man made this and they put it on the older brother's foot, but he said, "I have no power. I am not a shaman."[3] Anyway

---

[1] The symptom of ga·n sickness.

[2] One form of na·t'o'ke·ge' is made in the shape of a cross, two sections of cane being tied crosswise.

[3] Refusal of a man who has just acquired a ceremony or power to admit that he has it, is not uncommon and may be due to several reasons; that he is not sure of it yet, that he is self-concious about doing something with which he is unfamiliar, and that he does not want to accept too readily and cheapen his power. Even experienced shamans sometimes hesitate, though not for the first two reasons. In their case it may be for the third reason or because of the labor involved, or again due to the personal relationship with the people requesting his services.

they kept on trying. Four times they made na·t'o'ke·ge' and put it on his foot. After the fourth time the older brother said, "All right, gather wood and pile it in four places. Then take the sick one and wrap him in yucca leaves from head to foot." Now the boy made a drum. "Don't go away, don't get scared," he told them. He started to sing. Then they heard bullroarers in four directions. The earth rumbled and the sky also. Then all kinds of ga·n came down. The clown came also, carrying blacktail deer fawn. He held his bullroarer up, then he swung it and made a noise. Then ga·n held up their wands (knives). Then they all cut the yucca off the sick man. All the people there were made to line up in four circles about the fire. After the ga·n cut all the yucca off the sick man, they went with him to the east, then they took him to the south, then to the west, and then to the north. Now they went round the fire four times.[1] After that the sick man got well right away. The ga·n had come to that place from their own home. They had brought their sons and daughters with them. When the man was cured, they all danced there, the ga·n and the people. They made a circle four times around the fire, all dancing. The ga·n youths danced with the Apache girls, they flirted during the ŀe·datc'itc'uc.[2] The ga·n girls danced and flirted with the Apache young men also. This was all at night. Till midnight the ga·n people and the Apache were dancing together. While they were still dancing it dawned. Then the sun rose and when it rose the earth shook. Then the old women and old men built fires all around where they were dancing and sat by them, watching.[3] After the sun rose the people were dancing up high, off the ground about four feet. Then more of them were dancing off the ground, and the old men and women watched them. They were still dancing upward. Way up high they danced. Now the old men and old women said something to their daughters as they were still dancing upward. "Come back! Come back!" they said. They were so far up that they could just see them a little, and soon they could not even hear the drum beats. In a little they could not see them any more. Then these old people were running about the fire, crying. All the people who had been dancing went with the ga·n to where the ga·n lived. This way all the old people were left behind.

My yucca fruits lie piled up.

---

[1] The ceremony as given today closely resembles this description. The cutting off of the yucca is like cutting away the sickness.

[2] The social dance in which couples dance a few steps forward then a few steps back, side by side and facing the same direction. Dancing is one of the principal occasions on which courting takes place.

[3] As they commonly do.

19. *A GA·N BECOMES RAVEN OLD MAN'S SON-IN-LAW: *THE GA·N
DISAPPEAR FROM TSE·GOTS'UK[1]

Long ago people, all kinds of birds and animals were people then,
were living up to the north of here somewhere. Hawk people were
humans then. They did not know that ga·n people were living
down in the earth, below. Then Raven Old Man was there with the
Raven people. He had children and one of these was a beautiful
daughter. The ga·n people below knew about her. The old man and
his family were in their wickiup. Soon they heard something drop
outside. Raven Old Man heard it. "What is that, cibi·lsis (a buckskin pouch hung over one shoulder and resting on the hip on opposite
side) maybe ?" the old man said. The girl went out and found two
pack rats. She brought them in and they ate them. Four days
after this the old man heard something drop outside. "Go and see
if cibi·lsis is there," he said, though all the time he knew his own was
in the wickiup. So the daughter went outside and found two rabbits.
She brought them in and they ate them up. Four days after that
they heard something drop again. "Go out and see if cibi·lsis is
there," the old man told his daughter. She went out and found two
jack rabbits. "Here are two jack rabbits," she said. "Well, bring
them in and we will eat them," the old man told her. Then four
days later something dropped outside. The old man sent his
daughter out to see if it was his pouch. When she got outside she
found a black-tailed deer fawn. "Here is a black tail deer fawn,"
she said. "Well, bring it in," the old man told her. So they did
and ate it up. Four days after that something dropped once more
outside. The old man sent his daughter out to see if it was his pouch.
She went out and this time it was a black-tailed deer with two points
on his horns. They butchered and ate him. Then four days later
something dropped outside again. "What's that, cibi·lsis ?" the
old man said. He sent out his daugther and she found a big black-
tailed deer. They butchered and ate him. Raven Old Man was very
thankful for that. Four days after that the old man heard something drop outside. He sent his daughter out. "See if this is cibi·lsis
that has dropped there," he told her. So the girl went out and
found an enormous black-tailed deer, the kind that is all fat and in
good shape, like you get in the fall. They butchered and ate it.
Raven Old Man was thankful for this.

Then Raven Old Man said to this daughter. "Well, daughter,
this is what I have raised you for. We have eaten a lot of meat from
someone.[2] Build a new wickiup over to one side here and we will
find out who it is who is doing this," he told the girl. The new
wickiup was built and standing not far off. No one was in it. The
old man stayed with his family in their dwelling. Soon they saw

---

[1] Told by Francis Drake.

[2] By accepting many gifts such as this, a family was more or less obliged to
grant the request which would follow.

someone in the new wickiup. The girl went over there. She stayed there with that man. He was her man now.

After they had stayed together for quite a while, the man and woman went out for a walk together. Then the man told his wife, "I belong to the ga·n people." Soon they came to a sulphur wheat bush. He started to kick it from the east side, then from the south side, then from the west and last from the north. The plant came up by its roots. In the hole that it left, the top of a spruce tree stuck up through. The man told his wife, "Step on this. Don't be afraid." But the woman shut her eyes and stepped on it. Then they found themselves way down below, where the ga·n people lived. After they reached the bottom, they started to walk to the place the man's people were living. The woman had never seen people like this before. There were many of those people there. There were houses also, good ones. All kinds of farm crops were growing. There were corn drying racks.[1] The crops were in all stages of growth; some were up just a little, some were half way up, some high and some harvested already. The woman's husband had many sisters and so she had a lot of sisters-in-law. The man's mother was there. She tested her daughter-in-law.[2] She gave her a metate and mano and some corn to grind. "Let's see you grind some corn," she told her. But this woman could not grind corn well. She ground it but could not break the kernels up. For this reason the man's family did not like her. She was not strong enough and could not grind corn.

One day after they had arrived there, a ga·n came to them. He caught hold of the woman's hair and held her head back. "I want to see my relative-in-law's face. If she is pleasing I will go hunting for her," he said. Several of the ga·n did the same way. The last one was Gray ga·n (the clown) and he said, "Well, she is all right. I will go hunting for her like the others." The men who went hunting just brought in sinew. There was no meat, only a big pile of sinew there. Then one of the man's sisters was sent with the woman to bring in a horse, so they could ride back to Raven Old Man's place. In a short distance they came to some bears. The woman saw them and was frightened. She started to run away, but her sister-in-law called to her, "Come back here. They won't harm you. They are good 'horses'. They are gentle." But the woman would not listen and ran back to the camp. Her sister-in-law got the 'horse' and led it back. They saddled it up for the man and his wife. The woman's mother-in-law told her, "Don't look back on your way out. Don't look back till you get on top. Don't think why this is. I don't want you to look back. Don't do it!"

---

[1] Frames on which to hang corn to dry.
[2] This testing of a daughter-in-law was not uncommon and might even be used as a reason for marital separation.

The woman got on the bear, but her husband did not go along with her. She rode to the top almost. Then she thought to herself, "I wonder why she didn't want me to look back. I will try it." So she looked back; just a glance. As soon as she did that the bear started to roll down the hill. Clear to the bottom they tumbled. The old woman saw it and ran to her. "I told you not to do that. Now why did you do it?" she said. When she was going up she had had just a load of sinew, but now after the fall, it had all turned to meat and meat was scattered along the trail where they had fallen. The old woman carried the meat up to the top for her daughter-in-law. They packed the bear up again so that she could take it to her father. She went on alone from there, without her husband.

When the woman came close to her home, her mother, an old woman, saw her riding the bear. Raven Old Man and all his children became frightened and ran off from camp. "Don't ride down this way," they said. She unpacked the bear all alone, put the meat up and turned the bear back. But her husband got mad because he heard that his horse had been struck by someone up there.[1] On this account he did not return for two days and nights. Then in two days someone was seen walking to the wickiup where this man had lived with his wife. Raven Old Man sent his daugher. "You better go over and build a fire," he told her. She went over to her wickiup. The man, she found lying on the bed. He was very thin and bony, not like her husband. His legs and arms had white stripes about them, like those on a bob-cat's tail. The woman went back to her father and told him, "That man is not my husband. He is too thin for that and besides he has white stripes about his legs and arms." But her parents told her, "Maybe it is the same man and he has grown thin." "Why should he have white stripes about his arms and legs? I know it's not he," the woman said. Raven Old Man said, "Well, I believe he must have gone stalking antelope and has painted his legs and arms to look like an antelope." "No, I know my husband better than you two. It is not he," the woman said. She did not like this man, but her father sent her over to him and so she went, staying there all that night.

The next morning this man went hunting. When he came back he brought some dried meat. It had been roasted already. The following morning he went hunting again. Raven Old Man told his son, "Follow this man and see where he gets this dried meat. Don't let him see you." So the son did this. After the man had gone a way, his follower saw him stop and set fire to an old pitch-pine stump. On the side that the smoke blew, the man went. The snot started to run out of his nose and it was this he was taking and making into dried meat. The son came home and told his father about it. After that Raven Old Man would not eat any more of

---

[1] Though mounts were sometimes beaten, this was infrequent and people spoke harshly of those who did it.

this dried meat. "That is why it was salty," the old man said. This man was from the Mosquito people. That is why he was so thin. All things were people in those days.

The man went to sleep with the woman that night. Her real husband from the ga·n, knew, who it was that had his wife. On account of this he shot them with an arrow of red stone that night. The arrow went right through both of them. The woman used to get up early, but she had not yet appeared at her father's camp. When the sun had risen high up, Raven Old Man sent one of his small daughters over to see what was the matter. She just looked inside the wickiup and thought that they were still asleep inside, so she went back again. She told her father, "Well, they are still in bed." About noon, the little girl went over there again. She came back and told her father, "They are still in bed." "Well, go over there and uncover them," he said. So the little girl went inside and took the covers off. When she did she saw that both of them had bled at the nose. When she came back and said that they were dead, Raven Old Man and his wife started to quarrel. "You know I told you he was not her husband. You sent her over to him all the same. Now she is gone," they accused each other.

Then the Raven people were no longer there where they had been living. But ga·n people were still living down below in the earth. Many ga·n died down there. Though it is just as if they travel together with lightning, yet they died there. On account of this, ga·n people began to search for a place where they would not die; where there was life without end. From here on for a bit the story is dangerous to recount, but I have to tell it to you just the same.[1] They moved to a place halfway between the earth and the sky. There Mirage made an earth for them and they lived on this. But still they died there. They went through the sky to its other side, but still they died there. From there they came down on earth to ntca'na·sk'id (a place somewhere about 35 miles east of Macnary, Arizona). Wherever they had lived above, they had always had their agricultural crops with them. These were their food; corn, beans, and squash.

Then there were a poor people living near that place (ntca'na·sk'id), the Hawk people. They were of the 'iya'°a̧iye clan. They were called Hawk people because the relatives of this clan are hawks.[2] There were people of the na·dots'usn, bisza̧·ha, ndi'nde·zn and destci·dn clans there also. They were all a very poor people. At dusk one day, they saw a light far off. They asked each other, "Who is up there? Who has made that fire?" because everyone

---

[1] It contains power and so is dangerous. Through the misuse of such power misfortune might befall those involved in the story telling.

[2] Each clan or group of related clans has a related bird or animal. Occasionally they are referred as "Hawk people", "Bear people", etc., though this is done more as a joke than seriously.

was at home and they could not think of who might be out there. They tried to mark the fire, so that they might go there in the morning and see what it was. This is dangerous, this story that I am telling you, but I tell it to you just as I heard it. It is very holy, this part of the story, and if you or anyone should laugh at it, there is danger of you or that person's mouth and eyes going crooked. There is danger of this happening to me on account of telling this tale. One time there were two men, one blind, the other lame. The blind one carried the lame one on his back. They came this way to a group of people. When the people saw them coming, they laughed at them. The blind man clapped his hands together and part of the people became blind. The lame man drew up his leg to his body and then part of them became lame. That is the way with this story. We must not laugh at it. It is the same way with the songs of the ga·n curing ceremony which have to do with this part of the story.[1]

The next morning these people sent one man over to where they thought they had seen the fire, but he could find nothing. Again, that evening, after sunset, they could see the same fire. But the man who had been sent to investigate insisted that there was nothing over there. This time they cut a crotched stick and set it up in the ground. They layed an arrow in the crotch, pointing directly at the fire, so they would know just where it was in the morning. When morning came they looked to see where the arrow pointed. A man went over there to try and find something, but he could not find even a blade of grass that had been stepped on and bent, or a broken twig. It was two times that they had made trips to find this fire without results, but that evening they could see the fire again in the same place. They had left the arrow there from the night before, and it still pointed right to the fire. So in the morning they sent a man over to try and find something. He went and looked about for a long time, but found no ashes nor any blades of broken grass. Halfway to ntca'na·sk'id he went. "I have found nothing," he told the people when he got home. The next morning they sent someone over to search for the fourth time. He went to

---

[1] The narrator insisted that the story, as he knew it, did not mention the blind man and the lame man, but said these two were only mentioned in songs of this ceremony. They appeared to the poor people, who laughed at them and were punished in the above manner. But on the arrival of these poor people at the camp of the ga·n as described below, the ga·n sang songs over them and cured them. Another old man, Joseph Newton, says that there is a White Mountain myth concerning ga·n in which these two, one blind and the other lame, who were brothers, went about among the people, causing it to rain hot water on them if they laughed, and other such things. They belonged with the ga·n, and it was partially through them that the ga·n curing rite was obtained, he says. This is reminiscent of a Navajo myth of similar plot, which Mathews gives as origin myth for a branch of the Night Chant (Washington Mathews, The Night Chant, Memoirs of American Museum of Natural History, Vol. VI).

the same place the others had been. Then after a short distance he stopped and sat down, for he saw many people there, and many crops of all kinds and in all stages of growth; some just up, some ready to harvest and so on.

The ga·n people saw this man, where he had dropped down in the grass. They talked among themselves: "Someone has been sitting over there for a long time. Let one go over there and see him." So one went over towards him. He came as close as from here to the wickiup over there (20 yards). He did not say anything; just stood and looked at him. The man from the poor people had two eagle tail feathers sticking up in his hair. His privates were covered with the shredded inner bark of juniper. The ga·n went back and told his people, "That man has some inner bark from juniper to cover his privates." "You better take back two buckskins with you, one for him to cover his shoulders with and one to wear about his waist," they told him. So he took two buckskins over to the man and told him to wear them, one about his waist and one about the shoulders. The inner bark he had covering his privates he threw away. "Lets go back to my people," the ga·n said. They went. They gave this man some food: corn and squash. He had eaten of ga·n food now. After he had eaten, they talked to him. "Where did you come from?" they asked. The man pointed to where he lived. It was a long way back there. "Well, you are poor people. It's not right that you stay there. You better come here and live with us. We have lots of crops just going to waste," they told him. They gave him some corn and he started home with it. When he arrived, he had the corn with him and the people there ate it. This man told his people what he had seen. "I saw lots of people there. They were good. I have my belly full now. I ate all I wanted there and the chief of these people told me; 'You better come and live with us, because you people are poor.' He told me to tell this to you." The man could not sleep that night for thinking of all the ripe crops he had seen and the food he had eaten. The people were very hungry where he lived. They got up in the morning and moved away from tse·gots'uk (a place) where they had been living. When they arrived at the new place, the crops were all given to them. "Let them eat all they want," the ga·n said. They did eat all they wanted and now they had big bellies.

Thus these two peoples had lived for a long time together. Their children had become acquainted. The men went hunting together. The children played. They let them eat all they could from the farms, for the crops on them grew the year around, in all four stages, from just sprouting to ripeness. These people were the ga·n and Hawk peoples. I know the place they lived. I passed through there when I was a soldier in the U. S. army, on the way to Ft. Wingate. The children played together and some ga·n children became sick from the hawk illness. Their eyes became swollen and

closed, they scratched like hawks and their faeces were white like
that of hawks. Then the Hawk children became sick from the ga·n.
They became unable to walk, as if paralyzed.[1] The two kinds of
children were able to cure each other by one touching the other
where it hurt. When they did this they became well immediately.
But the ga·n chief heard about it and did not like it. The ga·n had
found the place where there was life without end. That is why they
had spread these sicknesses among the people, because they had
found a good place. Then Talking ga·n was chief. He went up on
top of ntca'na·sk'id every morning and talked to the people from
there. "We have done nothing here for a long time. It is better
that we go to tse·nodǫ·z surrounded by fire and tse·na·sbas surrounded by fire (places). Here it is as if we were herded together in a
pasture. We would like to have some meat. We want to move to
a place where people never die." That night they all collected
together to talk it over. They gathered this way every night from
there on.

All the ga·n people were divided into different kinds, just as we
are divided into various clans. There were Black ga·n, ga·no·waṇ
(meaning unknown), He Carries Pitch, Yellow ga·n, Weak ga·n,
Hairy On One Side Of His Face, Big ga·n, Red ga·n, Hump Backed
ga·n, and Gray ga·n. All these had daughters. They wanted to
know who would leave his daughter behind. They asked each one
if he would let his daughter stay behind with the Hawk People, but
all liked their daughters too well for this. So it came back to Black
ga·n, who was like the chief of these people,[2] "Well, I guess I will
have to leave my daughter." But he never told his daughter or
anyone else that he was going to leave her. He made a doll of turquoise and one of white shell. He hid these before they were going
to move.

The ga·n people spoke to the Hawk people. "We are going to
leave you now. Look after our crops for us. We will be gone for
sixty days. Then we will be back." Now they left. When they had
gone about half a mile, the mother of the daughter of Black ga·n
said to the girl: "Did you put your doll in the burden basket ? Is
it there ?" "No, no doll here," said the daughter. "Well, you better
go back for it. We will go slow for you," the mother said. So the
little girl started to run to the camp. She found the doll right away
and ran back to join her mother. There was a large lake ahead.
She followed the trail of her people. In a little way the tracks came
to the edge of the lake and all went into the water. A lot of grass
had been trodden down by the people passing over it. The little
girl went around to the other side, but could not find where they
had come out of the lake. So she went back to the old camp. The

---

[1] These are the symptoms of hawk and ga·n sickness.
[2] Black ga·n and Talking ga·n are always spoken of as the two leaders among
the ga·n.

Hawk people saw her and said, "What is that little girl doing over there?" They went with her to the lake, but they could not find where tracks came out of the water. They took her home with them. Every day she went to try and find her mother.

The Hawk people raised this little girl among them. After quite a while all the crops were gone and the people lived as before. They fed the little girl on wild seeds. The ga·n had made the crops grow and ripen by their wish alone. The little girl stayed at a ndiᶜnde·zn camp (clan). They raised her. She was big now, old enough to marry. So the man who brought her up said, "I didn't raise her for anyone else. It will be well for her to marry my son." That is the way it happened. After they had been married about a year, she bore a baby boy. The day he was born ga·n people came down from above and filled the wickiup. It was overcrowded, but ga·n said, "He never stops eating (even though full)," and this way more kept crowding in and shoving over to make room for others. The baby was the grandson of Black ga·n, who was lying outside, on his back. The ga·n picked the baby up and passed him from one to the other. Last of all they took him out to his grandfather. There he danced the baby up and down on his chest and sang; "cawa cawa ca." Then he said to his daughter, "Well, daughter, here is deer medicine. Put it inside the hood of the cradle, by the baby." But the baby's mother said, "No, I don't want it. You threw this baby away long ago" (meaning herself). So she gave the deer medicine to her husband's mother. Black ga·n had brought the deer medicine so that when the baby grew up he could kill many deer. But instead of this the deer medicine was given to the ndiᶜnde·zn (the clan of the woman's mother-in-law). On account of this ndiᶜnde·zn clan always used to kill big deer, very big ones, whenever they went hunting. This still was true up till about 1880, but there are hardly any of this clan left now.[1] Black ga·n gave his grandson a name; naba·dzisnda·he (captive taken in war), because the ga·n had left his mother behind among these other people who had raised her.

They lived on there. Then in a year more another baby was born to the woman. The ga·n people came there again, just as they had before. Black ga·n came there to see his grandson. He gave this second boy a name also, but I have forgotten it.

Then the boys started to grow up. They were so high and about ten years old, big enough to hunt birds. In the morning they went hunting. At sundown they returned home. After spending the night there, they went hunting again. Sometimes they would be gone for two days, sometimes for three or four. Then one man among the Hawk people became sick. They came to the mother of the boys about it. "My female relative-in-law, I wonder if you have anything to say that will cure this sick man. You might have

---

[1] Deer is also the "relative" of this clan.

something," they said. "I don't know anything. You people have known me since I was a little girl, left here and raised by you. If I knew something I could go ahead and say it over that sick man now, but I don't," she told them. Finally she said, "Well, ask those two boys. They are gone for a day or sometimes three or four days at a time. I believe they go to the ga·n, because they are relatives to them. You people better go after a deer. Run the deer down, don't shoot him. Bring the hide home and make buckskin of it. Then get some downy eagle feathers and turquoise. Tie these to the forehead of the buckskin and put it on the boy's foot. See what they will say." So they went hunting and got a big deer by running it down. When the deer was all in, they caught it without shooting, as there must be no arrow holes in the buckskin. They killed it, cut it down the belly and by the next day they had made it into a buckskin. Then they put turquoise and a downy eagle feather on its forehead and placed it on the foot of the eldest of the two brothers.[1] But he threw it to his younger brother, "Here is the one," he said. The younger brother threw it back to the other, saying, "You can do it." They did this several times and finally one said, "All right." When they had agreed to what the people asked of them, the boys told them, "Fix up a place; level it up so that there are no uneven places on the ground. We want a spruce tree put on each of the four sides and a pile of wood on each side also. Don't be afraid of anything you see, or run away." They knew that the people might fear the ga·n. "For the sick man, spread a buckskin and let him sit on it. Tie him all over with strips of yucca leaves and let him sit there."

Then it was sundown and now it was dark. All the people came to the dance ground. Lots of fires were all about it. Then the boy who had consented, started to sing.

"Holy power, here sounding (making a noise)."

As he sang they saw lightning appear over ntca'na·sk'id on the east side, then on the south side, then west and then on the north side. Then from the four directions the bull roarer sounded. It shook the earth and the earth rumbled back in response. The people saw the flashes of lightning and thought they were far off, but soon the ga·n came down, upside down they were, feet up and head down. They picked up the sick man who sat there, and tossed him from one to the other.[2] Before, no man was sick, but this man became sick and from then on there were sicknesses. That night the sick man was cured. The ga·n left at dawn. One of the two brothers went with them. I don't known which of them it was. Only one of the boys remained among the people.

---

[1] The requisite ceremonial gift for certain ceremonies is a buckskin with a turquoise tied to the forehead as described.

[2] The idea of the sick man being ignominiously tossed about greatly amused the listeners.

When the ga·n arrived back at their home, they came together
and talked about the youths and maidens. "We have many girls
and boys here. Those people whom we left have many boys and
girls also. It is not right for us to marry among ourselves. We
better go there and get some of their boys and girls," they said.
Then Black ga·n's grandson (the brother remaining among the
people) was going to make another dance at ntca'na·sk'id. This
time it was to be only a social dance. The ga·n people came to this
dance. It was just for pleasure and was not dangerous as it had been
before. Then as the dawn came, the dancers were raised up off the
ground. Many youths and maidens from among the ga·n and Hawk
peoples were dancing. The old people ran under them and said to
their sons and daughters, "Come down, come back," but they kept
moving upwards. Soon they were so high they could not hear the
singing any longer, only the sound of the drum. Then they could not
hear the drum any more. The people below lay on their backs in
order to look upwards. They could see the dancers there like specks
in the sky. They saw them a little while, then saw them no more.
This is how the good people were taken up above, to the place where
life has no end. Both the brothers were gone now. The woman who
was their mother went off for something and never returned. This
is the end of the story. This is the way that the ga·n curing ceremony started.

20. *THE MAIDEN FROM WHOM THEY DISAPPEARED INTO THE WATER:
INSIDE ELK'S BELLY[1]

It is worth a great deal to hear about holy power and learn it.
When a man wants to learn holy power, he goes to a person who
knows it, then he listens all night long until sunrise. They never
tell stories like this in daytime. This is so the Sun will not see them.

On the other side of the White Mountains, at dziłna·hodiłe, there
our people used to live, long ago (northeast of White Mountains).
One of the men living there said, "Later on there will be something
bad that will happen to us." Someone had told him this, as if the
word had come from some other place. He was told to make a sweat
lodge and to have all the people come together to hold a council.[2]
"We will have plenty of food to eat while we are holding the council," he said. This man who was the chief of that camp always
talked to his people early in the morning. He went up to the top of
the mountain there. At that time all the birds, eagles, hawks, all
of them, talked as we do now.

Now among all the birds and animals camped at that place where
the council was to be held, a great sickness came and spread. While

---

[1] Told by Bane Tithla.
[2] Any large meeting was commonly the occasion for a sweat bath. Food was
brought the men at the bath, by the women.

this was going on there were many people living there. If Hawk people passed near people or touched them, the people would get sick. Also if a ga·n brushed against people, the people would get sick. This is the way our people got their knowledge of how we can get sick from ga·n and how to cure sickness with the ga·n ceremony, also how we can cure hawk sickness with the hawk ceremony. This story is about the ga·n people from here on.

This was the time; while people were living on the earth with animals, that all kinds of sickness started. Since that time we have had sickness. Before that time people used to live well with no sickness. A man who had good health and lived long with no sickness and no trouble, was the first one to know what was going to happen to the people. Black ga·n (the man) told Hummingbird to go and see what was happening on the earth, up near the sky, in the clouds and try to find where the best place to live was; where they could live well to old age with no sickness. The last time Hummingbird went out to look for this place, he found where Gopher had piled up the earth at the mouth of his hole. Hummingbird flew down this hole to its very end. There he found where people were living in a good way, with no sickness. All was good. Then Hummingbird found them. This happened very long ago, at the time there was no wind, no rain, no clouds. For many years it was like this because something was going to happen. When they put a downy eagle feather on the ground, it would not move. Everything was absolutely quiet, as if it had stopped.

Then the head man, the one whom I spoke of before, was still there. He said that part of the people must move off, and one of them must leave their daughter (she must be about twelve years old) behind. He told them this every morning, "We will move off to a different country where we will live as long as life exists (life in general)." They told each family to leave their daughter on earth, but none wanted to leave their girl behind. They all wanted their daughters to go along with them. Then that chief who knew what was going to happen, said, "I don't want it to take so long; it must be done now. I'm going to leave my girl behind here." Then he said to his daughter and the others, "I want you to dress yourself up and pack your things ready to move." The girl did not know what was going to happen to her and the other people did not tell her. Then they all started to move out from that place. There was a big water in front of them and they went towards it. The girl was with them, but she did not know she was going to stay on earth. They traveled for about one mile and then in a little while they said to the girl, "We forgot about your little toys; little cups and dishes of pottery." They had not forgotten about them at all, but they told the girl that and sent her back after them. When the girl started back to get her toys, all the rest of the people went on to the big water. When they got to its edge, the water rose by itself. They could see a trail going in under the water and they all went in on this. When all were in under the water, it fell back and all those people were gone.

Then the river was as it was before. The girl came back. She did not know which way the people had gone. She thought they had crossed the river, so she wanted to cross it also. She followed their tracks to the edge of the river where they went in, but she could not find where they had gone, nor find where their tracks came out again. She began to cry and she went back and forth along the edge of the water, but could not find her people. From that time on this girl had good luck because she was left behind and God looked after her. When a story (incident) like this is finished, the shaman tells the man whom he is teaching, "Put your own mind to live like this and be in no trouble."

While the girl was still crying, Elk came to her and said, "What are you crying for?" The girl told him, "We were all close to the river and then they sent me back after my doll and playthings. When I got back, the other people had gone to the edge of the river. I trailed them here, but I can't find them anywhere. That's why I am crying." Then Elk said, "Maybe you had better get on my back and I will cross the river with you." The girl said, "If you go out in the middle of the river I think you will shake yourself, and if you do I will fall in the water." "No, I won't do that," Elk said, but the girl said, "I think you will." "If you don't want to get on my back, then get on my neck and put both your hands on my horns and we will cross that way." "If you go half way, you might put your head in the river with me," the girl said. "Then what shall we do? I say this way, but you say no. How will you cross? How about going inside my anus? That would be the best way to cross." Now the girl thought, "This will be the safest way to cross over." So she got inside Elk's anus. Then Elk went in the water. After a while the girl asked him, "Are you across the river yet?" because she thought that Elk must be taking her away to another country and not across the river at all. "No, not across yet," said Elk. "Well, I want you to paw the water with your front legs," she said. Elk did and she could hear the water splashing. Then after quite a way more, she said, "Are you across yet?" "No, a little way left yet," said Elk. "Then let's hear you splash the water." Elk splashed and she heard the noise. Further on she asked, "Are we across the water yet?" and now Elk said yes, they were across "Well, let me hear you stamp hard on the ground so I can tell," she said. Elk stamped on the ground and she could hear it.

This girl had done something in Elk's belly, but she came out all the same. Just after she came out, Elk died. She must have hurt Elk's belly.

Then that girl used Elk's meat. While she was there some snakes came out of the river to her. She cut open Elk's belly with be·cdjicdjine (obsidsian ?), then she used Elk's inside stomach and took all his guts out and gave them to the snakes, telling them to wash out the faeces. The snakes washed out all this and there was some fat left. The snakes ate all this.

While she was still there, she had good luck. Coyote came there and then the girl changed to a porcupine. When Coyote got there he asked for some meat, so she gave him some little scraps of meat. She thought Coyote would come back again later, so she put all the meat up in a tree. Pretty soon Coyote came back again. He had been far off where his family was and brought them all back with him. Coyote looked for the meat. There was some there and he looked up and saw it in the tree. Then he spoke to the porcupine, "ciɫna"a·c (my cross cousin),[1] my children want meat and I want you to give them some." Then the girl porcupine threw some old guts down to the ground which were no good. Coyote saw this and he stayed under the tree quite a while. Then Porcupine got angry at Coyote for acting like this. She thought she would fix him, so she said, "I want you to lie down under this tree with all your family and cover yourselves all over with a coyote skin blanket that has no holes in it. Be sure and cover yourselves well with it. I don't want you looking out from under the sides." So Coyote and his family did this and lay there, expecting something good. Then Porcupine took one of the big elk hip bones and threw it down on top of the blanket. One of the Coyote children was looking out from under the edge of the blanket with just one eye. When he saw the heavy bone coming, he yelled, "Here is something!" and he jumped out from under the blanket and got away. All the rest of Coyote's family and Coyote himself were killed. Then Porcupine got down out of the tree and ran around.

My yucca fruits lie piled up.

21. THE MAN WHO BECAME A GA·N[2]

Here is an old story which comes down to us from long ago, that I will tell you. You see this ridge here, dividing this canyon from the next one over to the east (ridge between east and west forks of Cedar Creek). Well, long ago they had lots of game on top of it, and the people used to go hunting up there all the time. There was one man living among the people here who was of the na·ɣodesgijn clan (notch between hills people).[3] He told the hunters, "If you kill a deer on that ridge, do not skin it there." But they did not heed him and went out hunting, killed a deer there and right away they skinned and butchered it. When this man found out about it, he

---

[1] This term is generally used by a man for male cross-cousins. Its use to a female emphasizes Coyote's eccentricity.

[2] Told by Alsus, on West fork of Cedar Creek.

[3] This clan was mainly concentrated in the area described.

told them, "I told you not to do that. Something bad will happen now. I tell you, if you kill a deer on that ridge, do not skin it next time." But they paid no attention to him and not long after that they killed another deer and her fawn. They skinned and butchered both right there. When the man found out about this, he said to them, "Why did you do that? Didn't I tell you that you should not skin the deer there? Now something is going to happen. After this if you kill a deer there, do not skin it." But the people did not believe him, for they went hunting again up there and this time further up in this direction (northwards), towards tłuk'a·'al'i̜· (an old farming site on west fork of Cedar Creek). Near here they saw a big buck and killed him. When they went to this deer they saw that one of his ears had been marked recently, just the day before. This had been done by ga·n people and the deer belonged to them. That is why they had earmarked it. Then the hunters had done a bad thing.

Some time after that the man who had warned them, was walking along the top of this ridge, going northwards. He came to a porcupine. He mounted the porcupine and rode it like a horse. The porcupine took him along up the ridge and as they went the man dragged the toes of his moccasins in the soft ground once in a while. He did not know where he was being taken and wanted to leave some sort of tracks on the ground that the people might be able to trail him, if he did not come back. After they had traveled some distance this way, they arrived at the mouth of a cave which is in the other side of this big bluff that you can see above here (north side of the bluff about a mile or two above the farming site mentioned before). The man rode the porcupine right into the cave and when inside he dismounted. Then the porcupine pushed him on into the passage leading inward. He went into the cave and followed a sort of tunnel for almost a mile, which finally took him out on top of a mountain. There on this mountain ga·n people were living and the man stayed with them.

Quite a long time afterwards the ga·n came among the people at tłuk'a·'al'i̜· to dance.[1] ga·n came there from the four sides, all gathering at that place and dancing. The man who had gone away and lived with the ga·n used to have a small dog. This dog was still there among his people at home. While the ga·n were dancing there, it ran up to one of them and jumped up on him, playing about his feet as if glad to see him. This ga·n was his master and he knew him. He had come there with the ga·n and was now himself a ga·n. At the end of the dance, the people came to him as they had found from the dog who he was. They wanted him to return and live with them as he had before, but he spoke with them, saying, "No, I cannot come back and live with you now. What would I do with

---

[1] Though at present men are dressed up as ga·n dancers, long ago the ga·n themselves used to dance for the people.

this hair on my face here," and he tugged at the growth of hair on the side of his face. He had turned into ni·k'izditluk (hairy on one side of his face, a type of ga·n), and so he could never get rid of this hair. He departed with the ga·n and never again came back to his people.

22. *MAKING A CHIEF: SUN AND THUNDER: SUN AND DARKNESS[1]

Long, long ago they called a council in the Sun's house to see who should be made chief. Coyote wanted to be chief that time so he went there. They said, "All right you will be chief if you can read this paper here," and they gave Coyote the piece of paper to read. Coyote looked at it and tried to read it, but all he did was to keep saying, "sisi, sisi, sisi" that way, so they said, "Go out in the hills, Coyote, and there you can be chief." So that is where Coyote went and why you still can hear him hollering there.

Then Mocking Bird wanted to be chief, the one who always talks too much, so they told him to go ahead and see if he could talk well enough to be a chief.[2] He started in to talk, and he talked pretty well, too, except that he kept copying things that he had heard other people say in his speech. So they said, "All right, you talk this way, copying, so from now on you will talk this way in the trees," and this is why Mocking Bird is always talking in the trees.

Then Gopher wanted to be chief. "I will be a good one for chief because I am as if in charge of everything in the world here."[3] But there was a whole crowd of people there and they made fun of Gopher. "Chief with sacks on each side of his face," they said, "we will know everything that you are eating now." No one wanted him for chief, so he got mad and went outside. There he gathered up all the wind, the clouds, the rain and made them into a ball and stuck them in his sacks (cheek pouches). Also he took all the plants and grasses from all over the earth and put them in his sacks. Now he went under the earth and left these people.

When he left, the world was absolutely still and there was not a breath of air. You could stick an eagle's downy feather in the ground and it would not move at all. Then those people tried to locate Gopher and get him to bring back everything on the earth that he had taken. (Hummingbird goes out by himself and looks all over the sky and earth and finally finds Gopher under the earth where everything is growing and there is a lot of rain, etc., just as in the ga·n myth. But no ga·n were mentioned in this story. Hummingbird did it on his own.) Gopher said to Hummingbird, "You people

---

[1] Told by Palmer Valor.
[2] Good speech making is one of the requisites of a chief.
[3] Gopher's remark about his being "in charge" is typical of certain Apache types; chiefs, powerful shamans and also self important men whom others do not take seriously. It is a phrase of self assertion.

laughed at me when I wanted to be chief, so now if you want me
to come back you will have to make a dance for me for twelve days.
If you do this, on the morning of the twelfth day at sunrise I will
come back to you." (So Hummingbird goes back and lies there
and breaks wind because of his gorging. After four days he tells the
people what Gopher said, just as in the ga·n myth.) Then the people
started to make that dance as Gopher wished. They danced for
twelve days and on the morning of the twelfth day, just at sunrise,
Gopher came back on the earth. At the same time that he came
back there were clouds in the sky, wind and rain, and all the plants
were growing again.

Then the Sun and Black Thunder were talking together and arguing which one raised most plants on this earth. Each said it was he
who raised the most plants. "It's not you who raises the plants,"
Sun said to Black Thunder, "it's I." So Black Thunder said, "All
right, you say you are the chief of this thing, so let's see you plant
something and maybe you can raise it by yourself." So the Sun
planted corn, but when the corn got about a foot or so tall, it all
dried up and died because there was no water. Then the Sun said
to Black Thunder, "You are right after all, you are the one in
charge of the plants, so let's see you plant something." So Black
Thunder did plant corn, but when it got about two feet tall the corn
leaves turned all yellow because there was a lot of thunder and rain
all the time and too much water. Then Sun and Black Thunder
talked about it. "We were both wrong. The way it is is this. We
should help each other and that way it will be all right." They
planted corn again and when it got about two feet high, the leaves
started to twist. This meant the corn was getting dry, so Black
Thunder made it rain and the corn grew again well. Now the Sun
looked at his field and was glad. This way he raised lots of crops,
because Black Thunder and he worked together. "From now on
this is the way we will do, helping each other. As long as the earth
rests here we will raise lots of crops," they said.

Then Sun and Darkness started to talk to each other. "We will
be both the same way," they said. Then Sun said, "From noon
still sundown I will always be with some of these people and they
will go down with me, the nde·ziz (dead people's bodies)." Then
Darkness said, "I will do the same way when I am home. At dawn,
when darkness goes, there will always be some nde·ziz who go with
me."

This is a very big earth and there is always lots going on here,
across the ocean, everywhere, and so this is why the Sun and Darkness talked this way. This means that every day and every night
some place on this earth, people die.[1]

---

[1] This is a regular belief, and it is said of Sun and Darkness that they take
people with them.

23. *ROAD-RUNNER YOUTH MAKES MULBERY MAN[1]

Long ago they say. Just as here 'at Bylas, there were lots of people living together at a place. There Road-runner was living with his mother. Both were very poor and hungry, because they had little to eat. The other people there had lots to eat though. In those days all the different kinds of birds were like people, and that is the way this camp was.

Then their chief talked to them; he said, "All the boys and girls are to go out and gather different kinds of seeds." So the boys and girls were all out gathering seeds, lots of them. They had carrying baskets and seed beaters to knock the berries and seeds off the bushes with. They gathered the food like this all day, two together, a boy and a girl. Then at sunset they all went home with each other. When they got home the girls would cook the seeds up well and then take them to the camps of the boys they had been out with, and there they would eat with each other. The girls always used to choose the boys that they wanted to go out with when they went to gather seeds.[2] None of the girls wanted Road-runner and so no one would take him out with her. The way they used to do was this; all the boys and girls met in the middle of the camp and then they would pair off to go together for seeds. Road Runner went to this meeting and stood with the other boys. Then the boys and girls all paired up and started off. There was only one boy left behind who no one had chosen and this was Road-runner. There was nothing for Road-runner to do but to go home, and so he did. The next morning they all met again in the middle of the camps, but it was the same this time as it was before; Road-runner went, but he did not get chosen and was left behind again. The girls had brought their carrying baskets and their seed beaters with them to gather the seeds in. Road-runner had brought a seed beater with him, but the girls would have nothing to do with him. This way all the boys and girls went off and left him, so he went back to his home again. In the evening when the couples came in with the seeds that they had gathered, the girls cooked them up well and took the food to the camps of the boys, where it was eaten. Road-runner's mother just had to stay in her camp without food.

Some time after this Road-runner had a message from God about something that he was to do. "Go and cut a stick of wild mulberry; make it so long, and also make it smooth. Then take it to the river and put it in the mud along the edge of the water. Leave it there for four days." Road-runner did as he was told to do. He fixed the

---

[1] Told by Bane Tithla.
[2] Boys and girls who were courting formerly went off in groups to gather seeds, making a social event of it. Old people often mention this. Notice that the girls choose the boys. Girls commonly make public advances to boys and girls, never boys, choose a dancing partner of the opposite sex.

stick of wild mulberry good and smooth and the right length. He went to the river bank, where he put it in the mud and left it. Quail Girl was the best one of the girls who went with the boys to gather seeds each day. She was the only one in the whole bunch who had any good looks. Road-runner was thinking about her now. The next day Road-runner went to where he had put the mulberry stick in the mud to see what was happening. When he got there he saw that the stick looked a little like a man. He went back home after he had seen it, and stayed there all day. In the evening the other boys and girls came in, bringing the seeds that they had gathered. These they cooked up and ate together as usual. They were all having a good time there. Only Road-runner was very poor and unhappy. None of the men or girls liked him. The next morning Road-runner went to the river and looked at the stick he had put there. This time it looked almost like a real man and one end of it was turning into the head. After that he went home and stayed there. At sunset again, all the boys and girls came in in a long line, bringing their seeds to cook. They had lots to eat and all had a good time. Every girl there had some boy that she was good friends with. The third day Road-runner went again to where he had that mulberry stick in the mud. This time the piece of wood was lying in the mud with legs, arms and hands and head already formed. The hair on its head was nice and long and hung to the middle of the back. Then Road-runner went home. In the evening the boys and girls came in, all in line, carrying their seeds. The girls cooked the food and took it to the boys in their camps, where they ate and enjoyed themselves. The rest flirted together and had a good time, but Road-runner was still poor and lived there without food. On the fourth day Road-runner went to river bank again to look at the piece of wood. When he looked he saw a young man there: good looking, better than any that were in all the camps. He would be the best looking one of all the boys at that place. He wore moccasins of good buckskin that were painted yellow and his buckskin shirt was painted yellow also.

Then Road-runner took this young man back with him to the camp. Nobody knew who the stranger was at all. Just like this, Road-runner went with him inside his camp. The next morning all the boys and girls gathered together to start out to get seeds again. Road-runner went over there because he thought that this time some girl might want him. For this reason he took a seed beater with him. All the boys lined up and Road-runner got right in the middle, where he thought he would have the best chance of being chosen. Then the girls started to pick their boys and go off with them in couples. Pretty soon a girl came right towards him, and as the other boys in front of him had already been chosen he thought this time sure he was going to be picked. But she skipped him and took a boy right behind him instead. Road-runner ought to have had enough sense to get out, but, he stayed and kept on hoping.[1] There were a lot of boys behind him and these the girls chose, till he was the only boy left. Then they were all gone and so Road-runner went back to his home. This is why our people always tell their boys not to do as Road-runner did when the girls do not like him, and try to force himself upon them: "If you do this you are liable to become the way Road-runner was," they say. That evening they all came home with their baskets full of seeds they had gathered with seed beaters. Then each girl who had been out, cooked up the food that she had brought in and took it to the camp of the boy she had been out with. There, with the boy and his parents, she ate it and everyone felt good. Road-runner was very poor, staying with his mother. All they had to eat was a few seeds that an old woman had given them. Though they were living among all these people who had lots to eat, they went hungry most of the time.

Mulberry Man was staying with Road-runner and his mother. In that camp there was nothing at all. Road-runner's mother had a big tʻusʼistɬuḷ (woven water bottle) without any pitch on it. When anyone was coming she would put Mulberry Man in this, so no one would see him. Thus the old woman who used to come and visit never knew this strange man was staying there. After she had gone Mulberry Man came out again and was with Road-runner and his mother. That's the way they did every time. Then some other people became suspicious that something was going on in Road-runner's camp. The old woman who had been visiting the camp also thought that something was being hidden from her. For this reason she came to the camp whenever she had an excuse, so she would have a chance to look around.[2] But Road-runner always stayed outside the camp and kept watch for anyone coming. If someone was getting close he would warn them in the camp, and Mulberry Man would hide in the basket. All the same that old woman had heard some one else talking in the camp, as if he were telling a story to Road-runner's mother. Thus she came to think that there was surely a man in the basket, who told stories to the mother when nobody else was around. But she did not say anything about it in their camp; she just kept watching. Then after a while the old woman said to the other people that there was a good looking young man in Road-runner's camp, and for some men to go there and find him. So some of them went there and looked for the young man. Road-runner had turned the tʻus that he was hidden in upside down, and though the men looked all over for him they could not find him. Finally they gave it up and went away. The old woman was very curious to see that young man though and so she kept on coming to Road-Runner's camp whenever she could. She

---

[1] Road-runner's social plight together with the thought of this ludicrous bird in such a position, always causes laughter.

[2] This a common ruse whenever undue curiosity is aroused.

kept on telling the other people that there was a strange young man in that camp. The people looked through the camp for three days but they could find nothing, because they did not think to look in the t'us that was turned upside down. On the fourth day the old woman went to Road-runner's camp, where she made an excuse of telling a story to his mother. This time she found out that the young man was in the old t'us, and so when she came away she told the other people that the man they were looking for was in the t'us. The people had a meeting about this. Road-runner and his mother went there. They heard the people talking about someone being in their camp. Then the men asked them straight out, "Who is that young man that is staying in your camp with you ? Where did he come from ?" But Road-runner and his mother said that there was no one except themselves in their camp and that nobody had been bothering them. "All the same there is someone staying there," the people said. "No, there is nobody that we ever saw around there," Road-runner and his mother said.

Now the men started to play shinney. "If the ball is knocked into your wickiup that will mean that you have a friend who has come to stay with you," the people said. So the men started to play shinney on a level place. Road-runner was playing to. He hit the ball away from his camp, but the others hit it back again. They kept on playing that way all day, back and forth. About sunset Road-runner got the ball because he was the fastest one. It was close to his camp when he got it and he hit it away as hard as he could, running after it. But he was all in and the other men knocked the ball into his wickiup past him. "Now we have knocked the ball into Road-runner's camp," the men said, and so they all gathered and went to the camp there. Here they found Mulberry Man and took him out of the basket. Now all the people saw Mulberry Man and they said to him, "The one that you are staying with is your brother. You stay with him; he is your brother." Every man there said this to him. Right then the chief talked to all the people and told them that they were to go out and gather more seeds again. But Road-runner did not want to go to where they were going to choose partners and so he just stayed with his new brother at home. All the girls chose boys to go with them, all except Quail Girl who did not pick anyone. On their way out some of the girls stopped at Road-runner's camp. They came close to the doorway and said, "Come on, let's go and gather seeds!" But Road-runner and his brother said no, that they would not go. Then Road-runner's mother said no also and so the girls went off for seeds. The next day they met again and the girls chose their boys. Some of the girls did not choose anyone and these stayed behind. The good looking Quail Girl did not pick anyone and so she stayed behind also. Then the girls that were left went to Road-runner's camp and stopped at the door. "Come on, let's go and gather seeds!" they said.

"No," Road-runner and his mother said. So the girls went off on their way. Then Road-runner said to his mother that he was feeling bad because the girls would have nothing to do with him before. For this reason he did not want to go now. "Because of this I made you for my brother. I had a hard time here. I and my mother were poor and that's why I made you, my brother. I made you myself."

In the evening all the boys and girls came home with lots of seeds and they all had plenty to eat. Three mornings the girls came for Road-runner and his brother, but they would not go. Then the chief talked about Road-runner, because he did not want to go and gather seeds with those girls. "It is because the girls did not want him before," he said. So the chief said to the girls, "If you go to Road-runner's place, ask him to go with you for seeds and if he will not go with you, catch hold of him and take him out. Just one girl grab him." The next morning the boys and girls came together and paired off to go and gather seeds. But some of the girls stayed behind and these girls came over to Road-runner's camp. Before this the good looking Quail Girl used to choose a boy right away, but now she did not do it and she was one of the girls who stayed behind. When these girls got to Road-runner's camp they said, "Come on, let's go and gather seeds!" But he would not go and so one of the girls went inside and took his hand and led him out. Then the girl and Road-runner were standing outside, so Quail Girl went in and took the brother's hand and led him outside also. They started off with the two boys and gathered seeds. When they gathered the seeds they beat them off the bushes with seed beaters. Then at sunset they all came home. Road-runner and his brother came also. The girls who had been out with them cooked up a big lot of the seeds and brought them to Road-runner's camp. There they made all kinds of food and ate lots. Road-runner's mother ate lots now. The next morning the boys and girls had a meeting again and chose partners. The girls who were left all went to Road-runner's camp again, and there got those two boys to go with them for seeds. Then Road-runner was very glad and his mother was glad as well. When the girls stopped for Road-runner and his brother and asked them to go for seeds, they did not refuse at all, but went right out. Quail Girl always picked out Road-runner's brother, because both of them were good looking. Road-runner went with the same girl that he had been out with the first time. This way those two boys got to be good friends with these girls. That day at sunset, they all came in in a long line. Road-runner and his brother went to their camp. Then the girls cooked up a lot of seeds and took them to the boy's camp in many baskets. Road-runner's mother had lots to eat and the old woman was glad on account of this. Road-runner was also glad now, because he had a chance to flirt with the girls.

It was some time later that the good looking young man, Road-runner's brother, got married to the Quail Girl who was so pretty. So the new couple built a wickiup for themselves and lived there. Then Road-runner thought that he would like to get married also. The young people kept on doing as they had done before, going for seeds. Each day the girls came by for Road-runner. One day Yellow Warbler Girl stayed behind with the other girls and went with them to Road-runner's camp. She had left her old sweetheart and had come to this camp instead. When the girls got to the door they said, "Come on, let's go and gather seeds!" Then Yellow Warbler Girl went to Road-runner's brother who was there and led him out by the hand. One of the other girls took out Road-runner also, but she did not do it because she really liked him and wanted to flirt with him, but only because he had a good looking brother. Later on Road-runner's brother got to be good friends with Yellow Warbler Girl. They often went to gather seeds together, which they brought home and cooked and ate at his camp. They had lots to eat there. After a while Road-runner's brother got married to Yellow Warbler Girl. Now he had two wives and had two wickiups in his camp.[1] This is the way he lived with his two wives. Then Road-runner talked to his brother. "I want you to let me sleep on one side of your fire, in your wickiup," he said. "No, I don't want you to sleep there," the brother said, and though Road-runner kept on asking, his brother still refused him.

In those days there were all kinds of birds living in the world, just as there are now. Road-runner was still going with the other girls when they went for seeds. He thought that he would like to get married, but those girls were only kidding him along and really did not like him at all. He was still asking his brother to let him sleep in his wickiup and finally his brother said, "All right, you can sleep in my wickiup."

The young people kept on going for seeds each day and all had lots to eat. Then after a long time Road-runner said to his brother, "I want you to give me one of your wives, so that I and she can be married." His brother said no to this, but Road-runner kept on talking, "I made you into a man by cutting you out of mulberry and putting you into the mud. That is the way you became a man and for this reason I want you to do as I ask you." When the brother heard what Road-runner said, he was feeling pretty badly that he should be talked to this way. The other people heard about it also and for this reason all the people at that place went away somewhere. Next morning Road-runner and his mother woke up and found themselves all alone. Every camp was empty. Then Road-runner and his mother were as they had been before all this happened; very poor and with nothing to eat.

---

[1] Plural wives generally lived in separate wickiups within the same camp cluster.

As all the people had left, Road-runner started out to follow their tracks. He kept on trailing them for a long way and finally came to where they had camped for the night. There they had made a dance at night. The fire still remained. He went on, still following the people. That evening he came to where they had camped for the night again. Here they had danced all night too and gone on again. Road-runner found all this, but still he was following them. Then as he was following them he had a message from God, as before. This time the voice said, "Why are you doing this?" Road-runner answered, "I am following these people because my brother was taken away." It was noon and as he was going on, the voice said to him, "They are going to have a dance again tonight. Your brother is having a good time with those people. In the evening, at the place where they are to have the dance, there will be an old woman who will go to one side by herself. That old woman will be the mother of the Sun. Sun is the one who made all these people go away. You are to go to that old woman and throw her flat on the ground and step on her. Then take all her bones out and put on her skin. Take the stick that she was walking with, a staff, and walk with it like an old woman down to the dance. Then when you get close to the dance, dance yourself where the people are lined up. Stop and sing this song right where the men are standing around the fire in four circles. When they hear this song they will open a place for you to get through and they will say that you are the Sun's mother. This way you will go right inside, next to the fire. You will dance round it and sing that same song."

After Road-runner heard this he started to follow the people again. Just about sunset he came to the old woman he had been told about, going along in front of him. He caught up to her and threw her down on the ground and tramped on her. When he had got her body soft by doing this, he took all her bones out and put on her skin. Then he took her stick and started out walking like an old woman· towards the dance. Just at sunset he got near and could hear the' drum. In a little way he got to the dance and the men saw him and said; "Open up there, because the Sun's mother is coming. She is a good dancer."[1] Then Road-runner was right up to the dance and so he started to sing that song. The men opened up right away and let him through and into the dance. He knew that his brother was dancing there also, so he danced around inside those four circles of people, looking for his brother. After a while he found his brother. He danced over close to where he was. Then he said to him, "Are you the one?" "Yes, that's me," the brother said. "Then hurry up and follow me," he said. Road-runner went to where he had come into the circles, through the men. When he got there he put his brother in front of him. This way they got out. His

---

[1] During social and other dances, jocular old women frequently clown by dancing individually.

brother in front of him ran the fastest now and he followed behind. Back of him all the men were following and trying to overtake them. Pretty soon he was far ahead and all the others were way behind. Then he took off that old woman's skin, and threw it aside. He said to the Sun, "This is your mother's skin," and he threw it back to him. Those men were still chasing him and he did not know what to do to get rid of them. Then he had an idea. He split each of his feet in three pieces at the end. From that place on they could not tell which way he was going. So they had to give up the chase right there.[1] This way Road-runner got back to his home safely.

My yucca fruits lie piled up.

24. THE MAN WHO PURSUED MOUNTAIN SHEEP[2]

A man started out to hunt from t'usila°edi!γuj (a place near Rice). In a little way he came on a mountain sheep and ran after it to catch it, but it got too dark and so he gave it up. Next morning he started in to trail the mountain sheep again. He did not come up on it and when it became dark he stopped again. This was just below Warm Springs (on the San Carlos River), and he could see from the tracks that the animal was almost played out. It had dragged its feet on the ground. In the morning he went down and trailed it into the canyon there. A short distance in was a big bluff and right at the foot of it there was smoke coming out from a cave. An old woman and an old man were living there. The hunter arrived at the cave, "Oh, there are some people staying here!" he said. "Yes, we stay here," the old woman told him. The hunter spoke to them of what he had been doing, how he had trailed a mountain sheep for two days. "I trailed it here, but I don't know where it has gone." The old woman said, "Oh, was it you who did that?" The old man was lying there with his testes and scrotum hanging down onto the ground from between his legs, behind. He was all in and it was he who the hunter had trailed for two days. The old woman told him, "This is the one you have run for two days. We have sent word out about you, up there to tse·nodo·z and to tse·nazdlad and to tse·ts'isgedolza[3] about how you ran this old man. So you better run from here home right now. I dont know whether you can save your life or not."

The hunter started running from there to his home. He came close to the Triplets and from the tops of these the rocks started to slide downards into the canyon, where the road goes through now. The hunter yelled and the mountain rumbled just like thunder.

---

[1] It is difficult to tell which direction a road-runner's tracks go, because of the peculiar shape of his feet.

[2] Told by Francis Drake.

[3] Places where holy beings and animals live.

They went at him, but he escaped. All sorts of dangerous animals were coming behind him. He did not see them, but he heard their voices as they chased him. He got past that place and now he started to yell for help. This man was a ba·tci[1] and he was not far from home. They must have heard him coming in the camp. That is how they managed to save his life. The people came running out to help him. From that time on it became a rule that a mountain sheep must never be pursued and for the same reason buckskin can never be made of its hide. You can only kill and eat mountain sheep. That is all.

25. *WOLF AND MOUNTAIN LION HUNT TOGETHER: *WHITE-TAILED DEER AND MESCAL TALK TOGETHER: *SACK AND POT TALK TOGETHER[2]

Long, long ago, Mountain Lion and Wolf were killing all kinds of animals in a contest to see who was the best hunter. So they said one time, "We will go out at dawn and see who is the first to get something before sunrise." They bet on the outcome. Mountain Lion said to Wolf, "I don't think that you will bring in anything, but I will bring in a deer." Wolf answered, "I am the one who will get the deer and you will get nothing." They started off to hunt. Just about sunrise, Mountain Lion brought into camp 'ide·ɫgije' and a little while afterwards, Wolf brought in ni·ya·ge'iɫgij.[3] Both these deer were big. Thus Mountain Lion was the first to bring in something, but Wolf said, "We are both the same." Mountain Lion said, "We are not the same, because I brought in my deer first." Then Wolf said, "You crawl along on your belly and hide yourself. That is why you have sores on your belly and on your knees. That is the way you hunt." Mountain Lion answered, "You chase the deer all over and get them hot. Then you kill them and eat the meat when it is hot. It is no good that way." The reason that these two hate each other so much is due to this argument and contest of long ago.

Then Mescal[4] and White-tailed Deer were talking to each other. "If someone gets hungry, they can come and get me to eat any time. If a poor man is hungry, he can build a fire and roast me," said Mescal. Then Whitetailed Deer said, "If some poor man is hungry he can come to me, stand there and shoot me, then butcher me, build a fire, and cook my meat to eat. Also he can put some of my meat in a pot and boil it to make soup. This is the way that the poor man can make himself full and go on his way." On account of this, these two got mad at each other and still are.

---

[1] Apache Manso
[2] Told by Bane Tithla. "Sack and Pot Talk Together" is very probably a European tale.
[3] These two terms are descriptive of the horns of the deer. The first implies the largest of bucks.
[4] nadaɫba' (small species of mescal).

Then Clay Pot and Sack were talking to each other. Sack said, "If a poor man has something that he wants to put away, he can put it in me and I will keep it safely for him. I will keep corn for him this way. He will look around for something to put in so that I can keep it for him. Thus he will have lots to eat all the time." Then the Pot said, "If a poor man wants to eat, he can boil ground corn and other things in me. This way he can get something to eat right away." Then Pot and Sack got mad at each other because of their argument. Both of them went up on top of a high rock. When they got to the top, Sack said to Pot, "Let someone throw you off here and maybe you won't break. If someone threw me off, I wouldn't be broken at all." But Pot answered him, "If some one should build a fire and put me on it, I would not burn up. Nothing would happen to me. But if you were put on the fire, you would burn up right away, you Sack." Now these two were mad at each other on account of the argument.

My yucca fruits lie piled up.

VARIANT 1. (*WOLF AND MOUNTAIN LION HUNT TOGETHER)[1]

One time Wolf and Mountain Lion were camped together. They were both very great deer hunters, but they did not know which one was the best hunter. This way they decided to see who was the most successful hunter. They both started out when it got dark in the evening, each going in a different direction. Wolf hunted all night long, and finally killed one deer. He brought it back to camp. Pretty soon Mountain Lion came in with a deer also. Mountain Lion had hunted almost all night, too, and traveled a great way, as had Wolf. Mountain Lion said to Wolf, "You wear your claws off when you hunt because you run so much." Then Wolf said to Mountain Lion, "You wear all the fur off your elbows and legs the way you hunt, because you crawl along so much."

VARIANT 2 (WHEN EVERYTHING TALKED: *WHITE-TAILED DEER AND MESCAL TALK TOGETHER)[2]

Long ago when a person found lice in his blanket or on himself, he would kill them with his finger nail. He would say as if the louse was saying it, "White metal (fingernails) coming together upon me," for this is the way Louse said long ago. But Louse said, "If you just throw me in the fire to try and kill me, I will not die. I will walk out again."

This was very long ago when all the birds, animals, and insects talked as we do. Even fire drill could talk and he said, "If you do

---

[1] Told by Charlie Sago, at the head of Black River. Also called "Wolf And Mountain Lion Belittle Each Other."

[2] Told by Palmer Valor.

this way with me, whirl me around between your hands, fire will start."

Then pitch walked up to that place. "My name is 'Not without (me) is it feathered,'" he said, "because they always use me to paint the bands on their arrows about where the feathers are put."

Miller Moth was going on his way. He said, "If I see a fire on my way, I will never come home. If I don't see any fire, I will come home safely." And that's the way he has done ever since. Whenever he sees a fire, he flies into it and kills himself.

Then Mescal and White-tailed Deer were talking together. They were arguing about which of them was the most useful. White-tailed Deer said, "I am good for everything." "No, you are not, I am more useful than you," Mescal said. "No, you're not, I am more useful than you," White-tailed Deer said, "No, that's wrong," Mescal said, "these poor people have to chase you till you give out before they can kill you and boil your meat. But I sit right here all the time, and if someone wants me, all they have to do is come here, cut me off, and roast me." Then White-tailed Deer got mad and said, "What's the matter with you, tsị'tłʼige (Sticky Wood?) that you talk this way?" Mescal got mad also and said, "What are you talking this way for, tʻanaʼnaʻtsʼiʼnoʻzị·he (He Wishes for More, as if he (man) wished there was more meat on White-tailed Deer)?"

26. GRASSHOPPER LOSES HIS LEG: HOW GILA MONSTER GOT HIS NAME[1]

Long, long ago, when all the people were living far to the north, at taḷbakọ·waʻ (camps by dance ground), there were Mexicans living with the ba·tci[2] at a place on tʻusila·ʼediḷγuj (Cutter Wash, at its junction with the San Carlos Valley). There used to be lots of them living there and you can still see the stone walls of their old houses (prehistoric pueblo ruins). Later on they all moved over to Tucson where they still are. Our people used to come down from taḷbakọ·waʻ to this place, tʻusila·, on hunting trips. One time a war party started down and came to this place. Here they got in a fight with the ba·tci and Grasshopper had his leg shot off. The war party started back to taḷbakọ·waʻ. When they got there, they said that Grasshopper was shot and killed by the Mexicans in the fight. "He is not killed, he got back this morning before you. There he is running around over there," the people in camp said.

Then Turtle and Gila Monster started off from taḷbakọ·waʻ to hunt. They traveled on down by tʻusila· and there some Mexicans

---

[1] Told by Francis Drake. Compare Goddard, ibid p. 135.

[2] The Apaches Mansos, the same people already mentioned in other footnotes, were a small band of Apache of doubtful origin. They are said to have spoken a dialect similar to that of the Chiricahua Apache. During the 19th century they lived at Tucson and Tubac and often joined Mexicans, Papagos and Anglos in campaigning against the Western Apache.

and ba·tci surrounded them. Turtle said to Gila Monster, "Come over here and stand by my shell, it is hard and you won't get hurt." Gila Monster went over to him and from that place he shot and killed a Mexican woman. Gila Monster went over to the dead woman and crawled under her skirt, between her legs. "What's this here, like meat coming together in two parts," he called to Turtle. Turtle said, "Because of this, your name will be łe·nenlai (two parts meeting) from now on." When he left taļbakǫ·waᶜ he had another name, but when he went back he was known by this new name and he still is known by it.[1]

27. *CAPTURED[2]

One time some ba·tci[3] were out on a war party looking for our people. They came up from near t'usila·'ediļguj (Cutter Wash, just above Rice) and traveled north near where our people were living around tł'uk'a·gai (Fort Apache region).[4] There the ba·tci saw a boy and girl gathering seeds together. They ran at them, but only caught the girl. The boy got away. The ba·tci took the girl back with them to t'usila· (Cutter Wash).

The boy went to his home. Then he asked his mother to fix up enough food for two days. She cooked up a lot of old time food for him, seeds and other things and put them in a sack made of the skin of a small deer. Then he started off to that place where the ba·tci had caught the girl. From here he trailed them south, down to near t'usila·. He got there in the evening about dusk and went into the ba·tci camp. Here he met one old woman. He spoke with her. "It looks as if no one was here, grandmother," he said. There were no ba·tci there but that old woman. The old woman said, "All the people have gone to the place where they are dancing." Then the boy said, "I have been out hunting all day and I am hungry." Now the old woman cooked some stew for him and he ate it. Then she gave him a good Mexican blanket, all striped in colors, for the night and told him to return it to her in the morning.

The boy left her and and when he got out in the brush a way, he stripped, left his clothes there with the blanket, and only took his quiver on his back and his bow. Then he painted his body all over with white, and around his eyes he painted a black circle. This was so the ba·tci could not recognize him. Then he started off for the place where they were dancing. He could hear a drum over there and he went towards it. All the ba·tci were there. The boy stepped out and started to dance around by himself. The ba·tci, when they

---

[1] Individuals not infrequently acquired names in just such incidents as this.
[2] Told by Francis Drake. This story usually follows "How Gila Monster Got His Name."
[3] The Apaches Mansos.
[4] The Apache claim that the Gila Valley between Solomonville and Coolidge Dam was not yet occupied by them at the time of this tale.

saw him painted up the way he was, started to holler.[1] The boy
kept right on dancing. Some of them said, "Oh, he is such and such
a man," and they called a name. He kept right on dancing. At the
end of the song he sat down and rested. Then he was dancing again.
The ba·tci were talking among themselves and wondering who this
was dancing there. He looked like a stranger all right. The boy
kept looking around all the time and finally he saw her. A lot of
people were there. Then he knew it was his girl for sure; she was his
sweetheart. He took a little rock and wet it; then he threw it at
the girl and hit her. The girl picked the stone up. "This stone is
wet," she said. The boy came near and whispered to her, "This is me,
here, my cross-cousin."[2] The girl said, "You can't do anything to
help me; they keep me tied with a rope all the time and at night
they sleep on the other end of it so I won't get away." The boy took
his knife and threw it to the girl. "Here is my knife," he said. Then
the boy told her, "When you cut the rope go out in the brush and
hide there and wait for me, way over at that place." The girl cut
the rope and threw the knife back to the boy who stuck it in his
belt and started to dance again.

Then the ba·tci said among themselves, "That man is not one of
us." They were getting ready to take him. He sung for a little
while and then he sneaked off in the brush to the place the girl was
waiting for him. He told her to go ahead, and he ran back to where
they were dancing again, which he should not have done. There he
shot one arrow at the ba·tci. They hollered, "That man who was
dancing with us doesn't belong here at all," and everyone scattered
from the dancing place. The boy ran back to the girl and they
started off for home together.

They traveled up to the northeast as fast as they could. Just
before they got to tse·na·dje·he[3] the girl gave out. But they managed
to get to tse·na·dje·he all right. Here they cut some poles and
laid them against tse·na·dje·he and then laid more rocks over the
poles. They crawled in under and hid there. The ba·tci were following them from where they had run away. The boy and girl sat in
that place and made a prayer to tse·na·dje·he. Pretty soon the
ba·tci came up. They had trailed the two this far, but could not
find the tracks any further. They were looking all around for the
tracks, in the canyon and on the ridge. There was a whole crowd
of them gathered there on the trail. Some of the ba·tci boys started
to sing. They sang that they were lonesome for the girl who had
gone away. "You are gone away now back to your home,"[4] they

---

[1] When an individual shows off by dancing before a crowd, applause is voiced
by shouts and calls of the spectators.
[2] Marriage with a distantly related cross-cousin was very frequent.
[3] The name for a shrine made of piled up rocks. It is also a place name in this
tale.
[4] A love song.

sang. The girl and boy inside tse·na·dje·he were holding up one of the poles, and the girl started to shake this now so that one end of the pole shook a little. The ba·tci said, "That girl is far away now so we might as well go on home." They started back. As soon as they were gone, the boy and girl crawled out and started on their way again.

The two finally got back to where their people were living. Then the other people said, "You didn't go down there to get that girl for nothing. You might just as well marry her now." The boy said, "I never had it in my mind to marry this girl. I just brought her back because she looks nice and she always talked well with me. I don't want to hear you people talking that way any more." This way the boy did not marry that girl.

My yucca fruits lie piled up.

VARIANT[1]

Long ago they say. There were 'inda·[2] living at nit'egutci· (old San Carlos), lots of them. Then the 'inda· started off from where they lived. Then the 'inda· came to Dewey Flats, and they lived there. This way there are still the remains of their houses at Dewey Flats to this day. You can still see where there was a great house at that place, and this biggest house belonged to their chief. Then one time the 'inda· started off from that place and went northward. They were headed north to where our people were living at that time. With our people was living one good looking young man. There was also a beautiful and good girl. This boy and girl were great friends together.

The 'inda· came there and surrounded our people and tried to get them. But the people all scattered out in the brush and got away safely. Only one girl got caught and this was the good looking one who was the friend of the boy. Then the 'inda· started off with this girl to kinte·ldas'an̨ (broad houses standing, Dewey Flats).[3]

After the 'inda· had gone, all the people came together again and only that one girl was missing. The boy who was her friend felt very badly about this, so he told his mother, "Grind up some corn for me. I am going on a journey. Tie the corn meal up in a package." Then his mother did as he said, and in the morning he put the corn meal in his pouch and started off. When he got near Dewey Flats he sat down on the opposite side of the river and watched. He could see the 'inda· on the other side of the river and they were dancing.

---

[1] Told by Bane Tithla.

[2] A term for White People at present, but originally meaning enemy. It is still used in the latter way as in this tale and sometimes used to refer to inhabitants of prehistoric ruins.

[3] These are the large group of prehistoric ruins at Dewey Flats, on the Gila river. The name of the place refers to the ruins.

Then he got close to where they were dancing and made ready for what he was going to do. He took some dle·c (a white earth paint) and painted it all over his face. Then he tied his hair up on the top of his head in a knot with some grass. Now he took his quiver with the arrows in it and stuck it in his belt on one side and on the other side he put his bow.

It was dark now and he crossed over to where the 'inda· were. There were lots of them there, lined up round the fire where the dancing was going on. The boy went close to them. In the firelight they saw him and because it was dark they thought he was one of them. There was one girl dancing there and it was the girl who had been captured. This was why the boy had come to that place, so that he might help the girl. The 'inda· when they saw him, said, "Make way for him; there he is coming now; let him dance." It was a custom with these 'inda· for one man to go out and dance by himself, and that was why they said to make room for the boy. That girl was standing right behind where he was dancing, with her hands tied behind her to a stake. Now the boy who was dancing had a knife of obsidian with him in his moccasins. The captured girl was a good girl, with a good dress on. There were jingles on the dress. The boy started to dance and now he sang a song: "Open up, open up, make room," he sang in his song. He kept on dancing round about and danced in front of the chief's house, then he danced close to the chief. He had not yet seen the girl that he was looking for and that was why he was dancing around looking for her. He wondered where she could be. Then as he was dancing he came close to the girl and saw her. As he danced he said to her, "Are you the one?" but he was careful not to look at her. The girl heard him and said; "I am the one." Then while he was still dancing he said to her; "There is room for you to get away while I keep on dancing." But the girl told him, "I am tied up here. How can I run away?" So he threw the obsidian knife to her and told her; "Cut the rope and when I dance back you start to run away." He said this because he had it in his mind to shoot the 'inda· chief who was standing there.

Then the girl said, "I have cut the rope off all right." All this time the two had been careful not to let the 'inda· see that they were talking together, so the boy kept on dancing. Then the boy said to the girl, "All right, come on and follow me." He turned and shot the 'inda· chief with his bow and arrow. The rest of the 'inda· got scared and ran away. Then the two started to run for the river and got across it. The 'inda· chased after them with torches in their hands, but the two got away. After they had gone a way the girl said, "I am tired because I have these heavy clothes on." So the boy told her to take them off and she did. This way they were able to travel better. The 'inda· followed them till they lost their tracks, and then they gave up and went back to their home.

All the relatives of the girl who had been captured, thought she had been killed by the 'inda· and they were crying and mourning for her. Then the boy and the girl got close to their home again, after their escape. The boy told the girl to go straight back to her home and this way she returned to her relatives safely. All the girl's relatives were very glad that she was back again. Then her father and mother talked about what had happened, and that boy. They thought that now the boy had brought her back, he would marry the girl and so they went to the boy's camp to get him. But when they got there the boy said, "No, I am not going to marry her."

Maybe the 'inda· who captured the girl were ba·tci.[1]

"My yucca fruits lie piled up.

28. *THE OLD WOMAN AND BABY WHO WERE ABANDONED[2]

There were lots of camps together at that place. When the people moved away from there, they abandoned one old woman and a new born baby boy. When they left the old woman they told her that they would be back there in two days, or maybe tomorrow.[3] After all the people had gone, the old woman started to look around among the camps. She heard a baby crying and she went to it and got it. It was the one the people had left. She fed him on mescal mixed with water.

After a while this baby got older and stronger. Then he started to sit up. Later on he started to crawl around. Now the old woman set two sticks up in the ground a distance apart and tied a pole between them, up off the ground. This was for the baby to hold on to and learn to walk.[4] He used this quite a while and then he got so he was running around by himself. Later on he started to run faster. When he got a little older, the old woman made him a little bow and arrows to learn to shoot with. This way he got so he could shoot birds. He was about ten years old now, and the old woman was getting very old and feeble. She said to him, "cixwi·ye' (my grandchild), I am getting too old and feeble now and I can't do anything to help you any more. When you were a baby

---

[1] This sentence was in answer to a question as to whether the Apaches Mansos were involved or not. This tale together with the stories of "Grasshopper Loses His Leg," "How Gila Monster Got His Name," and the part in the creation myth told by Bane Tithla about the binda·yeiɣa·ni fleeing southward to nit'egotci·and na·ye'nezɣane taking refuge under Turtle's shell form a closely associated group of mythical events. In them are concentrated most of the few allusions in White Mountain mythology to prehistoric peoples and ruins. In one tale at least, the Mexicans and Apaches Mansos are described as the inhabitants of prehistoric ruins. There is possibly some confusion here of those two peoples and prehistoric enemies of some kind.

[2] Told by Francis Drake.

[3] When people became too old and feeble to travel, they were sometimes abandoned in this manner.

[4] A method still in use.

your parents went off and left you here. You had better go and try to find them as I am going to die soon. Here is dzoꞌ.[1] Stick him in your headband at the side of your ear, and he will always tell you what to do. I will die soon and that's why I am telling you this." This place was far north of where Fort Apache is now, way, way up there.

The boy left the old woman and started off. In a while he came to the place where the people had first camped after they abandoned the old woman and himself. dzoꞌ told him that the people had moved away from here so many years ago. He kept on going from one old camp site to another and at each place dzoꞌ would tell him how long the people had been gone. Whatever the boy thought he would like to have, he got. This way he got rats, rabbits, or young deer to eat. He had a hard time getting to his people, but he finally came to the place where they were living. Before he left the old woman had said to him, "Your mother's name is this and your father's name is that way," so the boy knew his parents' names.[2]

When he got to the camp, he said to the people there, "I have come over here to where my mother and father are living. Which is their camp?" The people said they did not know who were his mother and father. Then he spoke their names and told how the old woman had raised him. Now the people said to him, "Your mother and father are camped right over there, over at that place." The boy went to that camp. When he got there he said, "I have come to where my mother and father live." The woman said, "Who are you? What people do you come from?" "You are my mother. Long ago you left me and an old woman in that camp back there. The old woman raised me and just before she was getting ready to die, she told me who my parents were and sent me off to look for you," the boy said to his mother. "We left one baby and one old woman at that place, but the old woman could not have lived more than two days and I don't think that baby could have lived at all," his mother said. She would not believe this boy. "Well, my mother, I have come a long way to get to you, so don't talk that way. I am hungry, so cook something for me," he said to the woman. But they kept on arguing back and forth all night long. The next day his people moved their camp away on account of him, but he followed them. "You are my mother and you are my father. I am getting hungry; cook something for me. I want to eat," he said to them. But they said to him, "What kind of people are you? You talk too much. We don't know who you are," and they left him and went to another camp and stayed there all night. The next morning they came back, but the boy was still there. "My mother, I am hungry. Cook something for me," he said to the woman.

[1] A kind of supernatural power.
[2] Names and clan are the principal means of identification.

But his parents said, "We don't know you boy. You have made a mistake about us."

They did not want this boy at all, so the other men there said they would take him out hunting for deer. They all started out with the boy and came by a big yellow bluff. There was a cave in the foot of this. They told the boy to go and stand by it. Of the rest, some went up on the top of the bluff and some up its end to hunt. They carried a cedar bark torch with them, and now they set fire to the grass all round the foot of the bluff where the boy was. The fire started toward the boy. Then dzoʻ said in the boy's ear, "Take me and draw a line on the ground with me." The boy did this and whenever he drew on the ground with dzoʻ, it became just strips of bare earth, wide apart. Then he went on up to the top of the bluff. The people said, "That boy is too smart for us. We don't know how to do anything with him."

Then the boy went again to his parents' camp. "My mother, I am hungry, so cook something for me," he said to the woman. But his mother told him to stay away. Then he spoke to his father, "My father, give me something to eat."[1] But his father said, "What kind of a person are you? You are not my son." Then dzoʻ said in the boy's ear, "There will be a heavy wind that will blow rocks." The wind started to blow hard, it blew rocks about. "heˑ, my son, stop this wind," said his father. "Stop this wind, my boy," said his mother. "That's enough," said the boy, and the wind stopped. He stayed there one night and still asked for food. But his mother just talked the same way, "We are tired of you trying to fool us and make us ashamed,"[2] she said. Then dzoʻ said in the boy's ear, "There will be a heavy rain with big hail stones." It started to hail great big hail stones. All the people started to cry. "heˑ, my boy, make this hail stop," his father said. His mother said, "Make this stop, my child." "That's enough," said the boy, and the hail stopped. He stayed another night there. "My mother, I am hungry. Cook something for me," he said. But his mother said, "You chase us all around and keep asking for something to eat. Go away." Then dzoʻ said in his ear, "There will be rain coming down like hot water." It started to rain hot water. All the people said, "This is too hot." "heˑ, my son, make this stop," his father said. "Make it quit doing this way, my boy," said his mother. "That's enough," said the boy, and the hot rain stopped.

Then the people all moved away to get rid of this boy. In the morning the boy went to his mother and said, "My mother, I am hungry. Give me something to eat." His mother said, "Stay away

---

[1] Note that this is the only direct appeal the boy made to his father. All the other times he mentions the mother. Besides being in charge of food and cooking, it is generally thought that children are closer to the mother than the father.

[2] Ashamed of abandoning a child.

from us! We don't want you here. You do all kinds of bad things. You make wind to blow stones, you make big hail, and you make it rain hot water. We don't want you." Then dzoᶜ said in the boy's ear, "They will all turn to rocks." Where they were dancing they turned to rocks; where they were grinding seeds they turned to rocks; what they were cooking turned to rocks; everything turned to rock. The boy walked around in this place and there were lots of rocks all over. This is the end and those rocks are still standing there.

29. THE ABANDONED CHILDREN[1]

Long ago they say. Porcupine, a woman, was living with her two children, one a girl and the other, the younger one, a boy. She was a widow and was the only one of the children's relations still living. They were living in a camp like this one of mine here. Later on this widow started in to gamble at tse'dił (a dice game played with three sticks). Both her children were still small, but they followed her all the same, wherever she went. Then that woman said to her children, "You smell. Stay away from me." She kept on telling them to stay away from her. Finally she abandoned her children, ran off some place and did not come back.

At the same time one old woman and her son were living at that place by themselves. This old woman saw the two children the mother had abandoned. The little girl was coming along with her brother and both were crying. The son of the old woman told his mother, "Let them stay with us," but she said no. Still the boy asked her to let them stay with them. But the old woman said, "I told you these two smell too much, and that's why I don't want them here." The boy kept on asking his mother and saying, "But those two children are getting too poor. That is why I want them to live with us." Then the old woman said, "All right, call them over." So the boy called them. When the two children got there, they washed them all over with warm water.

Then these two children had been living with the old woman and her boy for quite a while. They were growing up and getting tall. The two boys went out together to hunt, along with the other men. They killed deer all right. The girl was tall and strong. She gathered all kinds of wild seeds, fruits and mescal and brought them into camp. Now she was getting lots to eat and they had lots of food on hand. They were all living well. Later on the girl was old enough to marry and the old woman's son was old enough also. They had all the food they needed on hand, so the old woman made them marry and they lived together.

After they were married, the boy hunted and killed lots of deer. They had lots of meat on hand. The girl also gathered lots of

---

[1] Told by Bane Tithla.

seeds and mescal and other foods. This way all the people who were living close by came there and were given lots of food. They all felt good over this.[1] After a while people who were living far off heard about it and they came there because they heard that this family was giving away lots of food to eat. Then that woman who was the real mother of the two children and who had abandoned them long ago, heard about this. So she thought she would come there to see for herself. She heard they had lots of food and that was why she wanted to go. But her two children felt badly about the way their mother had acted and they did not want to see her ever again.

Lots of people went to their camp and that woman followed behind. She got mad because all the other people were in front of her and she said, "You have no children there. You travel fast, but I am the one who has children there. I ought to be the one in the front. Pretty soon that woman got to the camp. Then her daughter had a baby. The woman sat far off from the camp and called to her daughter,[2] "My child, bring that baby to me." The daughter got mad, when she heard this because her mother was asking for the baby. She heard what her mother said all right, but she would not go to her. The people that the woman came with were given lots of food. The woman tried to get her daughter to come to her all that day till sundown, but she would not go to her. They would not give her any food either. Then that woman called to them, "Why don't you just throw me the scrotum," so the daughter put some rocks inside the scrotum and threw it at her mother. It hit the woman on the head, but it did not kill her, only knocked her over. The woman picked it up and walked under a tree. There she started to cook and eat it.

My yucca fruits lie piled up.

30. HER BROTHER BECOMES HER HUSBAND.[3]

One time a man and his wife were living together in a wickiup. This man's wife became sick. Her husband tried out for her all kinds of medicine, but she could not get well. All the different shamans sang over her, but still she did not get well. Then they held a ga·n dance for her, but it did not cure her.

The husband sat down there and began to think. It seemed as if there was nothing that could be done for the woman. Over beyond the camp was a little hill and his wife told him to carry her up on that hill, as she would like to be there, on top. So the

---

[1] Note the typical stress on diligence in procuring food supplies, also the pattern of the rich and industrious giving away food.
[2] She wished to avoid her son-in-law, the common practice.
[3] Told by Bane Tithla.

man started carrying his wife and got to the top of the hill with her just at sunset. After she had been there a while, she told her husband to carry her back to camp again. After that, very often she would ask her husband to carry her to the top of this little hill and leave her there for a while. Now she had been this way for a long time. This woman was not sick, she was just lying about it and pretending that she was sick. This way she kept on telling her husband to carry her to the top of the hill every day, leave her there for a while, and then come back and get her.

There were two men around that place. Both these men wore turkey feather caps[1] and both looked well. One of them was this woman's own brother. When the woman's husband carried her to the top of the hill she would tell him to go back and stay at home for a while, then when it was sunset to come and get her and take her home again. That's the way she was doing it. The husband did not like all this, and by his camp he sat down and looked over toward the hill. Pretty soon he saw those two men, wearing their turkey feather caps, coming up on the other side of the hill. When the woman saw the men with the caps, she stood up and went to one of them. Then she started off a little way and stopped under a tree. Now her husband had come around where he could watch what was going on. The man the woman had gone to, came to her under the tree and lay close with her there. It was this man's own sister that he was lying with. When the husband saw this he just went off home. When he got there he sat inside his wickiup and thought about all this. He did not like it.[2] That woman's brother was good looking and this was the reason she had pretended to get sick, so she would have the chance to go with her brother this way.

After the woman had been with her brother a while, she came back on top of the hill and sat there as before. At sunset the husband did not want to go and get his wife on the hill. When it came evening the woman hollered to him, "My husband, come here and take me back to camp!" But the man would not answer her and just sat there. When it started to get dusk the woman began crawling back to camp, pretending, and still calling for her husband, "Come and carry me home!" After a while the woman stopped and hollered again. She kept on calling and calling, but the man would not answer. After a while he heard her getting closer. There was a mano lying there and he picked it up and laid it down close by where he sat. He was thinking that he would hit his wife on the head with it when she got close enough. Now the woman said, "My

---

[1] Buckskin caps surmounted by bunches of small turkey feathers and two eagle tail feathers.
[2] Incest is a heinous crime and closely associated with witchcraft. The description of the investigation and punishing (except the dancing) are identical with actual cases occurring in the past.

11

old man always used to carry me back. What's the matter with him? He must have heard something." Finally she got to the entrance of the wickiup and when she did, the man took the mano and threw it at the woman, but she dodged it. The woman got up and ran away from the camp.

After this happened, that man told all his relatives about his wife having lain with her brother. He told everyone about it. Now the chief there heard of it and said, "Bring this woman here to me!" When the woman had come there to him, he said, "Let all the people come here and meet," and all the people did. There was a big crowd, and that woman was right in the middle. One of the men with the turkey feathers caps was there, but he was not the brother of this woman. The brother was not there. Then the chief sent a man to tell the brother to come, but the brother did not want to come. So the chief said, "Have him come here right away," and so the brother had to come. When the brother got there, the husband said to his wife, "Take off your clothes, all of them," and so the woman took off her clothes. Now her husband put a belt around her with metal jingles attached to it, hanging down in front. He tied a mano to each of her legs, just below her knees. When he had fixed her this way, he ordered her to dance right there before all the people. "When you dance, go to the man you have been lying with. Dance and sing towards him," he told her. So the woman started to dance and the manos kept bumping against her shins as she danced. The dangles from the belt kept hitting her between the legs. This way the woman danced around towards where her brother was. She came around in a circle towards him. When she got close, she danced back and forth in front of him, facing him (natcuɫge·de). As she danced, she sang, "Let them kill us both," and she sang her brother's name. Now all the people said, "She has just pretended to be sick so she could go out and lie with her brother. She must be a witch and we are better to kill both of them."

Right there they killed that woman and her brother. That's the way it was. Since that time this is how people have done. If some one sees a man and woman going together this way, who are brother and sister, they report it and hold a meeting about it. If the two deny that they have been doing this way, they tie them up in a tree by the wrists, with a hair rope, and while they are tied this way ask them again about what they have been doing. If they still won't admit it, they build a fire under them. The rope on their wrists stops the blood from flowing. When they can't stand up any more, they will admit it and then they are killed.

My yucca fruits lie piled up.

31. *HE BRINGS BACK A MOUNTAIN[1]

Long ago they say. Long ago there were some people living up at tⁱuk'a·gai (white canes)[2] and also some people living right here, where Bylas is now. Among the people here was a girl, and up at tⁱuk'a·gai was living a boy. This boy and girl got to know each other. After a while they were well acquainted and liked each other. Then after a long time they got married. The boy's people went out hunting deer and bear and other game. They killed lots. This was all brought to the girl's family, and they had a big feast on the meat. Then the girl's family gathered a lot of mescal and all kinds of seeds and fruits and berries, prepared them and carried them up to tⁱuk'a·gai for the boy's people.

After quite a while the boy and the girl came down here to live. Then the girl's people talked about the food that the boy's family had given them from tⁱuk'a·gai. Then they gathered together all the kinds of seeds and fruits and mescal that grew down here and sent the boy and his wife back to tⁱuk'a·gai with these. In those days tsisizin (rock standing)[3] was down here and belonged in this country. Up at tⁱuk'a·gai they had none of the kind of wild foods that grow down here. tsisizin had all these kinds of foods growing on it that belong here. So the girl's people picked the whole of tsisizin up and moved it to tⁱuk'a·gai where it is today. Then the people up there had all those kinds of foods which grow down here and ate them.

In those days the Triplets[4] was up at tⁱuk'a·gai. On it were living lots of deer and mountain sheep. So the people at tⁱuk'a·gai got together and talked about this mountain. They decided to move it down on the Gila River for the people living here. So they did and the Triplets is still here. Then the people down here went on it and hunted lots of deer and mountain sheep and got lots of meat. But the people from those days were all scattered by the water coming (the mythical deluge).[5]

My yucca fruits lie piled up.

32. THE ORIGIN OF CURING CEREMONIES[6]

This is how ceremonies started among us for the curing of sick people. It is the way that we got all such ceremonies. Long, long ago the earth was made. Then the one who made the earth also

[1] Told by Bane Tithla.
[2] The Fort Apache region.
[3] Saw Tooth, a sharp peak a little southwest of Fort Apache.
[4] Three peaks just east of New San Carlos.
[5] This tale is the explanation for the existence of vegetation and animal life on those two mountains that does not belong in the area in which the mountains are, but instead in the country from which they were mythically taken. There is a difference of about 2000 feet in elevation between the two areas, hence the variation in animal and plant life.
[6] Told by Anna Price.

11*

planned so that there should be a piece of land for each person, that he could live on and call his own. Our people were living in one such spot on the earth. They made their beds there, but they could not sleep well and did not like that place at which they first lived, so the one who made the earth told them to move to a new place. They moved and there they slept well and liked it and lived in a good way.

Then two men among them became sick. They were weaker and grew worse day by day. But the people did not do anything for them. At that time they did not know about sickness and how to cure any kind of illness, as they do now. They had none of these ceremonies for specific sicknesses at that time. Then the one who made the earth said, "Why don't you do something for those two men who are getting weaker all the time? Why don't you say some words over them?" But the people could not do anything for them, as they had no knowledge of curing ceremonies.

Then, at that place where they were, four men were standing; one to the east, one to the south, one to the west and one to the north. They belonged among the people at that place. Then the one who made the earth spoke to one of these men, telling him, "Everything on this earth has power to cause its own kind of sickness, makes its own trouble and does things. There is a way to cure all these things."[1] Now that one who had been told, knew about all this. Then those four stood there. Then on the first night the one standing on the east side began to chant a set prayer[2] all by himself. On the second night the one on the south started to drum and sing lightning songs. Then on the third night the one on the west chanted a set prayer. On the fourth night the one on the north began to drum and sing lightning songs.[3] What they did they did not concieve in their own minds; it was bestowed upon them by the one who made the earth. They said that it was as if the knowledge of what they should chant in the set prayers or sing in the lightning songs, had suddenly been transmitted to them from outside and immediately they knew all about it.

Then the one who made the earth said to these four, "Why don't you go to those two sick men and say some words over them and make them well?" So those four went to where the two sick men were and worked over them, and they were cured. From that time on we had curing ceremonies and knowledge of the different kinds of sickness that may be caused by various things. That is the way that all curing ceremonies started.

---

[1] This is the concept of causes of sickness.

[2] Set prayers are like the words of songs but lack the chorus phrases and meaningless syllables. They are chanted in a monotone and are traditional.

[3] The two types of curing shamans are differentiated from each other; the lightning shaman who sings with a drum and gains all his power by personal contact with the source, and the shaman who practises a ceremony mainly derived traditionally.

33. *COYOTE STEALS ABERT SQUIRREL'S FIRE[1]

Long ago everybody did not have fire, only a few. Abert Squirrel was chief of the fire owners. The others of his band were Raven, Turkey, Buzzard, Eagle, Red-tailed Hawk, and all the other hawk-like birds. This band, with Abert Squirrel as their chief, were the only ones who had any fire. They kept it up in the tops of the pine trees and would not let anyone else have any. To this day Abert Squirrel has brown markings along his sides. He got these from lying close by the fire when they used to keep it up in the pine trees.

Those other people who did not have any fire were too cold all the time and they needed fire. Slim Coyote was one of those who had no fire. One day Slim Coyote decided to get some fire. He came to the bottom of the big tree in which Abert Squirrel was living. He gave Abert Squirrel 'iḷgac (used witch power on him) and made him very sick. He lay on the ground. Abert Squirrel was pretty sick from Coyote's 'iḷgac. Then Coyote called up to Abert Squirrel's band in the trees, "Here is your chief lying sick. He is a very smart and good man; why don't you come down here and make a dance for him to cure him?" Abert Squirrel's band said, "That is a good idea. We will make a dance to cure our chief," and they all came down and started gathering a lot of wood for a big fire. Just before they started the fire, Slim Coyote went off and got a bunch of dry inner bark. This he tied under his tail and came back to where they were giving the dance. All the people who did not have fire were there to see the dance also, but Abert Squirrel's band would not let them come anywhere near the fire. Then they started to dance. There were thirty-two of the fire people dancing around the fire in a circle. They made all the people who did not have a fire stand back. If any sparks blew away from the fire, the fire people would reach out, catch them, and put them back in the fire. Coyote tried to go out and dance near the fire, but they made him get back.

Then the fire people said to one another that as long as Slim Coyote was the one to suggest the dance for Squirrel, it would be all right for him to dance close to the fire. "All right, come and dance!" they called to Coyote, but they made the rest of the crowd move back. Slim Coyote started to dance around the fire. As he danced, he sang, "I dance back and forth beside the fire." He kept on dancing around the fire, very close to it. Pretty soon he stuck his tail in the fire. "Look out, you'll burn your tail!" said the fire people. "My tail won't burn," said Coyote, and he kept on singing and dancing with his tail near the fire. "Your tail is on fire," said the fire people. Slim Coyote looked around and saw his tail on fire. He gave a big jump over the fire people. They tried to catch him.

---

[1] Told by Francis Drake. Also called "Abert Squirrel Angry about Fire".

He jumped over them. Then he gave a great leap and jumped over everybody and started to run away. The fire people chased him. As Slim Coyote ran he shook his tail from side to side and set fire to the dry grass and brush and pine needles. Some of the fire people stopped to try and put these ground fires out. The others kept after Coyote. Pretty soon Slim Coyote gave out, and he said to Poor Will, who was one of those who had no fire, "Take the fire and keep on going, my cross-cousin." Poor-Will took it and flew away. The fire people chased him now. As he flew he went from side to side, setting more brush and dry grass on fire. Then the grass and brush was burning all around. The fire people were flying away and scattering. Slim Coyote stood there looking at the fire. It was crawling along the ground like snakes, spreading everywhere. This is how fire was first obtained.

34. *THE WINNING OF DAWN[1]

Long ago it was dark all the time. Then all animals talked and acted like people. The animals were divided into two bands. In one band were all those animals that crawled and had poison, like snakes, bugs, or lizards. Bear was chief of this band. In the other band were the good animals, and their chief was Slim Coyote. They had no stars, moon or sun then, but Slim Coyote's band wanted these and daylight. Bear and his band wanted it to stay as it was, dark all the time. Slim Coyote and his people decided to play Bear and his band at hidden ball, to decide which group should have their way about the daylight. The two bands arranged to play the game. If Bear's people won, it was to stay dark and they would kill Slim Coyote and all his band. If Slim Coyote's followers won, it was to become daylight and they were to have sun, moon, and stars as they are today. They would have the right also to kill Bear and all his band.

The game was started, Bear's people sitting with him on one side of the big fire, and Slim Coyote's band on the other side. One of Slim Coyote's band yayi'i·'i· (he sees over and down)[2] was very good at the game. As they played, Coyote would sing, "Dawn, dawn, let it dawn," and it would start to grow light in the east like dawn. Then Bear's turn would come, and he would sing. "No dawn, no dawn," and it would get dark again. This way they went on. Coyote started to win. When Bear sang it didn't get dark any more. When Coyote sang the world got lighter all the time. The game was getting close now, and each band put guards out around the gamblers to keep them from leaving. If anyone went out to

---

[1] Told near old Summit by Charlie Sago. Also called, "They Played Hidden Ball."

[2] The term is usually applied to Road-runner; he is supposed to be able to see behind the canvas held up to hide opponents actions.

urinate, they were made to come right back. Pretty soon Bear said,
"I am going to my camp to get my tobacco pouch before we finish
the game." "No," Slim Coyote's people said, "you must stay here
till the game is finished." Bear said, "You will kill us all anyway,
as you have almost won the game. Let me go and I will come right
back," so they let him go. When Bear got to his camp he put his
moccasins on wrong, right for left, and left for right; then ran away.
As soon as Bear left, Slim Coyote's band started killing Bear's people.
They killed all but a few. Yellow Rattlesnake hid himself in the
sand, close to the fire, and so was saved. Black Rattlesnake
crawled into a crack in the rocks and tried to hide, but they found
him and shot him where he lay, with arrows. All this happened far
to the north, and to this day you can see the arrows sticking in
the crack of the rock where Black Rattlesnake was killed. Bear
ran off into a swampy place, because they were after him. Here
he hid in the mud and was not found. Because of the way Bear
acted at that time is why he is still so mean and ugly today. From
that time on the sun rose and set, and they had daylight and moon
and stars at night.

VARIANT[1]

Long ago the world was dark all the time. They had no day at
all. In those days the animals talked and acted like people. They
were divided in two groups. In one band were all the good birds
and animals: Road-Runner, Duck, Quail, Turkey, Dove, Gopher,
Pack Rat, Squirrel, Chipmunk, Antelope, White-tailed Deer,
Black-tailed Deer. In the other band were all the bad people like
Horned Owl, Black Bear, Big Bear, Yellow Bear, White Bear and
all the snakes.

These two bands got together and decided to play kenat'a·ha
(hidden ball)[2] to see if they would have daylight instead of
darkness all the time. The bad people wanted it dark; the others
wanted daylight. They made thirty-two counters. Whichever
side should win those thirty-two counters would win the game.
Then they started to play. One band sat on each side of the fire,
opposite. Each band had a blanket up in front so that the opposing
side could not see where they hid the ball. The place they were
playing was in a canyon, right below an overhanging cliff. Both
sides took their turn at hiding the ball. yayi'į·'į· (he sees over and
down)[3] was the best on his side. He could guess every time where
the ball was hidden. He would lie on his back and tell where the
ball lay, just as if he could see right through the dirt. This way he
got the ball for his side. He would go right over an pick it up every
time. Bear was the same way on his side. It was as if he could see

---

[1] Told by Francis Drake.
[2] The game here is the variety played without moccasins, in the loose earth.
[3] Road-runner.

right through the dirt. This way they kept on playing back and forth. Slim Coyote was there also. He was not on any side, but just went from side to side to help whichever was losing. Now the good people started to lose. Bear got the ball back right away, every time. The good people could not guess where Bear hid the ball and they did not know what to do. They said to Gopher, "You are smart, let's see what you can do to help us." Gopher went down under the ground where his side had hidden the ball and tied his rope to it. When Bear came over to find the ball, Gopher just pulled the ball away with his rope, and Bear grabbed into the dirt where the ball should have been and found nothing. Bear's side was still getting the best of it. They commenced to sing. They made up a song about Turkey, about how his neck was long and red. Then they sang about Road-runner, about the orange spots on the side of his head and how his tail pointed down to the ground. They still sing these songs when they play kenat'a·ha today.

Pretty soon Bear's side started to lose. Bear knew where the others hid the ball all right, but when he would look there it would be gone. Gopher would pull it away with his rope. Then Coyote started to sing and dance. He sang for dawn to come. At the end of the song he would holler and it would get light in the east. Bear sang for it not to dawn, to stay black as it was under his tail. Then it would get dark again. Now the good people were getting the best of it. They made up a song about Bear, how he was crying about his bad luck. Then they sang about Horned Owl, how his legs were covered with hair, how his nose was hooked, about his yellow eyes and the two tufts on his head which stood up like ears, and how he looked frightened. Bear said to Owl, "My cross-cousin, they sing bad about us."[1] Now the cliff above them was beginning to reflect light. That cliff and the place where they played is still there. The Tontos[2] know about it. It is in the Northern part of their country. The good people now won all the counters. Turkey took them and shoved all thirty-two down in his moccasin tops. That is why Turkey's legs have that flat bone in them to this day. The sticks turned into that bone. Then they all got sticks and started to fight the other band. They killed Bull Snake, Red Racer, and tried to kill Gray Rattlesnake, but he hid in the sand. Black Rattlesnake got in a crack in the rocks. They tried to set fire to him and kill him, but could not. They shot arrows in at him and you can still see those arrows sticking in the rock to this day. Horned Owl flew up and hid in a hole in the rocks, way up in the cliff. They shot arrows at his feet, and by hitting the soles of his feet they killed him. They killed Black Bear and Yellow Bear. White Bear got away, and so did Big Bear. And this is the way they won daylight.

---

[1] The animals singing about each other amuses the Apache because they are animals.

[2] "Northern Tonto" is probably meant.

35. *COYOTE STEALS SUN'S TOBACCO*[1]

Slim Coyote was living with the Indians. One day he started out to the Sun's house. When he got there, Sun was not at home. His wife was there and Coyote talked with her. "nde· (man)," he said, "where is my cross-cousin, the Sun." Sun's wife said that he had gone out and was not home yet. "I came to talk with him about something," said Coyote. Then Coyote saw Sun's tobacco bag hanging up on the side of the dwelling. "I came to smoke and talk with my cross-cousin,"[2] said Slim Coyote, "so give me a smoke while I am waiting for him. He won't mind, he is like my cross-cousin." Coyote was talking to Sun's wife as if she were his mother-in-law.[3] Sun's wife handed him the tobacco bag. Coyote took it and filled a little buckskin bag that he had with him. This little bag he hid on him. Then he rolled a cigarette. This way he got off with a lot of Sun's tobacco without Sun's wife knowing. He hung up Sun's bag again. Then he told Sun's wife, "I came to talk with my cross-cousin but he hasn't come back yet, so I guess I won't wait after all." Coyote started home.

Pretty soon Sun came home. "Who has been here and gone again," he said. "Somebody who said he was your cross-cousin," answered his wife. (She tells in full what happened.) Sun was very angry. "I'll get that fellow," he said. He went out to the front of his house where Black Wind Horse was tied, and saddled him up and set off after Coyote. This Black Wind Horse could fly and when he traveled he made a noise like lightning. A light rain started to fall and covered up Coyote's tracks, but Sun could still see the ashes from Coyote's cigarette, and he followed him by this. It kept on raining. Pretty soon the tobacco Coyote had with him, started to grow. Soon it was putting out leaves; then flowers. At last it got ripe and dry and the wind scattered the seeds all over. When Sun saw this, he gave up chasing Coyote and went home.

When Coyote got back to where he was camping with the people (Apaches), he kept his tobacco for himself and would not give any to the others. The people kept asking Coyote for a little smoke, but he would not give them any at all. The people got together and held a council about Coyote and how they could get his tobacco away from him. They decided to pretend to give Coyote a wife. They told a young boy to dress up as a girl and pretend he was going to be Coyote's wife. They told him just what to do. Then they told Coyote, "We are going to give you a wife." Coyote said, "You

---

[1] Told by Francis Drake.

[2] Cousin, where it occurs in White Mountain myths, always implies cross-cousin. There are no terms for parallel cousin other than those for siblings. Coyote always uses the term "ciłna' 'a·c" (male cross-cousin to male cross-cousin).

[3] Coyote's behavior and assumption of kinship here is ridiculous and amusing to Apaches. First he treats Sun as a cross-cousin; second he addresses Sun's wife by a mother-in-law term but does not observe avoidance, etc.

are trying to fool me." "No, we are not lying," they said, "We are
going to give you a wife." They set up a new wickiup for Coyote and
got everything ready. They told the boy who was to dress as a girl
not to let Coyote touch him till just before dawn, so that Coyote
would not find out the truth. They made a bed in the new wickiup
and Coyote felt so good he gave them all his tobacco. Just about
dusk the boy dressed as a girl went over and sat down beside Coyote
in his new wickiup. Slim Coyote was so excited he could not stand
up, but just kept crawling around on the ground. Coyote was
impatient and he said, "Why don't you come to bed? Let's hurry
and go to bed; I want to go to bed now."[1] The boy just sat there
and wouldn't do it. After a while, when Coyote had said this
several times, the boy lay down by Coyote but not close to him.
Coyote said, "I want you to lie close," and he tried to touch the
boy. But the boy said, "Don't!" and pushed Coyote's hand away.
This kept up all night and the boy would not let Coyote do anything.
Just before dawn Coyote made a grab and caught hold of the boy's
penis. He let go right away and jumped back. "Get away from
me; get back from me; you're a boy, not a girl," he said. Then
Coyote got up and called the other people. "You lied to me," he
said, "You didn't give me any wife at all." "Give me my tobacco
back," he yelled, but they would not do it. This is the way the
people first got tobacco.

36. *COYOTE'S DAUGHTER (BECOMES) HIS WIFE[2]

Coyote had a black belt with red fringes. He also had a turkey
feather cap with two eagle feathers sticking up. He was traveling
with his daughter. They came to a river and started across, wading.
Coyote said to his daughter, "Your dress will get wet, so lift it up
a little way." The girl did this. Pretty soon Coyote said again,
"Lift your dress a little higher, it will get wet," and the girl did so.
Then he kept on telling her to lift it a little higher until she had the
dress up to her belly. Then Coyote looked and saw his own daughter
(her private parts). She looked pretty good to him. When they
got across the river, they went on to Coyote's camp.

Then Coyote pretended to get sick. He lay down as if he was in
a very bad way. Then he made believe he was going to die. This was
all in one day. He said to his wife, "I am dying now. Over where
they are playing hoop and poles there will be a man standing, right
at one end of the course. He will be dressed just as I am now. That
is the man I want my daughter to marry. After I am dead, wait
and destroy the wickiup over me. I was always afraid of rocks.[3]

---

[1] Coyotes impatience amuses listeners.
[2] Told by Francis Drake. Compare Goddard, ibid p. 138.
[3] Probably refers to burial under rocks, the customary way.

Then leave some red paint beside me." When he got through talking, he made believe he died. His children started to cry for him. They destroyed the wickiup on top of him and went off, leaving him there.

Just as soon as they had left, Coyote jumped up, crawled out from under the wickiup and ran to the place where they were playing hoop and poles and stood there. He got there before his family did. Then he saw his wife and children coming. His wife talked with her daughter. "There is the man you are to marry," she said, "Go and fix up a new wickiup for yourselves." So they went and fixed up a new wickiup for the man and the girl. That evening the man and the girl went to the wickiup and lay down together. That way Coyote lay with his own daughter all night. He was married to her now.

Next day his wife said she was going to wash him up with yucca. Coyote had some lice in his hair and he told her to look for them. Coyote also had a mole on the back of his head. He laid his head on his daughter's knees and she started to pick off lice. After a while Coyote fell asleep there. Then the girl came to the mole on the back of his head. When she saw this, she thought, "This is my father." She slipped herself out from under Coyote quietly, so as not to waken him, and then stepped easily over to her mother's camp. When she got there, she said, "My mother, that man I have been married to is my father. I know because of that mole on the back of his head." Then the old woman got mad all right. She said, "He was dead over there a long time ago." She took up a big rock and went over to where Coyote was lying asleep. Just before she got ready to throw the rock on him, he jumped up. "It seems to me you are not glad to see me, my mother-in-law," he said to his own real wife. "What's the matter, mother-in-law, what are you trying to do?" His old wife said, "You were dead long ago over there, and now, Coyote, you marry with your own daughter. You had better not stay around here any longer. Go some other place!"

Coyote started off and came to another camp where they were playing hoop and poles. "Look, here comes the man who married his own daughter," they said. Coyote turned around and started off in another direction. The next camp he came to they said, "Here comes the man who married his own daughter," and Coyote turned around again. Then he went a very long way to a camp far off. When they saw him, they said, "There is that man who married his own daughter," and Coyote turned back. Then Coyote started to wonder who it was who was telling everyone about him. "Wind, you're the one who is talking about me," he said. Then he climbed up a hill where wind was blowing. When he got there, he put his hand back and spread his anus apart with his finger. The wind blew inside it and he closed it again. Then Coyote traveled on to another camp and no one said anything to him. He said to himself, "I knew you were the one doing this, Wind."[1]

37. *COYOTE KILLS HIS CHILDREN[2]

Coyote started to trot along. While he was on his way he met Turkey and her children. When he saw them the mother turkey was in front and all her children were following in a line behind her. Coyote thought this looked nice, with all the little turkeys in single file, so he said to Turkey, "Why is it, my cross-cousin, that your children always follow you in a line like that?" Then Turkey said, "I put a little hole through my children's bills and tie a string through it and then from one to the other this way. What string is left from the front one I put around my waist and lead them along. When they grow larger I don't use the string any more, but my children still follow that way and it looks better." Then Coyote said, "Now that you have told me how you did it, I am going back home before I forget and do the same with my children." So Coyote started off home. When he got there he said to his children, "I have good news for you that I heard from Turkey. I'm going to make a hole in your jaws and tie a string through from one to the other. What string is left I will tie around my belly. This way I will lead you in a line. When you are older you will do it naturally, without any string, just as Turkey's children do." Then he pierced a hole through the lower jaws of his children and put a string through them. His children hollered and cried, but he did it all the same. When it was all finished, he took his children outside and told them to line up with him at their head. Then he tried to make his children walk in line after him, but it hurt them so that they fell on the ground and were dragged along behind. Coyote kept on dragging them till they were all killed. He took the string off his children and left them to hunt for Turkey, because it was Turkey who had told him about this. He was mad about it and was going to eat all the turkeys up. But before he got there, Turkey saw him and flew up into a tree and sat there. Coyote came under the tree and sat down. "My cross-cousin, come on down with all your children. I want to see you walk in line with them as you did before," he said. But Turkey would not come down because she thought Coyote would kill her and her children. "My children have been walking all day and they are tired so I will sit here till sunrise and get down then," Turkey said. "I want you to come down just for a little while so I can see you line up," Coyote pleaded. But Turkey said, "No, I will stay here all day and not come down." Coyote was having a hard time of it so he gave up and left.

---

[1] People listening to the story often exclaim in disgust at Coyote's incestuous deed.
[2] Told by Bane Tithla.

While he was on his way he met Deer and her two fawns. They looked good to him, the little deer with white spots all over them. "My cross-cousin, how did you put spots on your children like that? It looks good to me with spots all over. I think my children should wear them also," Coyote said. Deer told him, "I put my children in a hole and then at the mouth of the hole I build a fire of juniper wood and back it in with rocks. Then I go over the hill and stay quite a while, till the fire is burnt down. When I come back I find my children spotted from the ashes. That's the way I always do it." Coyote said, "I'm going to do the same with my children." So he went on home to where his children were. He told them, "I have good news for you. I want you to wear white spots on your body just like I saw on Deer's children." Then he took his children to where there was a rocky hole close by, and put them inside it. He started to gather up juniper wood and pile it at the mouth of the hole. Then he set fire to it and went off over a hill and stayed there a long time. When the fire was all burnt up he came back to the hole. He looked down into the hole where his children had been burnt all over their bodies. Their lips were burnt away so that Coyote could see their teeth. "You are laughing at me now, but when you come out you will look nice," Coyote said. He went down into the hole to take them out but he found his children were all cooked and dead so he left them there.

After he had done this he was very mad at Deer for telling him to do this way. He said to himself, "I'm going to find Deer with her two young children and I will kill and eat all of them." So he started off. After a while he found Deer with her two children. He told them to stop, that he wanted to tell them about something. This was the way Coyote always did when he was going to kill some one. He said to Deer, "There are liable to be people hunting deer in here and they may set fire around in a circle so the deer can't get out. Then they will kill all the deer. I want you to cross out by here because this will be the only place you can escape if a fire should be set. That is why I have come to tell you this." Then the deer and the two children deer went to that place. Coyote left and circled around in front of them. Then he shot an arrow of willow wood ahead of the deer and from where the arrow lit, fire started. Coyote ran back as fast as he could to where he had told Deer to pass by and escape. Then he hid and peeped out, watching for Deer. When Deer came by Coyote shot at her from hiding, so she never saw him. When she was shot Deer started to walk slowly and in a little way stopped and lay down. Then Coyote went to her and said, "My cross-cousin, I told you not to walk but to go fast. That's why you have been shot. I told you there were lots of people hunting deer. I thought you understood me, but I guess you didn't do what I said. Now you are shot." Coyote had done all this himself and was lying. "Over there is good shade. I will carry

you to it and doctor you there. Maybe you will get well," Coyote
said. Deer said to her children, "This Coyote, when he packs me
over there means to kill me and he is going to kill you when he has
killed me. If he kills me, then one of you run one way and one the
other so Coyote won't catch you." Coyote carried Deer over to
the shade. His arrow was sticking in her side. Coyote said, "I
am going to try to suck the blood out of your wound where it has
gone into your stomach. That is the only way I think you will get
better." So he sucked on the wound, but all he was doing was
sucking the blood out so he could drink it. When he had drunk
nearly all the blood he just let the rest bleed out on the ground.
"Now I am going to sing over you," he said to Deer. "Big Medicine,
big medicine, get dry and soft." Then he started over again and
sang as before. Deer was just about dead so Coyote jumped on her
neck and bit her. After he bit her he turned and went for the two
deer children. But before he got there, they each went a different
way. He tried to catch both of them but he could not do it, so he
gave up and came back.

My yucca fruits lie piled up.

38. *THE BERDACHE COYOTE STORY[1]

Coyote was living with the Black Bird people. Black Bird was
a good looking young man and the girls all liked him. Coyote did not
look like much, and the girls did not like him at all. Black Bird had
a sweetheart who lived far off. He was about to marry this girl,
and so Coyote always went with him when he went to visit her.
The girl lived at the foot of some hills. When Coyote and Black Bird
went there, they went up on top of one of these hills and Black Bird
played on his flute. They heard it in the girl's camp at the foot of
the hill. The next day the two went back to the same place and
went up on top of the hill where they played on the flute again.
Some men are good at playing on the flute; some are better than
others. Black Bird could play well. Then that girl's mother heard
the flute. "My child, what was that? Over there I heard some nice
whistling. What was it?" They sent someone over to find out
what the sound was and they found the two fellows on the hill and
brought them back to the camp. Then the girl's people asked,
"Why are you here?" and the two answered, "I was looking for this
girl. I want to marry her." Coyote thought he was going to get
married to the girl himself. He thought the girl liked him a lot.[2]
"All right, tomorrow I want you two to hunt deer. The first one to
bring a big deer in will marry my daughter," the father said.

---

[1] Told by Bane Tithla. The name alludes to Coyote's failure to perform the
tasks of a man (procuring meat).
[2] Coyote's illusions and the following mistakes he makes because of them,
are considered very funny.

Early next morning, before sunrise, Black Bird started out to hunt. Coyote started out also, but he did not go very far before he came to a rat's nest. While he was there, he hunted rats. He killed some as quick as he could and hurried back to the girl's camp with them, because he wanted to get in first. But Black Bird had killed a black-tailed deer, just at sunrise, and he brought that in and dropped it in front of the girl's home. Coyote brought in his big rats also, but the girl's people would not take them and threw them back to him.[1] Only the deer would they use, and they started to cut it up. Then Black Bird was married to the girl.

The girl's father and mother both said to make a wickiup for the new couple, a way off from the old camp. So by evening they had a nice new wickiup made for them. Inside they made a good big bed where Black Bird was to sleep, but for Coyote they made a little rough bed on the opposite side of the wickiup, about big enough for a dog to lie in. When Coyote went into the new wickiup, he saw the good bed for Black Bird. "That's the one meant for me," he said, and jumped on to it. So Black Bird went to the poor bed that was really meant for Coyote. Then they brought a good basket to eat out of for Black Bird, but to Coyote they gave an old, old basket all worn out. Each one was sitting on opposite sides of the fire and when Coyote saw the good basket of food on one side of the fire he jumped over to it. "The good things are meant for me. That no good stuff is meant for you," Coyote said to Black Bird. Now both ate their food, and when Coyote finished he went over on the best bed and lay on his back and crossed his knees.[2] At sundown the people took all the cooking and food outfit back to the other camp.

When it got dark the girl came over to lie down with Black Bird. She came and sat outside the wickiup for a while. Inside the two men were lying, one on each side of the wickiup on the two beds. When it was time to go to bed, the girl got up, came inside and went to where Black Bird was and sat down near him. Then Coyote got up when he saw the girl go to the other bed. "That bed must be for me. That's why the girl went over there," he said, and he went over and sat down beside her. When he did that, the girl and Black Bird got up and went to the good bed. Now Coyote felt bad while he was sitting there, because he thought that it was he who was going to be living with that girl. Later on he said, "That first bed must be for me after all," so he jumped over on it again. When he got there, the girl and Black Bird went back to the little bed again. Now Coyote lay back on the good bed and crossed one leg over the other. The newly married couple were just ready to go to bed across the wickiup when Coyote jumped across beside them and

---

[1] Refusal or acceptance of game from a suitor, may mean refusal or acceptance in marriage.

[2] Coyote's reclining in such a postion is amusing.

said, "That's my bed. They made that for me to lie on." Then the
other two just went back to the good bed again and lay down together.
Coyote, lying by himself on the little bed, felt bad about not lying
with the girl himself. As he lay there he covered himself with
a blanket and pulled it up over his head. Then he pretended to
sleep and snore because he thought he would try to see something.
If the couple did anything, Coyote was going to try and watch
them. He turned over on his side towards them and the fire. Then
he pretended to sleep soundly, but he really raised the edge of
the blanket up carefully and peeped out, all the time pretending to
snore.[1] This is the way some people still copy after Coyote right
here in Bylas. At night they cover over with a blanket and pretend
to sleep, but what they are really doing is peeping under the edge
of the blanket or through a hole in it to see what some couple is
doing on the bed across from them.

Black Bird and Coyote lived on there together for some time.
When Black Bird killed a deer, he would bring it to his father-in-
law's camp. The new couple, with Coyote, were all sleeping in the
new house. Every night Coyote was doing the same thing, pretending to go to sleep, but really watching the other bed. He burned
lots of holes in his blanket so he could see well. Later on the others
found out what he was doing and they saw how he had made the
holes in his blanket. But every night Coyote watched and thought
about what they were going to do all the time.

Then one morning Coyote told Black Bird, "My cross-cousin,
I saw a big deer track yesterday. I want you to help me get that
deer. You go ahead and wait, and I will drive that deer up to you
so you can kill it. Let's go now! The place I saw the tracks was
right by two buttes over there. Go and hide between them, and
I will drive the deer to you. I know this deer will go between those
buttes." So Black Bird started off and went far between the two
buttes. When he had gone, Coyote started to run as fast as he
could to get around ahead of where Black Bird was going. He got
there and hid behind a bush. After a while the man got there and
thought that here would be a good place to hide for the deer. When
the man got near, Coyote jumped out at him and hit him with an
old dry coyote hide like his own. As soon as he did that, Black Bird
turned into a coyote. Coyote turned into the shape of Black Bird
and became good looking, as the other had been, but Black Bird
was only a coyote now.

In his new form Coyote started back to the camp. He was thinking that he would lie with that woman all night tonight. Just
before sundown he got to camp. There was lots of food there, all
kinds of seeds, and they gave it all to Coyote because the woman
thought this was her real husband, Black Bird. When she gave

---

[1] Another part which always gets a laugh.

him the food he ate every bit there was in the baskets and even licked
them out till not a thing was left. Then the woman gathered up
all the baskets and took them back to her mother's camp and told
her mother about it.[1] "That man, my husband, never ate much
before, but now he ate all I gave him and licked the baskets out
also."[2] It made her mad for this to happen. Her mother said,
"That man ran far off on the mountain today and that must be
how he got hungry. That's why he ate so much. Don't worry
about it!" Just then Coyote was pointing his arm at the sun. He
wanted the sun to hurry up and go down right away. He kept
thinking about when the sun would go down and it would get dark.
He went outside and looked at the sun steadily. Finally it had gone,
but the woman had not come back yet. Coyote thought to himself,
"Why isn't that woman back. I wish she would come right away."
Coyote was having a hard time. At last the woman came back and
sat down by the doorway. Coyote said, "What's the matter with
you, why don't you go to bed right away?" But she still sat there.
Then Coyote said, "I want you to come to bed right now, I said."
That woman thought to herself, "My husband never talked to me
like that before." Later on the woman lay with Coyote on the bed.
In a little while Coyote tried to lie on top of her, never getting off
at all. He did this way with her all night and never got off her the
whole time till morning. In the morning the woman went to her
mother's camp and told her, "That man, my husband, never did
like this before. He did this all right, but not for the whole night.
Last night that man lay on top of me all night and never slept at
all." But the girl's mother said, "Your husband must not have seen
you for a long time. He just wanted it badly. It means nothing
else." That morning the woman brought Coyote food and he did
the same way as he had done the night before. He ate everything
in sight and then licked out the baskets. Then he said to the woman,
"I'm going out to hunt today. I will bring in a deer about noon, so
you stay here." Coyote started off to hunt. After a long way he
crossed over a mountain and on its other side were lots of piñon
trees. There he stopped and started gathering piñon needles off
the trees. When he had a lot, he made a pile of them and set them
on fire. Lots of smoke came up. Coyote ran about the fire and stuck
his nose close to it. Soon the snot from his nose started to run and
get long. He picked it off and laid it to one side. Then he kept on
about the fire, every little while picking the snot off his nose till
he had a pile of it. Then he packed this in a bundle and started
home with it. When he got to camp, he told the woman, "I killed
a deer over there and left the skin to dry out, but here is the meat."
The woman took his pack to her mother's camp. There they used

---

[1] During the first few months of marriage, the young wife does not cook at
her camp. Her mother cooks for her at her own camp.
[2] It is not good form to show such greed.

the meat and cooked and ate it. But it did not taste right. It was too salty. "What's the matter with this meat? It's too salty and tastes different; not like meat," the woman said. Coyote answered, "I found some salt and spread it on the meat to preserve it. That's why it's salty." Now the woman started thinking to herself.

"Tomorrow I will hunt again," Coyote stated. In the morning when Coyote started off, the woman followed him. Coyote went far off to the same place he had been yesterday and piled up piñon tips in a big heap and set fire to them. Then he did the same as he had before. The woman in hiding was watching him all the time. What ran out of his nose, the thickest part he put to one side. That was snot. Coyote kept piling this up. He had lain on that woman all night and because of this she did not like him. That's what made her follow him. Coyote started to pack and tie up his load. The woman hurried back ahead and got to camp before him. There she told her mother what she had seen and how Coyote had built a fire of piñon tips and run around it and collected the snot from his nose and how he had spread it on one side to dry. "That's what we have been eating!" she said. When Coyote got home, he said to the woman, "Take this pack to my father-in-law." "No, you had better eat that yourself," she said. Then her mother said, "We don't eat that stuff. Before this we used to eat fresh deer meat, but this man is dressed just the same and looks the same as ever."

While all this had been going on, Black Bird who was turned to a coyote, said to himself, "When Coyote hit me with that hide I turned to Coyote." Then Black Bird went to where some other people were living. Here he told them just what had happened and how Coyote had acted. The people told Black Bird, "Wolf chief knows about this kind of thing. Go to him and he will make you right again. He is the only one who knows what to do for this." So Black Bird set out for Wolf chief's camp. While he was on his way, he ate grasshoppers and lizards just as Coyote does. When he got to Wolf chief's camp, he told Wolf chief, "While I was out hunting with Coyote he hit me with a coyote hide. Now I am a coyote and here I am traveling." "All right, now I will fix you up," Wolf chief said. He put a big pot of water on the fire to heat. When the water got pretty hot, Wolf chief walked around it. After that he threw jet hoop over the man's head and it dropped to the ground around his body. From the top of his head to his neck, the man became as he used to be. From the south side Wolf chief threw turquoise hoop over him and it dropped to the ground about his body. Now he was like a human to his chest. From the west side Wolf chief threw red stone hoop over him, and it dropped to the ground about him. Now he was a man to his knees. Wolf chief went to the north side and from there threw white shell hoop over him, and it fell to the ground about his body. Now he was all man again and the coyote hide that had covered him dropped to the ground.

Then Wolf chief said to him, "Coyote is out hunting somewhere. Go back there to where you think Coyote will pass. Hide in front of him and as soon as he gets near you, hit him with this coyote hide and he will turn to Coyote again. You are a man now and this is the only way you can go back to your camp again."

While this man was being cured by Wolf chief, he learned the coyote ceremony, the songs and all. These he brought back to use among his people, and that is how we got the coyote ceremony. That same day this man did to Coyote what he had been told to do, and Coyote became himself again.

My yucca fruits lie piled up.

39. *THE JACK RABBIT GIRLS TOSS THEIR EYES UP[1]

Coyote was trotting along, going to where the Jack Rabbit people lived. When he got near the Jack Rabbit camp, he met two Jack Rabbit girls. They were playing with their eyes, pulling them out of the sockets and throwing them up in the air and then running under and catching their eyes in their sockets again. Coyote stood there and watched them for a while. Then he wanted to try this himself; take his eyes out and toss them in the air and catch them again in his head. So Coyote got the Jack Rabbit girls to show him how to take his eyes out. Then he threw them high up in the air near a tree. The Jack Rabbit girls told him to be careful that his eyes did not catch in the tree and stay there. But his eyes caught on the tree and hung there. Then the Jack Rabbit girls ran way and left Coyote. Now he had no eyes and was blind, so he was crying to himself.

Coyote could not do anything without his eyes. Then he smelled pitch on the wind that came to him, and he pointed his nose into the wind and sniffed. Then he started off, up wind, following the pitch scent with his nose. Now he was nearly there. It was some old women boiling pitch to paint on a water bottle. He got to them, and they said to him, "The Jack Rabbit people always do that way, throw their eyes in the air and run under and catch them again. But why did you do that too. They told you your eyes would catch in the tree. We are going to try and work on your eyes for you with this pitch here." Then they made a pair of eyes out of pitch for Coyote, just the same size as his real eyes and stuck them in his eye sockets. "Now go outside and look around. If you can see all right with them, come back here inside the wickiup where it's dark, till your eyes look better. Go push the blanket at the door aside and look out." Coyote did. Far off there was a big mountain called gọgiceda'na·tsuk (bear grass in yellow line (on ridge)) and Coyote looked at this, saying to himself, "I see that

---

[1] Told by Bane Tithla. Also called "Coyote's Eyes Are Hung Up from Him."

12*

mountain all right as I used to," and he went back in the wickiup
again. This is why Coyote has yellow eyes, like pitch, to this day.

Later on Coyote's new eyes were all right and he started off
towards where there was a large patch of canes growing thickly.
The tips of the canes looked like downy eagle feathers to him. His
new eyes were bad and that's why he thought he saw people dancing
here. When the wind blew over the canes they moved back and
forth, as if people were dancing. Coyote went there and started to
dance around by himself, although he thought he was dancing
around with lots of people. Then he set off to a camp and when he
got there, told the people, "Over there are lots of people dancing.
They all have downy eagle feathers tied in their hair. I joined in
that dance and have just come from there a while ago. I want you
all to go back with me to that dance. Dress up good and paint
your faces and take a bath and come on." So now all those people
got fixed up and set off with Coyote for the dance. After a while
they got there. "Where is the dance," they asked. "Over there,
they are all dancing with downy eagle feathers," Coyote said. "No,
that's not a dance. It's only canes growing there," they told him.
"No, they are people," Coyote said, and he went over there and
started dancing by himself again. Those other people who had
come back with him, did not want to go over there with the canes.
Coyote could not see well yet, and he really thought those canes
were people. He had lied to the others, so they all went back home.

When they got back to camp, Coyote asked them for some water.
They brought him some, but he said, "That's rotten. I don't want
to drink that. Give me some better water." So they poured out
the water, though it was good, fresh and cold. Then Coyote said,
"I want a virgin, a pure one, to give me some water.[1] I want her
to go and get this water and bring it fresh to camp. That's the way
I want it, when it has just been brought." Coyote said this because
he saw a nice looking girl there, and she was the one he wanted
sent for the water. So they sent her off to get it. Coyote had it
in his mind that when the girl went for water, he would follow
her. When she started off, Coyote went another way so he could
meet the girl. They both got to the water at the same time. Coyote
thought he would try something. He said, "Your relatives have
given you to me. That's why I want you to leave your water bottle
here, and I will take you home with me." Now the girl started
off with Coyote. When they had gone a little way, the girl saw a
deer. "There is a deer over there," she said. "Where?" "Right
over there." "I can't see it. I will shoot it with my bow and
arrow. This arrow will follow whatever I shoot at, anywhere it
goes." Coyote shot and killed the deer. He went to it, but he
would not skin or butcher it so the girl had to do all this work for

---

[1] A girl who has never known a man is requisite in certain ceremonies.

him.[1] After this, they went to a shady place and sat down. Coyote laid his head in the girl's lap. "There are lots of lice in my hair because no one has picked them out for a long time," he said. So now the girl started to look for them. Pretty soon it got hot and the sun shown in Coyote's eyes. The pitch got soft and started to run out of them. The girl saw this and pulled herself out from under Coyote's head carefully and did not disturb him. Then she got up and ran off from him. When she ran off, Coyote heard the tinkling of the decorative metal dangles on her dress and followed after her by the noise. When he followed her like this, she got scared and took off the dangles and threw them onto a xucntca·gi (a species of cholla cactus). Coyote was close behind her and he heard the jingling on the xucntca·gi. He thought surely it was the girl, ran at it and grabbed around it with both arms. The stickers went into his body all over. Then Coyote said, "You are my wife. you set lots of spines into me. I have them all over my body now."

My yucca fruits lie piled up.

40. *COYOTE HUNTS WITH BOBCAT.[2]

There were a lot of camps together at that place. Big Wolf, the Snakes, Bobcats, all were camped there. Coyote started out to go there. He was going to visit Bobcat. When Coyote got there he stayed quite a while. At that place the people always went out hunting and brought in lots of deer. They only gave Coyote a little meat though. This way he had not much to eat and got hungry.

They all started out to hunt. Coyote and Bobcat together went in an opposite direction to try and get some meat. They headed toward a spring at the foot of a sand wash. Down this wash came a big cow trail, so much used that it was wide enough for a wagon. They followed this down and got to the spring. On one side was a piñon tree with its limbs jutting out towards the trail. Bobcat climbed up in this to wait, sitting on a limb. Coyote watched him and wanted to know what he did this way for. Pretty soon a cow started coming down the trail to the spring. When the cow got right under the limb where Bobcat was lying, Bobcat jumped down on her shoulders and hooked into her shoulders on both sides with his claws. Then the cow started to buck and bellow and jump around. A way off she fell down and Bobcat killed her. Then he started to butcher her. Coyote went to Bobcat but got only a little piece of meat. He was angry about this. After Bobcat had butchered, he packed all the meat on his back and started home with it.

Coyote stayed there by the spring. Coyote thought he would try something, so he went to the tree in which Bobcat had been and

[1] This is man's work, but Coyote was lazy.
[2] Told by Bane Tithla.

managed to scramble up it and out onto a limb over the trail. Then
he crouched, waiting. Pretty soon some cattle were coming down
the trail to water. Coyote watched them. When they got about
under him he jumped down on one big steer's back and tried to do
like Bobcat, but it did not work. The steer started to buck and
Coyote was thrown off. Then the steer turned and went for him,
and Coyote just barely got out of the way in time and into an old
hollow log lying there. Now the steer stood there and watched and
would not let him out of the log. Coyote stuck a long stick out at
the steer and tried to frighten him away, but it was no use. Finally,
about sundown, he went off and left him. When he was sure the
steer was no longer around, Coyote came out of the log and started
home to camp.

My yucca fruits lie piled up.

41. *BADGER CARRIES DARKNESS: *COYOTE AND BOBCAT SCRATCH EACH OTHER[1]

Coyote was traveling along. Badger always used to carry darkness
on his back. Coyote met him. "My cross-cousin, what's in the bag
you carry?" he asked. He was hungry and he thought Badger
had food in his sack. Because he thought there was food in there,
Coyote wanted to stay around where Badger was and maybe get
something to eat. So the two traveled on together for a way. Then
Coyote was thinking he would offer to carry the load and let Badger
rest. After quite a while Coyote said, "My cross-cousin, you look
tired. You have a heavy load there. Why don't you let me carry
it and you rest?" "No, I'm not tired. I always travel this way,"
Badger said. After a while Coyote said again, "My cross-cousin, I
think you are tired. Let me carry the load for you just a little
way and you rest for a while." "All right, you carry this, my bed,
if you want. I know you are thinking it's something to eat, but
it's not. I carry this always. I'll let you have it, though." "I'm
just saying this because I want to carry it for you and because you
are giving out. I will carry it a little way," Coyote answered. So
Badger took his pack off and gave it to Coyote and they started on
again. After a while Coyote said to Badger, "I want to stop to
urinate behind this bush. You keep on ahead and don't bother to
wait for me." So Badger went on ahead. As soon as Coyote got
behind the bush he started to untie the pack, as that was all he
wanted to do in the first place. When he untied the pack, it started
to get dark. Darkness was all coming out. Coyote got scared and
hollered after Badger, "waͅ·'a, my cross-cousin, I'm having a bad
time here. It must be that you are packing bad things with you.
I can hardly see at all." Badger came back and said, "I told you

---

[1] Told by Bane Tithla.

not to open my pack. Now you have done it and started this. I already told you that there was no food in it. You have done something bad." Then Badger spread his arms and gathered in all the darkness and shoved it into the sack again, tying the mouth tight. Coyote felt mad on account of being fooled and said "You just carry badness."

Badger went on by himself. After a while he met Porcupine. The two sat down and told stories about old times. Badger said, "I was living when the sky fell out onto the earth," and he set his pack down. "That's quite a while ago but I was living before that," said Porcupine. "I was living when the sky and the earth were rubbing together. Do you know about the time when that happened? Which of us is older now?"

Later Coyote started on his way and met Bobcat. They stopped to talk to each other. Then they said, "Let's scratch each other's back in turn and see who has the sharpest claws." Bobcat said, "I have no claws," He had claws all right, but they were sheathed so you could not see them. "Let me see!" said Coyote. Bobcat let him look and it seemed as if he had no claws at all. Then Coyote let Bobcat look at his claws and there was far more of them showing than of Bobcat's. "If I scratch your back nothing will happen. It will just pull a little hair and skin off you. But if you scratch my back, you will rip me right down," Bobcat said. "I want you to scratch me first," Bobcat said. "No" Coyote said, "you come first." Finally after a long argument Coyote thought it would be all right to do it first, because he thought this was going to be an easy game for him. He told Bobcat to sit up so he could scratch him from neck to tail. When he was ready Coyote raked him down the back as hard as he could and pulled a lot of fur and hide off Bobcat's back. "'eye'ya·, you hurt me, my cross-cousin, on my back," Bobcat said. Coyote just laughed at him and thought it was funny. It really did not hurt Bobcat at all, but he made believe it did. Now it was Bobcat's turn, and Coyote sat with his back to him. "My finger nails are not long, you will just barely feel them," Bobcat said. But when he got ready, he unsheathed his claws and gave Coyote a terrible rake with them, all down his back, taking off hide and flesh. Coyote jumped up and yelled, "You have killed me, my cross-cousin!"

Further on Skunk and Bear were sitting together, telling stories. Bear said to Skunk, "You stink too much where your rear end is." Skunk said, "You stink too much where your rear end is." They argued about it for a while and then said, "Let's see who is the worst one to stink. We will both try it and see which is the best at this." Skunk said, "I think that I am the best one. Come here and smell me." But Bear said, "When I break wind it is the most powerful. I think I am best." They kept on arguing, each saying he was the best one to make a bad smell. "It will knock you over,

the smell I make," each said. "All right, you try it first!" said one.
"No, you try it first!" Finally they agreed and Skunk said, "I will
put my head close to your buttocks so I will smell you well." Bear
started now and blew out hard, all he had, ką+, ką+, ką+ it went
and made a terrible smell. Skunk stuck his nose in the ground and
shook himself. He got out of the way as quick as he could. After
a while he recovered and came back, saying, "My cross-cousin,
I think you are the best. You smell the worst, but I will try all
the same to make a worse one." So Bear put his nose by Skunk's
buttocks. Now Skunk started to squirt and blow out at the same
time. It was terrible and when Bear smelt it he stuck his nose in
the ground. It was as if he had had his senses knocked out. It
pretty near killed him.

My yucca fruits lie piled up.

42. COYOTE AND BOBCAT TRICK EACH OTHER: *COYOTE CARRIES OFF BEAVER[1]

Coyote started on his way. He was traveling in a good country,
along a river. After a while he came to where Bobcat was lying
asleep in a cool, shady place and there he stopped. In those days
Coyote had a short snout, not long as it is now, but Bobcat had a
long snout, not short as it is today. Coyote said to him, "What's
the matter? Why are you sleeping?" When he said this, Bobcat
never woke up, so Coyote reached over and pushed Bobcat's nose
back into his face with his hand. That's the way Bobcat's nose looks
now. After Coyote did this he called to Bobcat, "My cross-cousin,
why are you sleeping here where no one is? Wake up!" Bobcat
jumped up and sat there under the tree. "I must have slept a long
time," he said. Then he wanted to blow his nose and he reached for
the end of it, but he just closed on air. No nose was there. "What's
the matter with me?" he yelled. Coyote said that was the way he
found him asleep when he came along.

Then Coyote started on again. Pretty soon he got to a good
shady spot where it was very nice. It looked so good that he lay
down and went to sleep. While he was asleep there, Bobcat came
along and saw him. Coyote's nose was none at all then, just teeth,
but Bobcat grabbed it and pulled it out long as it is today. When
he did this, Bobcat said, "Why are you sleeping here? No one else
is here. Wake up!" Coyote woke up and got up. He had to blow
his nose and reached for it. Then he found he had a great long nose.
"What's the matter with me? I have a long nose," he said. Bobcat
said, "I saw you with your nose long while you were sleeping.
Something must have happened to you, I think."

---

[1] Told by Bane Tithla.

Coyote started off on his way. After a while he came on Bobcat asleep again under the shade of a tree. Coyote took a long stick and stuck it in Bobcat's anus and kept on screwing it in till it got to the stomach where there is a kind of fat. He twisted the stick back out so that some of the fat was on the end of it. Then he said, "Wake up, my cross-cousin, I have been sitting here watching you a long time." Bobcat woke up. Coyote took the stick and said, "Here is some fat for you that I got from some people coming back from hunting. You must be hungry now." When Bobcat got up, Coyote gave him the fat and he ate it all up. When he was all through, Coyote said, "You eat your own fat. You eat your own fat. Now I will call you 'You eat your own fat.'" When Bobcat heard this, he started to vomit and kept it up.

Coyote left and started on his way. After he had gone some distance, he found good shade and lay down there. Pretty soon he fell asleep. Then Bobcat came along and found him there asleep. Bobcat got a stick and did the same with Coyote as Coyote had done with him. Coyote ought to have known better than to start it anyway. When Coyote woke up, Bobcat said, "This is some fat I have brought for you from some people I met out hunting. I want you to eat it now. Coyote ate it all up and then Bobcat told him he had eaten his own fat. When Coyote found this out, he started to vomit and could not hold anything down. "I don't eat my own fat at all. I don't eat my own fat at all," he kept on saying.

Coyote started out from there. After he had gone a long way, he came to Beaver sleeping on the edge of a pond. As he lay asleep there, Coyote lifted him up and put him on his back and carried him to the top of a mountain. There Beaver was still asleep. Then Coyote woke him up. "Wake up, you are lying far off in the mountains asleep, a long way from water. I know that you live in the water and I don't see why you are sleeping here," he said. Poor Beaver woke up and saw where he was. He started back for his pond on the river. He knew this was all Coyote's doing. Beaver had a hard time getting back to the water, and Coyote kept chasing after him and making fun of him. All the way back Coyote never left him. He sat on top of him and did everything he could to make it hard. Beaver had a very bad time. "I am getting tired and foot sore," he said. But anyway Coyote kept on chasing him and teasing him. Finally Beaver gave out. There were big blisters on his feet but at last he got to the water. When Beaver went into the water, Coyote started off on his way again.

After a while Coyote came to a shady place by the river and lay down there. He thought this would be a good place to go to sleep. While he lay asleep there, Beaver came and builded in such a way that there were four bodies of water around where Coyote lay. Then he went to Coyote and woke him. "Why are you sleeping here? You are in the middle of water and all round you is water. It is

far to the mountains from here, where there is no water." Coyote
woke up and sat there looking around. He saw lots of water all
about him. "My cross-cousin, carry me across this river," Coyote
said. But Beaver answered, "No, I don't know how to take you
across. You had better go by yourself." Coyote asked again to
be carried, but Beaver would not give him any help. So Coyote
started out to swim. When he got in the water, Beaver swam up
alongside him and splashed water on Coyote with his hands. Then
he ducked him and even sat on him. Coyote had a hard time to
cross the first body of water, but he finally did it. He had three
more to cross, so after he rested he started again to swim across.
Beaver sat on top of him and threw water in his eyes and face.
He kept ducking him all the time. Coyote said, "Don't do that
way, please!" but Beaver never payed any attention and kept right
on pestering him. At last he got across the second body of water
and stopped to rest. Then Beaver said, "How did you get inside
these waters anyway?" Coyote got up and started across the
third body of water and Beaver jumped on him again. He sat on
Coyote's back and ducked him and splashed him all over. Coyote
kept on crying, "My cross-cousin, don't do that please!" but it did
no good. He had a bad time getting across that third body of
water. He rested a while and then went into the fourth body of
water. Beaver sat on his back and ducked and splashed him just
the same way. Now Coyote was about to give out and he pounded
with his front feet on the water (like a dog strange to water). He
had an awful time getting across and just made it. Beaver wanted
to keep him in the water and said, "What's the matter with you?
This is good for you."

My yucca fruits lie piled up.

43. *COYOTE TROTS ALONG[1]

Long ago, when all the animals were talking like people, Coyote
was living. He was traveling along. It must have been summer time
then. As he went along, he said, "I wish I was traveling with wet
sand under my feet." When he said that, under his feet the ground
was wet. A little further on he said, "I wish I was traveling
on muddy ground, so it would squeeze up between my toes."
When he said this, he was traveling in mud. A little further he
said, "I wish I was traveling in water up to my knees," and right
away he was going along in water up to his knees. Later on he
said, "I wish I was traveling in water up to my belly," and then
he was traveling in water up to his belly. Now he said, "I wish
I was traveling in water up to my neck," and when he said that,
he was traveling in water to his neck. Pretty soon he said, "I wish

---

[1] Told by Bane Tithla.

it would come to my ears," and then it came to his ears. Coyote was on his way to some people's camps. He said, "I wish the water would carry me to where those camps are," and the water carried him along to where the people from the camps he was going to, came down to get their water.

When Coyote got there, he gathered some tl'o'ts'o·z (a grass) and stuck some in his anus, in his ears, nose, mouth and eyes. Then he lay down. This way he was just pretending that he was dead, as if the water had washed him up there, so the Jack Rabbits would come close to him and he could catch them.

Then two Jack Rabbit girls came down to get some water. They saw Coyote lying there and stopped. "We all thought Coyote was like a white man. But here he is now, lying dead, with lots of worms in his anus and his mouth, ears, eyes and nose. So we are just as well to go near and look at him." They thought the tl'o'ts'o·z was worms. "If we make a dance around him, he will come alive maybe." The Jack-Rabbit girls said this just for fun because they thought that at last Coyote was out of the way and would make them no more trouble. Now they sang, "Jack-Rabbit stops and squats quickly," and danced as if they were pushing him. They sang and danced about him because they were glad he was dead. Then all the Rabbit People came there, because they heard the girls singing. They sang and danced back and forth in front of Coyote.

All kinds of Rabbit people and Rat people and Bird people, all the ones that Coyote was always after, felt good because they thought Coyote was dead. Next came Wood Rat and he sang, "I'm going through iron arrow points and that's why I have sore places on my belly." That's the way he sang to Coyote as he danced. Then Rock Squirrel came next and sang, "I'm always thinking about that North Country and I'm lonesome for that rocky point I know up there," all the while he was dancing to and from Coyote. Now Chipmunk came and sang, "When that big Coyote is on the ground, I always hide and whistle," as he danced back and forth in front of Coyote. After him came Mouse and danced in front of Coyote and sang, "I am inside the camps. I have broad ears and sharp eyes that shine bright."

Then all the small animals all over the earth were glad because they thought Coyote was dead. They all came there and danced and sang. Black Tail Deer came there and danced and sang also. He sang, "I'm a big deer, I go to water and stick my muzzle in the water till it comes to my eyes." Then Dove came and sang and danced back and forth in front of Coyote, "I pick up my red shoes and put them on," he sang. Then Mearn's Quail sang and danced, "Spotted quail, I'm spotted on the belly, my hair is cut short to my ears, no tail I have," he sang in front of Coyote. Next was Gambel's Quail "I always walk against the hill," he sang as he danced back and forth to Coyote. Now Red-shafted Flicker, "Red-shafted Flicker you might as well go home now," he sang as he danced. Pretty soon Skunk got to that place. He was on Coyote's side and sang to him, "My cross-cousin, wake up and bite lots of these birds and we will taste them again." He kept on singing, "I will squirt my water in the bird's eye and we will taste them again." When Skunk sang this way, Coyote jumped up and ran around, trying to bite the birds and animals. But he did not get any at all.

Then he chased one cottontail. After a long way Cottontail went in a hole. Coyote got to the hole and looked in. He hollered down it, "My cross-cousin, I want you to come out before I set fire to you with sulphur wheat." Then Cottontail said, "That bush is my feed." "All right, then I will set fire to you with tł'oʻdidjige (a grass)," Coyote said. Cottontail answered him, "That's my good feed." "All right then I will set fire to you with pitch," said Coyote. "That one is not my feed," answered Cottontail. "I'm going off to get some pitch and I want you to wait for me there till I get back," Coyote said. Coyote had to go far off to get pitch, and after he had gone, Cottontail came out. He threw his moccasins back in the hole and said to them, "If Coyote comes back here, I want you to talk to him, my soles," and then Cottontail left there. After a while Coyote came back with the pitch and hollered down the hole, "Are you still there, my cross-cousin?" "Here I am," Cottontail's moccasins answered. "I'm going to set fire to you with pitch now," Coyote said, and he started in to build a fire in the hole with the pitch. When he got the fire started, he said, "My cross-cousin, has that melted pitch run down to you yet?" "No, not yet," the moccasins answered. Coyote waited a while and then said, "Has that melted pitch run down on you like water now?" "A little way yet," the moccasins answered. In a little Coyote hollered, "Is the pitch on your body yet?" There was no answer this time, so Coyote said to himself, "It is on him now, sure," and he started in to dig. He dug hard and finally came to where Cottontail's moccasins were. When he found these moccasins had holes in their soles, he threw them to one side and went on.

After a while Coyote came to a tree. Right there somebody had set up a rabbit hide filled with sand to fool Coyote because they knew that Coyote was not smart and was crazy. That's why they had done it. When Coyote got close, he saw the stuffed rabbit skin. He jumped on it and grabbed it, biting and chewing on it. Then he found out he was chewing sand, and it was all over the inside of his mouth. "This is a sand rabbit. I don't want this," he said, and he threw it away. Now his teeth hurt. He kept on his way and after a while a rabbit came out in front of him. He saw it, but he said to himself, "I don't want any sand rabbit," and he wouldn't even look at it. This was a real live rabbit though. In a while Coyote got to where he saw a rabbit lying underneath a yucca plant. He did not take care about the yucca leaf points, but just made a jump for the rabbit. The leaf points stuck all in his chest and he never got the rabbit. Some time after that Coyote came to life again. When he was a little stronger, he looked down on the ground and saw his own blood there. "What's the matter with that rabbit. He must have lots of blood," he thought.

He got up and kept on his way. Then he saw a bird sitting on a tree. He wanted to catch this bird and eat it up. The bird said to Coyote, "I'm cold, my cross-cousin, I'm freezing, and I'm poor also. I want you to put me under your arm pit so my fat will get warm. Then you can suck the grease out of my body." Coyote took this all in and put the bird under his arm. Now the bird was getting warm and it said, "My cross-cousin, don't squeeze me so. Lift up a little." So Coyote raised his arm a little. When he did this, the bird was good and warm and flew away. He lit in a tree close by. Coyote went over there and said, "My cross-cousin, come down here," but the bird would not come, so Coyote went on his way.

Further on he came to Locust, who was resting on a tree limb. Coyote picked him off and was going to stick him in his mouth, but just before he did it, Locust said, "My cross-cousin, don't eat me up right away! Take me to where there is a crack in the ground. When I get good and warm is the best time to suck out my grease, and while you are doing that I will dance around your lip and go in your mouth. I want you to understand this." So Coyote took him over to where the ground was cracked and laid him down there. Then Locust told him, "Here is where I'm going to tell you a good story, so put your head down near me and listen. Before you eat me, lay me on this crack, open your mouth and close your eyes. This is the best way to eat me, and when I am hot you can suck all the grease out of me. Then while you are doing that, I will dance around your lip. That's the way you will chew me." Coyote listened to all this and believed it. Now Locust stood on Coyote's lips and danced and sang, "I am Locust, I am Locust." "Make your mouth wide," he told Coyote, and Coyote did. Now Locust was getting good and warm, but he still kept on singing and dancing. Then he was hot, "tc'id, tc'id, tc'id," and he flew right into the crack in the ground. Coyote snapped at him, but missed. Then Coyote said, "I was going to eat that bug a little while ago."

My yucca fruits lie piled up.

44. *COYOTE RACES WITH FROG[1]

One day Slim Coyote was traveling along. He met Frog. Slim Coyote said to Frog, "Come on, let's race together and see who is the faster." Frog said, "You must be making fun of me to talk like

[1] Told by Francis Drake.

that." "No, come on, let's race together!" said Slim Coyote. "All right," said Frog, "but first I want to go some place for a minute." Slim Coyote said he would wait. Frog went off and went to where the other frogs were, his people. He told them he was going to race Slim Coyote and that he wanted them to place themselves all along where the race was to be, at intervals. "Now," he said, "if Coyote is the loser, then the frog who has the place at the finish will say to Coyote, 'My aunt,[1] you are no runner at all; you are no man, only a boy,' and make fun of him."

Frog went back to where Slim Coyote was waiting, and they started to race. Frog took one jump and then another frog took his place, and then another for one jump and so on. This way Slim Coyote lost the race and the last frog said to him, "My aunt, you are no man, only a boy. I beat you racing. You are no runner." Slim Coyote answered, "My aunt, you are a good runner and you beat me. I have raced with lots of Apaches and other people, but you are the first ever to beat me." That's the way Coyote lost the race.

45. COYOTE AND BEAR CRIPPLE AND CURE EACH OTHER[2]

One time Bear was playing hoop and poles. He won from his opponent a quiver for arrows, made from bearskin. Coyote was present and said to Bear. "Hey, my cross-cousin, you have won that quiver for me." "No, not for you. You go about eating all kinds of things, cactus fruits and all. For that reason it is too dangerous to give it to you." But Coyote kept on begging for the quiver and so Bear finally said, "Well, you can have it, but you must be sure not to eat certain foods," and he called them off to Coyote. "You cannot eat xuctco' (a cactus), juniper berries, manzanita berries and mesquite beans.[3] If you eat of these, something will happen to you."

So Coyote got the quiver. He slung it over his shoulder, ready to go. He took his bow and put an arrow to it from the quiver. He practised, drawing the bow with the arrow a couple of times. Then he went off. On his way he passed many of the kinds of food which Bear had told him he must not eat. He thought to himself, "I wish I could eat some of those fruits." He kept on till he came to a mesquite tree loaded down with beans, all ready for eating. He could stand it no longer and climbed up in the tree and started to eat the beans. Then he heard his quiver, which he had leaned against the bottom of the tree, say; "ca," but he replied, "Keep still my quiver!" Then it turned immediately[4] to a bear. Coyote

---

[1] In derision.
[2] Told by Francis Drake.
[3] These are all foods of Bear. Food taboos in certain instances are common.
[4] Bears are often described as appearing from almost nowhere.

said to him, "Hey, my cross-cousin, shut your eyes and open your mouth wide and I will jump right into it, just as you want me to do." So the bear did this. Coyote jumped the other way out of the tree, and started running. After some distance Coyote was just about all in and ready to give up, so he used his evil power ('ini·jił) on the bear, "May your guts be all tied up in knots," he said. This caused the bear terrible pains, but he also used his evil power on Coyote. This caused terrible shooting pains through Coyote's pelvis. That is how they almost killed each other with their power. They could hardly walk and just managed to keep an even distance apart. Then Coyote asked the bear if he could cure him, so the bear fixed him up. Then Coyote fixed the bear up with his power. They cured each other.

46. *COYOTE READS THE LETTER AS HE SITS[1]

All the shamans were holding a council at the Sun's house. They were all there. When they were through holding the council, they got a paper from above. On it were written words, just like a letter. The shamans wanted to read the letter and know what it said. One of them said he would try. They had a chair there and they told him to sit in it and take the paper. The shaman sat down and took the paper. He looked it all over, but could not read it. Then another shaman sat down and tried, but without success. One after another they sat in the chair and tried to read the paper, but could not. Finally Coyote, who was a shaman, was the only one left. They said, "You ought to be able to read this paper, Coyote." Coyote sat down in the chair and took the paper. He looked at it a while and then started to read it. He rested his head on one hand and held the paper before him with the other hand. Coyote read the paper right off without trouble. He knew how.

47. HOW DEER HORNS BECAME HARD[2]

Long ago the horns of deer used to have a marrow just like a regular bone, with lots of fat inside. One time when Coyote was out hunting with all the rest of the people, they killed some deer and divided up the meat among themselves. But they only gave just a little to Coyote. He got mad about that. Then Coyote said, "This deer horn was marrow inside, but when I eat it, it's only bone that I feel against my teeth." Now the horns of the deer these people had killed all turned to bone and they could not eat them any more. This is the way I heard it.

---

[1] Told by Francis Drake. Also called "The Paper from Above Arrives at the Sun's House."
[2] Told by Palmer Valor. Compare Goddard, ibid 138ff.

48. *coyote brings in big owl's cap: how deer horns became
    hard: the bear woman: coyote determines death[1]

Big Owl was living north of here. He was always hunting our
people and killing them to eat. He had been doing this so much
that he had pretty nearly cleaned out all the people in that country.
Only where Coyote was living he had not come yet. A way off
there was a girl living, about twelve to fifteen years old, all by
herself. All her people had been killed by Big Owl, so now she
started for Coyote's camp. When she got there she told what had
happened, "All my relatives have been eaten up by Big Owl and
now I am all by myself. Whoever will kill Big Owl, I will marry
him." Coyote overheard what she said. This girl looked good to
him and Coyote began to think about where Big Owl lived and how
he could kill Big Owl, because he often visited him over there.

One morning early Coyote said he was going off to visit his cross-
cousin (Big Owl). When he left the sun was just rising. Right
away he got to Big Owl's camp. When he got there, Coyote told Big
Owl, "My cross-cousin, I am a good runner. I am the fastest one.
I started way far off, but I got here quick. The medicine I have will
make you run fast. If you like I will give you some." Big Owl's
wife was there at the camp also. She was Frog, the one who lives
by the river. Then she said, "You always say that you are a bad
runner. Wherever you go you see deer ahead of you, but they
always get away. You never catch them. You better let Coyote
give you this medicine to make you run fast." Then Coyote said,
"I think you don't believe me. I will just show you. Step outside
and watch." From that camp in one direction way off, were big
mountains and it was the same in the other direction. There,
before Coyote started, he shot an arrow of bear grass stalk to the east.
Then he shot one of bull rush stalk to the west. When his arrow
dropped over the hill smoke came up, because Coyote had set fire
to the arrow before he shot it. Big owl saw the smoke coming up
way over there and he thought Coyote had run over and made the
fire himself. Coyote wanted to make Big Owl believe this so he
could give him the medicine. Coyote always lied to everyone and
that's why he was doing it now. He was fooling Big Owl. Pretty
soon Coyote came back to Big Owl's camp as if he had run back
from where he pretended to have set the fire. Then he said, "I
told you so. You see, I have run over behind that big mountain
and set a fire there and am back already." Then Big Owl's wife
said, "Hurry up, this is true all right, I believe it. You go and get
this medicine and be a runner also!"

Big Owl wore a cap and Coyote kept thinking that this was the
only way he would be able to get that cap for himself. "All right,"
Big Owl and his wife said, "you give me medicine on both my legs

[1] Told by Bane Tithla. Compare Goddard, ibid p. 138 ff.

to make me run fast." Then Coyote said, "You better make a sweat lodge and then we two will go in it." When the lodge was made Coyote told him, "I want you to hang your cap in front of the doorway here. Then I'm going to show you how I will treat you. I have good medicine to put on your legs. We have to go inside the lodge, and then I have to put white ashes inside your leg bones. I will have to split your calfs and thighs to put it in." Coyote always kept in his mind how he was going to fix Big Owl. Then they went inside the sweat lodge and covered it all over, but first of all Big Owl hung his cap up over the doorway as Coyote wished. "I'm going to cut open your legs when we get hot. When you get good and hot I will have to put a hot rock under your legs to heat them." "If it doesn't hurt, all right, but if it hurts I will stop," Big Owl said as Coyote worked on his legs. "Don't do anything while I am working," Coyote said. After he had cut Big Owl's legs, he took rocks and put one under each of Big Owl's legs. Then with another rock he smashed both of Big Owl's legs. When he did this he jumped up and out, and took Big Owl's cap. Then he said, "That's the way I do with a man so he will never do wrong again." Big Owl's wife saw Coyote going off and said, "Where are you going? You were supposed to make my husband a good runner."

Coyote went back to where the other people were camped. Just before he got to the camp, back of a little ridge and just at sundown, he said over to himself, "mbuᵒize· ḷi·le, I have his cap here. I come towards camp." All the people stepped out to look at Coyote. They saw he had Big Owl's cap. Now the people agreed that Coyote was all right, and so they brought that girl to him and he married her.

After Coyote married the girl, he lived on with the people there for some time. Then after a while the people decided to go and hunt across on the other side of a big canyon near there. This canyon was a great many feet deep and it was called tse·yi'nogode·l (canyon). There must have been a great many deer on the other side of it. This canyon is northwest from here. They say there are pictures on a rock in the canyon. The Tontos[1] have seen this place and tell a story about it. Before the people crossed this canyon, Great Blue Heron straddled the canyon with his long legs and the people crossed over on him. That was the only way they could get across.

Then they commenced to hunt and killed lots of deer. Coyote went along with them, but they did not give him good meat, just old scraps and bones. In those times deer horns were all made of fat and also their bones were all fat. Coyote got sore because the people kept all the good meat for themselves and just gave old scraps to him, so he said, "From here on you people will kill poor deer." In those days all the deer were very fat. Then Coyote cooked some of

---

[1] Southern Tonto or Northern Tonto?

the meat they had given him. When he ate it he bit on bone. That's
how bones started, lots of them, in deer. After Coyote did this, they
all started back for home, the men going in front. Coyote fixed it
so that he took a long time packing up and starting. He wanted to
stay behind for some reason. When the people got to tse·yi'nogode·ł,
Great Blue Heron straddled the canyon for them again, and they
walked across on him. In those days all the animals could talk and
so the people told Great Blue Heron, "We used to give you all the
fat deer meat with no bones in it, but now Coyote cooked meat and
it has bones. We feel bad about this and on account of it we have
only a little meat to give you. Coyote is way behind and when he
comes let him get on your legs and when he is a way out, draw back
and let him drop so he will fall into the canyon." Now all the
people were across and pretty soon they could see Coyote coming.
Great Blue Heron straddled the canyon for him, but when Coyote
started out over the canyon he drew his legs back. Coyote yelled,
"My cross-cousin, don't do that!" but anyway he fell down into the
canyon and his pack fell with him. As he was falling, he spoke to
his bedding. "I want only you to get hurt." That's why, as he hit
the bottom, he was not hurt at all. The people from above saw
where Coyote had fallen. He was sitting there. When Coyote looked
up he could see the sky just like a little door way above between
the canyon walls. Only bats were flying around him. "My cross-
cousins, I will give my pack to you if you will make a trail up this
canyon for me to get out on," he told the bats. They said all right,
and all the bats started to work on a trail for Coyote. It was a good
sloping trail. When it was all finished Coyote went up it and got out
of the canyon.

The other hunters had all gone right back to their camps. When
they got there Coyote's wife asked them what had become of her
husband. Then they told her, "We saw him coming a little way
behind us. When we crossed tse·yi'nogode·ł Coyote got close to
Great Blue Heron and went out on his legs. Then he must have
fallen off into the canyon." Now Coyote's wife went to Great Blue
Heron on the edge of the canyon and asked where Coyote was. "He
has crossed already," Great Blue Heron said. He did not tell her
that Coyote had fallen down. Then she said, "I think you must
have drawn your legs back and let him fall," and she picked up a
rock and threw it at Great Blue Heron's legs and broke them.

After she came back to camp, she was anxious about her husband
and looked all over for him. Later on she turned into a bear and
started killing people. She got mean and was killing people in
that camp to eat, right where she lived. Her little brother was there.
He told some people about how his sister went away somewhere
every day. He told this to Chipmunk. Chipmunk said to him, "If
that girl wants to come and look for lice in your hair, you watch
her shadow, and if you see her shadow change to a bear, then jump

up and get your bow and arrows and kill her, for she will kill you if
you don't. Over there she buries what she doesn't eat, at the foot
of that pine tree. So run to that place and cover this over before
she kills you." A while after the boy had been told this, that girl
came there and saw her little brother had lots of lice in his hair.
"I want to pick them out," she said. So the boy said all right. But
he kept a close watch on her shadow while she was working. In a
little while he saw her shadow turn to that of a bear, with the hair
standing up and the front paws raised, all ready to bite him. He
jumped up and ran to the pine tree and hid. Then he shot an arrow
into the bear's body, but did not kill her. The bear ran after him,
but after a little way fell down. Now the bear said, "My little
brother, you have killed me," and she died.

From this time on the boy lived by himself, because before most
of his relatives had been killed by Big Owl and now the rest were
killed by that bear. Then Chipmunk told him, "You see those bones
lying there? I want you to gather all the bones and put them
together. Make them like a person standing up. After you do this,
then rub some fat all over the bones (human bones) and then they
will turn to a man again." So the boy did this for four days in
succession. He went there once every day. The first day he went
there and assembled the bones and rubbed grease on them. That
day as he was going to the place, he heard a person's voice, as if
someone was talking to him. But there was no one there. When he
was through, he came away. The next day he went back again. As
he got near he heard voices of children and men and women. It
sounded as if there were a lot of people. But when he got there,
he only saw some bones lying on the ground. He worked on the
bones again and rubbed them with grease. Then he left there
and stayed away. The next day he went back and when he got
near he heard men and women talking as if a crowd were there
playing the hoop and poles game. There were women and they were
hollering as if everyone was having a good time. But when he got
there, there was nothing but bones. He fitted these together again
and rubbed fat on them. Then he went away. Next day when he
got near this place again, he heard lots of people. The men's voices
sounded as if they were playing tse'dił (three stick dice game) and
haigo·he (four stick dice game). Boys and men and women were
having a good time. When he got there he saw lots of men and
women and children. They were all living as before. Now this boy
lived with these people.

Some time after that Coyote came there. He was always making
trouble. Coyote said he did not like this. This was bad. It was as
though these people had been brought back to life. Then he said,
"I'm going to look for a mano and a hair brush. I will tie them together and throw them in the river. If they sink down in the water
and then come back to the top again, that will mean that dead people

can come back to life. But if they just sink, people will be dead forever." He did this and threw the mano and hair brush in the river. They never came to the surface. When he did that, all those people who had been brought back to life disappeared and never came back.

My yucca fruits lie piled up.

49. *BIG OWL CHOPS OFF HIS PENIS[1]

Long ago they say. This is a story about Big Owl's penis. Up near tⁱuk'a·gai (Fort Apache district), there is a big rock called tse·sizių (rock standing up, Saw Tooth Mountain). Big Owl was going along to the foot of this rock. He was carrying his penis with him and following the trail over by ya·gọgaidje·łk'id (a place). He kept on toward tse·sizių, still carrying his penis with him. In those days it was very long, so long that he had to carry it wrapped around his body. Then he went on down to the river (White River). Across the river was a woman going down to tse·łkan'iska·d (a place), above the river on the ridges. Big Owl crossed the river, carrying his penis with him. That woman saw him then. She was very hungry and so she started down a ridge to Big Owl, because she thought that big load Big Owl was carrying might be something good to eat. When she got to him she said, "Big Owl, give me some of what you are carrying there." "What I'm carrying is no good to eat," said Big Owl. "Anyway give me some, I'm hungry," the woman said. "You can't eat this," Big Owl said. But the woman told him, "Give me just a little." "All right, turn around, bend over and lift up your dress," Big Owl said. The woman did so, and Big Owl unwrapped his penis from around his body. Then it became stiff, went way out to the woman and knocked her down on the ground. The woman got up and Big Owl wrapped his penis around himself again.

Then he started to think about this and sat down. "This is no good, the way I can do now, no good at all." Big Owl was thinking that his penis was too long and that he would like to cut it off. "I'll cut if off sure enough," he thought, and so he started up the side of the hill there to a big rock about the size and shape of this wickiup. Then he got another rock and carried it up on top of the big rock. On top of the rock he unwrapped his penis and let it hang down over the edge. He looked to see where would be just the right place to cut it off. He finally cut it off just between his legs. Now he thought it would be all right to go around this way and he liked it because it was nice and short. What he had cut off, he threw down to the foot of the rock so it was all coiled about the rock at its bottom. Then he got down and on top of it, all around, he piled up

---

[1] Told by Bane Tithla.

little rocks and also some dirt so no one would see it. He was all right just as he was, good and short, he thought, and so he went on his way. Before, he had to carry a heavy load, but now he had got rid of it and twisted it round the rock. Pretty soon he met another man and told him what he had done. This man had a long penis, just like Big Owl's. But Big Owl said, "I have a short penis, so from here on that's the way all men will be, because I am that way," and from that time on men had it the way Big Owl had made himself. The rock where Big Owl cut his penis off is still there and is called mbuʻbila·sidą· (owl his penis it sits) because of this story. You can still see the rock on top of the big one, with which Big Owl cut himself. Around the base of the big rock his penis is still coiled and piled on top of it are the small rocks and dirt he put there.

My yucca fruits lie piled up.

50. *TWO HILLS IN LINE[1]

Long ago they say. Big Owl was living on this earth just as a man does. His father was Sun and he was traveling over this earth doing lots of evil, killing many people. Big Owl had a great burden basket. Wherever he went he always carried this burden basket with him on his back. He went to hunt different people and kill them. Big Owl's wife was Frog. He had a son also, a big tall fellow.

One morning Big Owl started off to hunt some people. On his way he went between two mountains, one to the east, and one to the west. On the east mountain was a woman and also on the west mountain was another woman. The one on the east mountain hollered to Big Owl. Big Owl heard her and said, "Where are you ? Come over here. Let's lie down together". He stopped there and shaded his eyes with his hand and tried to see who it was that had hollered at him. This person, whoever she was, had hollered at him in a polite way, so he looked to see where she was. He thought it would be nice to go to where she was, so he started up the mountain towards the top. When he got up a way, the woman over on the west mountain called to him, "Big Owl, come here, I want to lie with you." Big Owl heard and stopped and shaded his eyes and looked over on to the west mountain. He thought that the woman must be calling him from the top of that mountain now. He thought she must have crossed back from the mountain he was on, as he was sure he had heard her holler before. He turned and went back down the way he had come and across, and started up the west mountain. Just before he got to the top, over on the east mountain, a woman hollered to him and said, "Where are you going ?" Big Owl thought it was the same woman.

---

[1] Told by Bane Tithla.

He was as if crazy, Big Owl was, and not very smart. All he thought about was killing people and eating them. When Big Owl was coming to these two mountains, the two women had seen him. They had talked together: "He is crazy and doesn't know much. I will go on top of that mountain and you go on top of this mountain and holler at him, first one, and then the other. That way I think he will never come to either of us," they said. So that's what they were doing now. When Big Owl heard the woman over on east mountain, he went back there again and started to go up. Then he stopped and shaded his eyes to look. "I think she is the one. I will go to her," he said to himself and started up again. When he was almost to the top, just before he got there, the woman on the west mountain called to him again, the same way. Now he stopped there and shaded his eyes to look back across to the other mountain. He was pretty near giving out from climbing up and down these two mountains. The woman on the east mountain who had called him was hiding only a little way from him, laughing at him. Big Owl thought there was only one woman, but there were two. He turned and went back all the way to the bottom of the mountain and started up the west mountain once more. When he was nearly to the top, the woman over on the east mountain hollered, "Where are you going? Come over here so I can lie with you." Now Big Owl was mad because it was almost sun-down. He thought this woman who was calling to him must have feathers and fly back and forth between the two mountains. So when he went back down and started up the east mountain, he kept looking at the sky as he went, to see if anything flew back over him. This way he did not look where he was going and fell over a xucntca·gi (cholla cactus). The stickers went all over his face and body. "'aihiʻ (ouch)!" he said. He pulled the stickers out of himself and it hurt. He was good and mad now and started off back home. As he was going off, those two women called to him to come back. But he had lots of stickers still in his body, and so he was mad and kept on his way.

When Big Owl got home, he said to his wife, "sisą· (my old woman),[1] I want you to pull these stickers out of me." So his wife began to pull them out. "Wherever you go it seems you know nothing. It's always this way," she said to him. Then Big Owl told his wife about what had happened. "sisą·, on my way between two mountains some woman called me to come to her. When she did this I started up one of the mountains to go to her. Then a woman called to me from that other mountain and said, 'Come over and lie with me here,' so I went down and up the other mountain. I got almost to the top when a woman hollered at me to come up the other mountain, so I did. This way that woman kept calling me back and forth all day between those mountains. I thought she

---

[1] Addressing his wife, as he habitually does, by this uncommon term, is one of Big Owl's characteristics. It causes considerable amusement.

might be flying beween the mountains, so I watched the sky on my way and that is how I fell into this cactus." Then his wife laughed at him and said, "You don't know much. I think you are not smart enough. I think there were two women there, and when you got close to the top of one mountain where a woman was, the other called you back. This way they called you back and forth because they knew you didn't know anything. That's the way. Everyone thinks you are crazy." "My wife, it must be you are right. First one woman called me, and then the other called me. That's the way I think. That's true. Make me some bread early in the morning and I will go to that same place. If they holler at me again, I will go right to the top of one mountain," said Big Owl.

So next morning he took the bread and started off for the two mountains. He thought those women would call him again as they had done yesterday. He went between the two mountains. "If they call to me, I am going right straight to the top of one mountain, even if the other one calls me back," he said to himself. Big Owl kept looking on both sides and listening. Then he thought he heard one holler and he started to climb up one of the mountains. When he got to the top he found the woman's tracks, where she had been yesterday. "ᵉ, if she was only here I would lie with her today," he said, and he lay down in the same place that the woman had been lying. "I would lie with her this way," he thought. From there he looked over on the other mountain. He went down the mountain and started up the other. When he got to the top he found the other woman's tracks, where she had been sitting. "Here, this is a good place. I would have been lying with her here yester- day if I had found her," he said, and so he lay down where she had been and moved his buttocks up and down. That evening he went back to his camp and said to his wife, "sisąˑ, you were right. Those women were on both mountains. I saw their tracks there today." "Yes, I told you those two knew you were not smart and were crazy," she told him. "From now on, wherever I go, if someone hollers to me that way I will go right to them. It doesn't make any difference if two people call me from different sides. The first one who calls me, I will go straight to her," and from that time on Big Owl was always careful and listened because he thought more women might call to him.

My yucca fruits lie piled up.

51. BIG OWL HUNTS "RATS": *PEOPLE TURN THEMSELVES TO GROUND HEAT: *BIG OWL EATS HIS OWN CHILDREN: *BIG OWL AND TURKEY MEET EACH OTHER[1]

Long ago they say. Big Owl was living with Frog, his wife. Big Owl was always out hunting. He had a great burden basket which

---

[1] Told by Bane Tithla. Compare Goddard, ibid pp. 137—138.

he always carried on his back. Whenever he killed any people he carried them home in this burden basket. He had a great pot to boil them in also. One morning Big Owl started off to hunt. His son went along with him. After a while Big Owl came to a wickiup. There were all kinds of cactus around this wickiup. The people living in it knew that Big Owl was not smart. Inside they were grinding corn on a rock. Big Owl said, "My son, it must be Pack Rat who is living here." He had a long stick and he stuck this inside the wickiup.[1] Within were a woman and some girls. When they saw the end of the stick come in, they all grabbed hold of it and started to pull. Big Owl pulled also, but the others were dragging him towards the wickiup. He thought that his stick must be sticking into a rat, maybe lots of them and this was why they were pulling so hard. He tried to drag his stick out, but they kept pulling him towards the wickiup. Then Big Owl called to his son to help him. When those people had almost all of the stick pulled into their wickiup and Big Owl was only holding the tip end, they let it go. Big Owl fell over backwards onto a rock and hurt himself. Then he turned to his son and said, "I told you to help me and pull out those rats. You didn't do it and now I am hurt badly." His son said, "You're not smart enough. There are some people living in that wickiup. I told you already, and that's why I wouldn't help you." Big Owl said, "You mustn't call them people while we are hunting them. Those are rats in there." "I told you people were living in there, but you wouldn't pay any attention to me," his son answered. Then Big Owl said, "I want you to go on the other side of the wickiup. I'm going to poke this stick in and these rats will run out to you." So he poked his stick into the wickiup, and when he did this, the woman and girls grabbed it again. Big Owl pulled hard and then shouted to his son, "Hurry up and come here! I have a rat sure now." His son came and both of them pulled on the stick. The people in the wickiup let it go and Big Owl fell on his back again and hurt himself. Now his son said, "You don't know anything. I told you that people were living there. They grabbed your stick and when you pulled, they let go and you fell over backwards." "You mustn't call them people. There is a rule that you mustn't call those you are hunting people. You have to follow this rule, because it is the only way you can get them," Big Owl said. Then he poked the stick in again, but he had a hard time, because the women and girls would not take hold of it. Big Owl said, "Those rats must be way back in their hole. Before, when I was pulling I told you to help me, but you would not help. You ought to have helped me and we would have gotten the rats out long ago. We had better let them go now and move on. We may see some other people on the way." So they started on again.

---

[1] The usual method in hunting pack rats.

After a while they came to where some people were camped. These people could change themselves to anything they wanted to, to a man or anything else. Now they said, "Let's change ourselves into tse"a·dande'e' (ground heat shimmering) so Big Owl will pass us by. He is not smart." So all the men and women took off their clothes and made a long line where Big Owl would pass by. Big Owl knew that these people were camped here and after a while he got to where the people were lined up. He looked and said to his son, "This, in a long line here, is called ground heat." His son said, "What's the matter with you? These are people, not ground heat at all." Big Owl told him, "You are not smart at all. You call everything people. Don't talk this way! If you keep on we will never see any people at all." But all the time these were people standing in front of him, with no clothes. His son said, "If I were you, I would call these people." "Don't call them people again. I told you this was ground heat." Then Big Owl started to walk up to the people in line. When he came to one of the women, he felt between her legs and also of her breasts. "This is ground heat all right. They are always the biggest between the legs," he said. He kept on right down the line doing this way till he got to a woman who was bleeding from her monthly. Big Owl said, "This is the best paint," and he took some and painted his face with it. After he had done this to all the women, he asked his son to do the same way with all of them, but his son said, "Not me, not me! I don't want to do that. You are very foolish when you do that way. When you touched the flow from that woman's monthly, that was no good. I'm afraid of that."[1] Big Owl and his son went on from there, but that day they found no people at all and came home at evening.

That night Big Owl said, "To morrow I will go by myself out hunting, because you, my son, will not obey me. You just do the way you like and talk about people all the time. That is no good." So in the morning Big Owl took his largest burden basket and started off. After he had gone a way, he met two boys. He told them to get into his basket. They did and he carried them along. About halfway from his camp was some water in a tank in the rocks. He wanted a drink, so he set his basket down and went to the water. While he was gone, the boys got out of his basket and rolled two big blue, heavy rocks into it. When Big Owl came back he thought the boys were still in the basket, because the two rocks stuck out like their heads. So he lifted it up and set it on his back again and carried it on toward his home. The two boys were still in the basket sitting on one of the big rocks. As Big Owl went along, he passed under a tree. Then the boys caught hold of one the of the limbs of the tree, lifted themselves out of the basket and got away. Big Owl

---

[1] The normal reaction. Sickness may be caused in men by contact with menstrual fluid.

never knew it and thought he had the two boys still, but he only had two rocks. This way he got back to his camp and set his basket down inside the wickiup. "My wife, here are two black-tailed deer fawns. I want you to butcher them and then boil them so we can eat them right away," he said. His wife looked in the basket and saw the two rocks. "You have only two rocks there," she said. "Don't call them rocks, I have two young deer there, real deer. Get the knife so you can butcher them."

They had a large knife that Big Owl used to kill people and eat them. His wife took this and tried to cut the rocks with it but couldn't. Then she said, "I tried to cut them but I couldn't, so you had better cut them yourself. I told you they were two rocks." Big Owl tried to cut the rocks, but he couldn't. Nearby his son-in-law was living. Big Owl told his wife to take these things to his son-in-law's camp and tell him to cut them and use them for himself. His wife took the stones over to the son-in-law's camp and left them outside the wickiup. "Big Owl brought these in. He wants you to cut them up and boil them so we can eat them," she said. So the son-in-law stepped outside and went to the basket where the two rocks were and saw them. "These are only rocks, not food at all," he said and carried the basket to the edge of the hill where he rolled the rocks out, down the slope to the foot. Then Big Owl's daughter went to her father's camp and said, "These two big stones, what do they mean. They are only rocks, so my husband took them and rolled them down the slope to the foot of the hill." Big Owl's wife talked to him and said, "Tell me just were you have been and what you did." So Big Owl said, "I met two baby deer and put them in my basket and carried them home here." Big Owl always called people deer, and women he called female deer. This is why he had called the two boys young deer when he met them. "Those two you called young deer, while you were on your way home did you leave your basket with them in it any time?" his wife asked. "Yes, sure. On my way I saw some water and wanted to get a drink, so I set my basket down and went to the water," he said. "That was bad to do. Those two people knew you were off drinking and so they probably set the two rocks in the basket while you were gone," his wife said. "Yes, that's right, now I understand about it," Big Owl said. "From there on did you go under any trees?" she asked. "Yes, that's right. Close to camp I passed under that tree." "I think those two boys grabbed the limb and lifted themselves out when you passed under," she said. "Yes, that's right, my wife. From now on I will never lay my basket down or go under a tree again," Big Owl said.

The next day Big Owl started off once more. While he was on his way he met two boys again. He told them to hurry up and get into his basket. They did and he carried them off. This time he was very careful to travel where there were no trees, and in an open

country where there was no water either. That's the way he got
back to camp all right. Then he said to his wife, "sisą· (my wife),
here are two baby deer that I brought for you. Get some water and
fix them to boil." So his wife filled the big pot with water and set
it to heat over a big fire. Then Big Owl said to his wife, "Let's go
outside. I want you to look for lice in my hair. Whenever I am
out hunting, the lice bite me so much that I want you to pick them
out now." So they went outside and sat in the shade. His wife
picked the lice out of his hair.

The two boys were in the pot in the house, where they had been
left to cook. The youngest one said. "I'm getting too hot now. This
water is getting warm." Big Owl had two sons also and they were
asleep in the wickiup, covered over by a blanket which reached to
their necks, leaving only their heads sticking out. Big Owl's knife
was lying close to their pillow. The oldest of the two boys in the
pot said, "We are getting warm now so we will get out." So they
did get out of the pot. The oldest boy went to Big Owl's knife and
then to the two sleeping boys and cut their heads off with it, just
where the blanket ended. They put the bodies of Big Owl's two
sons into the pot, but left the two heads just sticking out of the
blanket as if the two were still asleep. Then the boys who had done
this turned themselves to downy eagle feathers, and were blown out
the doorway. Big Owl's wife saw them being blown away and said,
"cahastį· (my old man) there are two good eagle feathers I see
blowing out of your wickiup. One was big and one was little. They
were together." Big Owl saw the feathers and wanted them. "The
big one is mine," he said. "You always want the biggest," his wife
said. "The big one is for me and the little one for you," she said.
"All right, you can have the big one and I the little one," he said,
and started to try and get them, but he missed both of them and the
wind kept on blowing them away over the hill. Big Owl came back
without them.

After quite a while, about noon, Big Owl thought that the meat
must be well cooked. He told his wife, "That meat must be done.
Go and get it and bring it out so we can eat. But don't take it all.
Save some for those two boys who are sleeping, so that when they
wake up they can eat." So his wife went in and brought out a lot
of the meat to Big Owl, but left some in the pot for the two children.
Then Big Owl started to eat. One of his boys had a little wart on
his hand and another on top of his foot. While they were eating,
the woman saw these and said, "My old man, this looks like
ke·la·t'axę·se (wart on the point of his foot; the name of one of the
boys)." "Don't talk like that about our children, because they feel
sick. Don't say this way about them," Big Owl said. So they
kept on eating the meat and drinking the soup. Then Big Owl
said, "Those two boys are still asleep. They have been asleep too
long. Go and wake them up and let them eat!" So his wife went

in the wickiup and took all the meat out of the pot. Then she
pulled the blanket off the two children to wake them, but all she
saw were the two heads lying there. These rolled off the pillow
onto the ground. The woman stepped outside to Big Owl and said,
"I told you ke·la·t'axę·se was in the pot. I showed it to you and
that was he. His head was cut right off there and his body put in
the pot. They are what we have been eating. I found only their
two heads lying on the bed, and when I pulled back the blanket
these rolled down onto the ground." Big Owl said, "I think you tell
the truth, but I will go see for myself anyway," and he went into
the wickiup and said, "You are right." His wife said, "Those eagle
feathers I saw blowing away, I think they were the two boys that
you brought home." Big Owl said, "You are right. We ate our
own children. I never tasted my children at all." He meant this
as if he had never eaten their meat and he spit it all out. Big Owl
did not know how to cry, nor his wife either. The two sat there and
thought about how to cry, "he·, my wife, how should I cry?" Big
Owl said. Then his wife said, "'etuł hictcago', 'etuł ('etuł I cry,
'etuł). Now how will you cry?" and Big Owl said, "'idicndi'i
hictcago', 'idicndi'i ('idicndi'i I cry, 'idicndi'i). In those days
no one ever cried about anyone, and so they did not know how.[1]
Now each of them cried his own way. After a while Big Owl said,
"What's the matter, są· (old woman)? Let's stop crying and later
on we will raise some more children. So let's stop crying." His
wife believed him, so she stopped crying.

Then they talked together. "We will go to tse'iłk'i·nagusgize
(rock spiral hole going in it). There I think we will raise more
children again," said Big Owl. So they moved from their old home
to that place. When they were settled there, Big Owl started out
to hunt. While he was on his way he met Turkey. "Where are
you traveling from?" he asked him. "I come from ts'iłtsugidaska·d
(ts'iłtsugi (a certain kind of tree) growing)," Turkey said. "And
where are you come from?" Turkey asked. "I come from tse'ił-
k'i·nagusgize. At that place is my wife. I want you to go there.
Tell her I met you here and told you to go to her, and tell her to
cook you in a pot. I don't want her to put your neck in the pot.
Also, while you are cooking I want her to put a flat rock on each
side. When you are well cooked I will get home and I'll be very
hungry. I'll take your head and pound it on a rock, and that's
the way I will eat it." "All right," Turkey said, and he started off
for tse'ił k'i·nagusgize.

When he got to Big Owl's wife, he said to her, "Big Owl told me
to come here and that's why I came. 'I have lots of sinew and
feathers at my camp,' he told me, 'and I want you to have these
roasted for me. Also break my bow up and arrows too, and roast

---

[1] These are ridiculous ways of crying.

them along with the rest. Then I will be hungry and it will be all roasted so I can eat it right away,' Big Owl told me," Turkey said. So Big Owl's wife believed him and got all those things and put them in the pot and started to boil them. She broke his bow and arrows and put them in also. After she had done this, Turkey said, "Big Owl told me to tell you to warm up some water for me, so I can get a good bath with it. Also, after that, I have lots of lice in my hair and you can pick them out for me." So Big Owl's wife warmed up some water and washed Turkey's head with it and when she was finished, both went outside and lay in the shade. There Big Owl's wife started to look for lice on Turkey, and he laid his head across her thighs. About noon Turkey thought Big Owl would be coming home in a while and so he said to Big Owl's wife, "When you have picked all the lice out, Big Owl said you were to lie with me for a good while." "Even if he did tell you, I won't do it," the woman said. "But he told me that you were to do it," Turkey said. "You lie about that. My husband likes me too well. He would not say that," the woman said. "I'm telling the truth about it, because Big Owl said this to me. If your husband came home and found out you hadn't done this with me, he would get after you," Turkey told her. So she said, "All right, I don't believe you, but let's start anyway." They went into the wickiup. Turkey lay with Big Owl's wife clear till sundown. Then he thought that Big Owl might be coming home soon, so he stepped outside and went on his way down to a lake where he stopped to wash himself. When he had done this, he climbed up a great big spruce, going to the top of it. "Big Owl can't do anything to this tree, so I am safe here," he thought.

Then Big Owl was coming toward his home. As he came, he called to his wife, "My old woman, take out the neck. I'm very hungry; the turkey neck. What's the matter with you? You never left my turkey neck here to roast for me." His wife told him, "I think you are not very smart. You sent Turkey to me and told him to tell me to gather all your sinew and feathers for you and also to take your bow and arrows, smash them up, and roast them along with the rest." "All right, you had better throw the sinew out," Big Owl said. "But that's not all. Turkey said I should give him a good head wash and bath all over, and then comb his hair and pick the lice out of it. After all that, you told him to lie with me and so I did it. He lay with me almost all day," his wife said. "He lied to you. I never said that. I told him to go to you and tell you to roast him for me and to cut his head off and put it on top of the pot when it was well roasted, then to put it on a rock, and I was to pound it up to eat when I got home. All right, I want you to go in the camp with me and I want to see how you look. I'll find out if Turkey has been lying with you." When Big Owl had seen his wife, he said, "He must have done this with you a long time. I

never did this much with you since we have been married. Where
did Turkey go ?" "He told me he was going to the water to wash himself," the woman said. Then Big Owl got mad. His wife got mad
also and she ran off and jumped into the river and left Big Owl.
That's how the frogs got into the water and are still living there.
Big Owl followed her and cried to himself on the river bank where
she had gone in. "'etuł, 'etuł, I have lost her now. She was good and
had a big one between her legs."

Then Big Owl got his knife and stone axe and bows and arrows
and started out after Turkey. He went down to the water and looked
into it. There he thought he saw Turkey in the water, but Turkey
was sitting in the spruce tree above and it was only his reflection.
But Big Owl thought it was really Turkey under the water and he
started to shoot his arrows in the water at the image. When he
shot all his arrows, then he threw his bow into the water at Turkey
also; then his stone axe and his knife. But there was Turkey, still
unhurt. He could see him in the water. After he threw all his
weapons in, he jumped in the water himself and tried to grab
around with his arms and catch Turkey. But he could not catch
him at all. He kept on doing this way under the water, till he gave
out and his eyes got red from water. So he came out and lay
down in the shade. Turkey, up in the tree, urinated and it dropped
down on Big Owl's face. Big Owl said, "What's the matter ? Water
is dripping in my face," and he looked up. There he saw Turkey
sitting. "he·, there above me is 'red anus'," he said. Then he told
Turkey, "Get down from there before I pull this tree up." Turkey
told him, "Right beside this is a great pine tree. Let's see you pull
that one up." So Big Owl went to the pine and pulled it out. Then
he came back and said, "Hurry up, get down there, or I'll pull this
tree up." "There is a big tree over here. Let's see you pull that
one up," Turkey said. So Big Owl went to it and pulled it out.
"Hurry up, get down here before I pull this tree out," he yelled.
But Turkey would not answer him, so Big Owl went to the spruce
that Turkey was sitting in and with one pull he uprooted the tree.
Just as it was going to fall, Turkey flew far off over the hill. Big
Owl followed and where Turkey lit on the ground, he found his
tracks. Where Turkey ran over ground Big Owl could not see his
tracks, but where he ran over bare rock he could see his tracks
plainly. Thus he kept on following him for a long way, till finally
he caught up with him.

When he caught Turkey, Big Owl ordered him to gather a lot of
rocks and a pile of wood and when he had done this, to set fire to
the wood and heat the rocks up. This was the way Big Owl thought
he was going to cook Turkey on hot rocks and eat him all up. He
thought he would skin Turkey first and put the meat on the skin.
He told Turkey to get some branches of tc'ilda'ditł'uge (a shrub) and
spread them on the ground so he could butcher him on them.

Turkey felt badly on account of this and while he was pulling up the bushes, he thought about it. Then he spread the branches on the ground. "Hurry up and lie down on top of them," Big Owl said. He took out his knife and was just starting in to cut Turkey's breast when Turkey said, "Wait a minute, you forgot about the rocks to pound my neck with. I want to get those two rocks for you first." "Yes, that's right, I forgot. Go get two big rocks for me so I can use them to break your head and also so I can crack your bones to get out the marrow. Go ahead, get them!" Big Owl said. So Turkey started out to get the rocks. While he was doing this, Turkey began to cry. He found some good flat rocks, but he kept on going further and looking. Finally he turned over a rock and saw under it Horned Toad. Horned Toad was making an arrow. Then he asked Turkey, "My grandson, why are you crying?" and Turkey told him, "That Big Owl sitting over there is waiting to kill me." Then Horned Toad said, "My grandson, wait, I want to finish this arrow first. I will give it to you.[1] Also I will give you my hat which Big Owl is always afraid of." After Horned Toad finished the arrow, he gave it and a bow to Turkey and told him to hide them by his side. Also he gave him his cap. Then with these Turkey started back to Big Owl, bringing the two rocks. When he got to him, he said, "Here are two good rocks I got for you." "All right, hurry up, lie down on the brush here," Big Owl said. Turkey did and Big Owl took out his knife, just ready to cut Turkey's breast. But Turkey said, "Wait, something is sticking in my back," and he picked out Horned Toad's hat and showed it to Owl. Horned Toad had told Turkey that when Big Owl was about to kill him, he must show him the hat. "He will be afraid of that hat and when he starts to run, you shoot this arrow and tell it to follow Big Owl wherever he goes." When Big Owl saw the hat, he stepped back. "I found this hat there," Turkey said. "Throw it away," Big Owl said. He kept on saying this and backing off. But Turkey held the hat in his hand and showed it to him. Pretty soon Owl started to run off. Then Turkey put the arrow to his bow and said, "This way arrow, trail after him wherever he goes, this one I shoot at," and he shot the arrow at Big Owl. While Big Owl was running he dodged around a tree, but the arrow followed him around the tree also. At the place Big Owl was living he went into the rock, but the arrow went right in after him and right under the soles of his feet. I think that's the way Big Owl was killed.

My yucca fruits lie piled up. There is another story pretty nearly the same as this one, but I don't remember it.

---

[1] Lizards are ritually associated with stone arrow points.

52. *COYOTE STEALS WHEAT:
*COYOTE'S FAECES UNDER HIS HAT[1]

Coyote was always in trouble. This was long ago when our people and animals and birds lived together near White people. Coyote was going around among the' camps visiting. He would stay in one camp a while and then move on. Then he stayed at Bear's camp. From there he used to go to the White man's camps and fields and steal wheat. He went at night and took the ears off the wheat, carrying them away. Every night he was doing this. The White man who owned the farm found out what Coyote was up to and trailed him from where he had stolen the wheat. When he located the path by which Coyote had come, he went back and all the White men held a council as to what they should do and how they should catch Coyote. They made a figure of pitch, just like a man, and stood it up by the trail where Coyote used to go into the field. That night Coyote went back to steal wheat again. When he got to the field, he saw the pitch man standing there. Coyote thought it was a real person and he said, "Gray Eyes," he always talked like a Chiricahua,[2] "get to one side and let me by to the wheat. I just want a little. Get over I tell you." He was close to the pitch man now, but the pitch man wouldn't move. Then Coyote said, "You won't move? If you don't move over, I will hit you with my fist and knock you over. Wherever I go on this earth, if I hit a man once with my fist, it kills him." Coyote thought this was a real man. "All right, then I'm going to hit." He did and his fist stuck fast in the pitch, clear to his elbow. "What's the matter? Why have you caught my hand? Turn loose. This other hand is worse yet. If I hit a man with it, it knocks all his senses out." Then Coyote struck with his other fist and this arm got stuck in the pitch also. Now he was just standing on his two hind legs. "What's the matter? I'm going to kick you now because you hold me this way. If I hit you, it will knock you over." Then Coyote kicked and his leg went into the pitch and stuck. Now he was standing on one leg only. "This other leg is worse yet and I'm going to kick you with it," he said. He kicked, and his leg stuck into the pitch. All his legs were held fast in the pitch and only his tail was left free. "This tail of mine, if I whip you with it, it will cut you in two. So turn me loose." But the pitch just held him. He struck with his tail and got it stuck also. Only his head was free. He was still talking with it. "Why do you hold me this way? I will bite you and if I do I will kill you. You better turn me loose before I do. I will bite your

---

[1] Told by Bane Tithla.
[2] This is the Chiricahua name for Whites, according to Western Apache. Frequently narrators in speaking Coyote's parts assumed a marked nasal voice which they say is a Chiricahua speech characteristic. It is done to make Coyote the more ludicrous. Relations with the Chiricahua Apache were not always friendly, as may be surmised.

neck." But the pitch did not listen to him. He bit it and got his whole mouth stuck and there he was.

In the morning the farmer came, put a chain around Coyote's neck and lead him back to the house after he had taken him out of the pitch. When he got to the house, he said to his family, "This is the one who has been stealing from me." The White people held a meeting as to what they should do with Coyote. Then they decided to put Coyote into a pot of boiling water and scald him. So they filled a pot with water and set it to heat, tying Coyote up to one side, by the house. Pretty soon Coyote saw Gray Fox coming along. Gray Fox was loafing around the house, looking for something to steal from the White man. He saw the pot boiling on the fire. Coyote called to him, "My cross-cousin, come here. I want to tell you something," Gray Fox started to come. He did not know Coyote was tied up. When he got there he saw Coyote was fastened. Then Coyote said, "My cross-cousin, there are lots of things cooking for me in that pot," though the pot was only to scald him in. "There are potatoes, coffee, bread, and all kinds of food for me. They will soon be ready and they are going to bring them to me. You and I will eat them. We will eat lots. For this reason I want you to put this chain around your neck while I go and urinate behind that bush." Fox said all right and he took the chain off Coyote, putting it on his own neck. Coyote left and when he got behind the bush, he ran off.

After a while the water was good and hot and the white men came to where Gray Fox was tied. "This one is little. What's the matter? He must have shrunk, I guess," they said.[1] They lifted him up and threw him into the hot water. His hair came out. Now Gray Fox was all red and without hair. They took off the chain and threw him under a tree. Gray Fox stayed there until evening as if he was dead. When it got dark and cold that night, he became conscious again. He woke up and said, "I must have slept very hard." Then he got up and started off. After a while he got to Bear's camp and asked Bear, "Where is Coyote?" Bear said that Coyote always went for his water just a little way above, at some springs. "Coyote always comes there at midnight," Bear said. Gray Fox told what had happened (he tells Bear all). "I let him put the chain on me and then he never came back. That's why I am chasing him. If I see him, I will kill him." Bear told him to go to the spring and hide, so Gray Fox hid himself there at midnight. Coyote coming to the spring, knew that Gray Fox's body would be all red. When Coyote got close, he said, "I see something red. I want to get a drink of water, but what is that red thing?" Gray Fox just kept still. When Coyote put his head to the water to drink, he intended to jump on him. Coyote started to drink and

---

[1] The gray fox is a smaller animal than the coyote.

Gray Fox jumped and caught him. Gray Fox said, "Now I'm going to eat you up and kill you." The moon was in the sky and it was shining down into the water. Coyote saw it and said, "Don't say this to me. Don't talk like that. This in the water (the moon's reflection) is 'ash bread'[1] and it's good to eat. If we drink all the water we can take it out and eat if for ourselves." Coyote was fooling. They both started to drink and kept on. But Coyote soon merely pretended to drink. Gray Fox drank lots. When Gray Fox was full of water, he got cold. Then Coyote said, "My cross-cousin, some White people left a camp over here and I'm going to look for some old rags or quilts to wrap you up in. Wait here for me." So Coyote started off and as soon as he was out of sight, he ran away.

It was near morning now and Gray Fox got mad. He started off on Coyote's trail. As he went along, he talked to himself, "If I see you again, right away I will eat you up." He had drunk lots and so while he was trotting, he kept breaking wind, "guł, guł, guł, guł." He didn't know what the noise could be, so he stopped and listened. "That must be White people coming after me," he thought. He started on again but kept listening and looking back. He couldn't see anything. After a long way he came to a place some White people had been camping. He thought he would look for some old gunny sacks. Then he saw Coyote. "Coyote is the one I am looking for," he said and he planned as to how he could get close to Coyote. Finally he sneaked up on Coyote and caught him. "I'm going to eat you up. You fooled me many times," he said. Then Coyote said, "Don't talk that way, my cross-cousin. I'm here looking for a sack. About tonight or tomorrow the ocean is going to come all over the earth and so I'm going to get inside a sack and tie it up over my head in order that the water will wash me up on dry ground. Why do you want to eat me when the ocean is going to come over the earth?" Gray Fox believed Coyote about the ocean, so he said, "All right," and let go of Coyote. Then Coyote said, "My cross-cousin, look for a good sack over there and if you find one, go inside it and tie the mouth up. If the ocean comes, we will float on top of it and when it sinks again, we will come back on the ground and start all over again." Gray Fox started to look for a sack. Pretty soon he found one and Coyote said, "You might just as well get in that sack now, because the ocean is close. I will tie you in. I want to do this for you and then I will do the same for myself." So Gray Fox crawled in the sack and Coyote sewed the mouth tight. While Gray Fox lay in the sack, Coyote looked about for a big rock. Finding one, he lifted it up and let it drop on Gray Fox. He aimed for Grays Fox's head, but he missed. Then he ran off. Gray Fox had his senses knocked out, but after a while he woke

---

[1] A corn batter wrapped in corn husks and steamed in a shallow pit.

up, tore a hole in the sack and got out. Then he said to himself, "I will get Coyote."

Gray Fox looked for Coyote all over the mountains. At last he found him sitting under a large rocky point. He came up on him and grabbed him. "Now I'm going to eat you up," he said. Coyote said, "What's the matter with you. You are not very smart and don't understand things well." Lots of clouds were in the sky and Coyote said, "I want to explain this to you. My cross-cousin, something bad is going to happen to us. That sky is going to fall down. All the people on this earth know it and are sitting under rocks. But I guess you could not have heard about it yet. They have been warned about sky." Gray Fox believed him. Coyote told him to watch out, as the sky was falling. "Try to put your hand against this rock here." Gray Fox did this and Coyote told him to wait, that he was going to urinate. When he got in back of the rock, he ran off. Soon, Gray Fox looked for him and saw that he was gone. Coyote went off to some other camps. But Gray Fox was still searching for him.

While Coyote was at the camps, he and Bobcat decided to go together to a place far off, where a White man was making some whiskey. They arrived at this place and Bobcat went to the White man to get him to come out of the house. While the White man was gone from the house, Coyote went in, stole the whiskey, and both he and Bobcat ran off with it. When they had gone a short distance, they stopped to drink the whiskey. After they had taken some, they commenced to feel good. Then Coyote said, "My cross-cousin, I feel good; I would like to holler." "No, we are still close to those White men. They might hear you," Bobcat said. "I won't holler loud, my cross-cousin," Coyote said. They stayed there, arguing and drinking and then Coyote wanted to holler again, but Bobcat said no. "I'll holler quietly," Coyote said. "All right then, holler quietly," said Bobcat. Coyote intended to holler softly, but he slipped and hollered loudly. The White men were looking for these two and they heard Coyote. They went all together to the place they had heard the voice. Bobcat was always smart and so he hadn't drunk much. He only felt good, but Coyote was really drunk. The White people surrounded them. Bobcat got up and jumped over the first White man. The second jump he went right over all the rest and got away. They came to Coyote and arrested him, putting chains on his legs, and took him to town. Later on Bobcat use to visit Coyote once in a while. Then on one visit, they arrested Bobcat also. They had them both locked in the guard house for quite some time.

One day, out in front of the jail, some white men were breaking horses. The two prisoners looked out and watched them. The horse they had they tried to saddle, but no one could get close to it. Then Coyote told the guard, "If I were they, I would saddle that

horse up right away." The guard went over and told the others
what Coyote had said. Then they said, "All right, we'll see. Tell
him to come out here." They let Coyote out. He went to the horse
and did lots of things to it. He knew horse power and this was why
the horse wasn't wild any more.[1] After he saddled the horse, he
got on and rode it. Coyote thought he would fool these White
people. He kicked the horse gently with his heel, but it wouldn't
move. Coyote was thinking it would be nice to have a good saddle
with taps and saddle bags. He told the White people to put on such
a saddle. They brought out a brand new one with everything on it,
just as he wanted. He put it on and mounted, but the horse wouldn't
move because he just kicked it gently. The horse would go all
right, but Coyote planned on fooling the White people. Then
Coyote said, "This horse is thinking about a nice white bridle and
bit and lines, all covered with silver. He wants to wear it." The
horse wanted to go but Coyote kept holding him in. They brought
a fine bridle, as Coyote had wished, and put it on the horse. Then
Coyote got off the horse and said, "I want you to fill the saddle bags
full of crackers and cheese. That is why this horse won't go. He
wants this. Also, I want to wear a good white shirt and vest and
big show hat, and a pair of white-handled pistols in a belt. That's
the way the horse wants it. Good silver spurs, the horse wants
these also." They brought all this equipment and Coyote dressed
in it. They filled the saddle bags. Now he got on the horse. Ahead
of him by the gate were some American soldiers. He kicked the
horse and started right for the soldiers as fast as he could. He made
it look as if the horse was running away with him. The soldiers
moved back and he went through them. They followed him, but
he never was caught. Now they knew how he had fooled them and
they looked all over for him.

Later he was traveling on foot again. I don't know what he had
done with his horse. He knew where some White people were
living who kept two good white horses. He went there because he
wanted to steal these. Early in the morning he arrived and drove
out the horses. He herded them to the top of a mountain. The White
man who owned them looked for them, but couldn't find them.
Later Coyote took these horses to some other White people, because
he thought he was going to sell them. Just before he got there, he
stopped and built a big fire. When it had burned down, he painted
the two horses all black with the charcoal. After he had done this,
he took them to the White man's house and told him to put the
two black horses in the shed so they wouldn't get wet if it rained.
He was afraid the color would wash off. "All right, I'll put them
in the shed," the White man said, and he gave Coyote lots of money
for them. Coyote took his money up on the mountains where he

---

[1] Men with horse power used it on bad horses to gentle them.

lived. After a while it rained on the horses and the black was washed off them. Then they found out that these were the two white horses Coyote had stolen, so they started out after him. American soldiers were out after Coyote.

Coyote was sitting by a spring under a walnut tree. He knew the soldiers were after him. He swept all the ground clean under the tree and took his money, placing it up in the tree on different branches. When he finished, he sat there beneath the tree and waited. Pretty soon the soldiers came, and Coyote said, "I'm going to tell you a story about this tree. This tree has money that grows on it and I want to sell it to you. It takes all one day for the money to grow and ripen on it." Then the soldiers said all right. Coyote told them, "I want you to give me all your pack mules if I sell this tree to you." Coyote was always thinking about food, and he thought there would be food in those packs. The White men said all right. "Well, today what grows in the tree is mine, but from tomorrow on, what grows in the tree will be all yours," Coyote said. Then he got a big rock and threw it against the trunk. When he did this most of the money fell to the ground. "See, it only ripens at noon. You have to hit it just at noon." He hit the tree again and the rest of the money fell to the ground. Now it was all on the ground and they helped him pick it up and put it in sacks. Then they turned all the pack mules over to him. He arranged it with the head officer so no one could say anything.[1] Then he started off. Coyote traveled till sundown and all that night, to another country. The soldiers camped under the walnut tree and the next day they waited till noon. Then the officer told the soldiers to hit the tree, as it was time for the money to be ripe. They pounded on the tree but no money fell out. Then the officer told the soldiers to chop it down, cut it into lengths and split it, for maybe the money would be inside. They did this, but they couldn't find even five cents.

Coyote kept on his way. That night one of the mules got hungry and started to bray. He didn't like this so he killed every mule that brayed. He continued till he had killed all of his mules. In the meantime the soldiers had gone back to the town. On his way Coyote came to a White man's house and bought a burro from him. He was always thinking about how he could swindle someone. Now he had another plan. Returned to his old home in the mountains, he put a lot of money up the burro's rear end; so much. Then he kicked the burro in the belly and all the money fell out behind. He tried it again and it worked as before. "This is the way I am going to do and I will sell this burro for lots of money," he thought.

---

[1] This reflects experience with Whites in which the Apache have learned that authority is strictly vested in one person whom other local officers, etc. must obey, a system considerably different from their own in which a chief did not enjoy unlimited authority.

So he put his money in the burro's rear end and started for town. When he got to town, he took the burro to the man in charge there and showed it to him. "This is a good burro. When he passes excrement money comes out of him. He does this every day." Coyote always talked like a Chiricahua. "Let's see this burro do it and we will know if it's true or not," the head man said. "All right, you will see for yourself. As long as this burro lives, he does this. The first money that comes out will be mine and after that the money will all be yours," Coyote said. "All right," they said, "this burro must be worth lots of money." Coyote started to kick the burro in the belly and all his money fell out. He gathered it for himself. "Now it's yours," he said. They payed him lots of money and he went on his way. "Next day, at the same time, he will do it again," Coyote had told them. So the following day when the time came they brought the burro out and got ready to get the money from him. They kicked him, but nothing came out. He merely broke wind. They kicked him all day till evening. Then they said, "We might just as well kill this burro and look inside him. So they killed the burro and cut him open, but there wasn't a sign of money inside, nothing.

After this had happened, a whole bunch of soldiers came to arrest Coyote. They followed him and on their way they packed much grain and other foods. Coyote, living up on the mountain, thought of how he could fool them again. At that time, none of our people ever lied. Only Coyote lied. That's the way Coyote taught us to lie and steal. Long ago we believed what a person said and that's how Coyote was believed. On his way Coyote saw the soldiers coming. Right on the side of the mountain was a little ridge, all white, running down. Out on the end of this he sat, behind where the trail crossed it. While he was there, he passed his excrement on the ground. His straw hat was old now and he set it over what he had done. Soon the soldiers came to him. He spoke to them and said, "Right here I have found gold. I want you people to stay away. Move back now. This place is gold. You have never seen this before. It is sticking up right out of the ground. That's why I put my hat over it. If you want to buy this gold I will sell it, but it is the richest gold. This is a good country here as well. What I want in trade for all this is your pack train." "All right," they said and they drove the pack train to one side. Then Coyote told them about the gold, "It's right in here, but I don't want you to lift that hat off it yet. If you do, it will turn into something else. If you do what I tell you, it will be all right. I'm going to drive the pack train over this ridge and then over another ridge. When you see me cross that second ridge, I want you to pick up this hat and you will find the gold." Coyote started off, driving the pack train. The Americans waited for quite a while, watching him go. Finally, they saw him go over the last ridge and out of sight. They

lifted up the hat. When they did so, there was only his faeces,
mixed with the grasshoppers and juniper berries he had eaten.
My yucca fruits lie piled up.

VARIANT (*GRAY FOX STEALS WHEAT)[1]

Gray Fox used to go where the White people were living and
steal wheat. He always came at night when it was moonlight. The
White people found out what he was doing and they didn't like it.
One White man made a man out of pitch and put a hat on him. He
looked like a real man. Then he set him up in the field at the place
Gray Fox always passed. When Gray Fox came along, he saw
standing there, this man of pitch. Gray Fox used to talk like a
Chiricahua and he said, "Hey, Gray Eyes, stand to one side and let
me by. I want to get some of that stuff growing in there for myself."
The pitch man didn't move. "Hey, do you hear me? Do you
understand? Move over and let me by." But the pitch man didn't
move. "What's the matter? Do you think I'm not a man?" Then
Gray Fox went close to him. "I tell you I want to get that wheat.
Get out of my way. If you don't, I'll hit you with my fist and knock
you down." Then he hit him and his hand stuck in the pitch.
"What's the matter? Why do you hold my hand tight? My left
hand here, I can kill a man with it. Before I hit you, I want you to
turn me loose." But nothing happened. Gray Fox hit with his
left fist and got caught. "Hey, what's the matter? Why do you
catch both my hands like this?" Now Gray Fox was standing on
his hind legs. "My leg is the worst one; worse than my hands.
When I kick a man, part of him goes one way and part the other.
You better hurry up and turn me loose." "All right then," and
Gray Fox kicked the pitch man and his foot stuck. "What's the
matter? You grab my foot. Turn it loose." Now he was standing
on one leg. "My left leg is worse yet. When I kick with it, you will
fly into pieces. You better turn me loose right away. All right then,"
and Gray Fox kicked with his left foot and got it stuck in the pitch.
"What's the matter. Turn me loose, you. You grab both legs and
both hands. My tail is the worst yet. When I hit a man with it,
part goes one way and part the other. You better turn me loose
before I hit you with it. All right then, I'll do it," and he hit with
his tail and got it stuck in the pitch. "Hey, what are you trying
to do. You hold both my hands, my legs, and tail. My teeth here
are the worst of all. When I bite a man with these, I bite him in
two. You better turn me loose. All right then, I'll do it," and Gray
Fox bit, getting his teeth stuck in the pitch. Now he couldn't talk.
He was held there.

---

[1] Told by Francis Drake.

In the morning, about sunrise, the White man came and found Gray Fox. He tied a rope around him and led him off to his house. "Hę hę+"[1] he said. When he got home, he tied Gray Fox up to the corner of the house. Then he put a kettle of water to heat on the fire, so he could scald his hair off. While the water was heating, Coyote came trotting along on the other side of the river. Gray Fox saw Coyote and whistled to him. Then he picked up some chips of wood and pretended to be eating them. "This is bread," he hollered to Coyote. Coyote came across to the place Gray Fox was tied. Gray Fox said, "You're too late. I just ate up all the bread. But go over and look in that pot. There are potatoes in it cooking for me." Then Gray Fox said, "I want you to take this rope I am tied with and put it about your neck. Then you can have those potatoes for yourself." "All right, but hurry up," said Coyote. The rope was tied around Coyote's neck and Gray Fox went off. He never came back. In a little while the White man's boy came to the place Coyote was tied. He hollered to his father, "The one that was tied here was smaller. Now this one is large." Coyote said, "That's the way I always do, change my size." Then the White man came and grabbed Coyote, tied up his legs, picked him up, and threw him in the pot of water. All Coyote's hair came off and he lay there as if dead. But later that night, he woke up again and started away. He had no hair and he was cold. His skin was all red from the water.

"You can't get away from me, Gray Fox, I'll catch you wherever you are," he said to himself. On the way Coyote passed by a den in the rocks where Bear was living. Bear saw his red body; "Hey, my cross-cousin, give me some red cloth," he said. "I have no red cloth. A white man threw me in a kettle of boiling water and all my hair came off. Gray Fox was the one who got me into this trouble. Where can I go to find him?" he asked. "Right below, where the two rocks come out to meet each other. Gray Fox always goes there for water about midnight," Bear said. Coyote went there and looked for the best place to hide. He hid right by the trail. He waited, lying down till Gray Fox should come along. Near midnight, Coyote heard Gray Fox coming. He was singing about how he had fooled Coyote. Then he saw Coyote. "Hey, what's that lying so still? It must be the red rock I saw on top of the mountain and it has rolled down by itself." Gray Fox came close and Coyote jumped at him. "I'm going to catch you and eat you up. You did wrong to me. Because of it, I got thrown in the kettle, lost all my hair and almost was killed. Now I will fix you." Gray Fox said, "Hey, my cross-cousin, don't talk like that about eating me up. Come on, let's go over here. There is some 'ashes bread' and we will eat it soon. Come on, and I will show it to you." Gray Fox

---

[1] The common expression when an individual catches someone in a misdeed, or has an enemy in his power.

took Coyote to the water hole and showed him the reflection of the moon. "I always drink all the water and then I get to the 'ashes bread' on the bottom of it." So they both started in to drink. Gray Fox drank a little and then he merely held his mouth to the water and pretended he was drinking. Coyote kept on drinking and drinking till his stomach was bulging and water was running out through his nose. His body was shaking. "My cross-cousin, you are getting cold." "Yes, I am cold all right," said Coyote. "Well, I know where an old woman has set fire to some dry wood. I will go there and bring fire for you," and Gray Fox started off. Coyote waited for him, but he never came back. Then Coyote started to trot after Gray Fox. He had so much water in him that he kept breaking wind, "bad, bad, bad, bad," he went as he trotted. Coyote thought to himself. "That must be some White people traveling along," and he kept turning around to look. Then he found out where the noise came from. "Yes, this noise is in my anus," he said and he started on his way again. "I'll catch you, Gray Fox," he said.

Finally he came to Gray Fox. As soon as Gray Fox saw Coyote, he started to point downwards at a rock and say, "'e', 'e', 'e', 'e'," Coyote said, "I'll eat you up now all right," and he made for him. "My cross-cousin, you always talk about eating me up. Don't talk this way. I heard the sky is falling down and that's why I am pointing at this rock. Point at the rock as I do," Gray Fox said. So Coyote started to point down at the rock and say, "'e', 'e', 'e', 'e'," like Gray Fox. Some buzzards sat close by in a tree. Gray Fox said to Coyote, "Put your hand to this rock and keep on saying as I said. I am going over and kill some of the buzzards to get feathers for you." Gray Fox started. Coyote waited for him, but he never came back. "All right, I'll get you anyhow, Gray Fox. You've fooled me long enough," and Coyote started out again.

After a while he came to Gray Fox. He was making a big basket out of tc'idnk'ų·je branches (a species of sumac). Coyote said, "I'll eat you now all right. You have fooled with me and lied to me lots of times, but I'll get you now." Gray Fox said, "What's the matter, my cross-scousin. You always talk with me this way. We heard that a great wind is going to come. All the other people are working here, making baskets in order to crawl inside them. That's why I am doing it. You better get busy and make one for yourself. The one I am making is as tall as I am when I stand up." Coyote said, "I don't know how to make these things." "Then when I finish this one, I will make one for you," Gray Fox said. After a while he said again, "Here, you say you don't know how to make these, so this one will be for you. I will make another for myself." "All right," and Coyote crawled inside. Gray Fox closed him in and tied the basket up tight. He turned the basket over and with a big rock, he pounded on it. "The wind has come," he said to

Coyote. "It's a very heavy wind," and every time he said this, Gray Fox would pound on the basket with a rock. Then he stood on top of the basket and danced on it. Gray Fox said to Coyote, "You are always getting after me and going to kill me. Now I'm going to kill you," and he picked up rocks and threw them on the basket. When Coyote stopped moving, Gray Fox went off and left him.

After a while Coyote came to and crawled out of the basket. He started after Gray Fox. "I'll get you Gray Fox," he said. He asked the bird people to give him some hair and they did. In about four days he had hair all over his body. Then he asked the bird people where they had seen Gray Fox. They said that he had gone to gather wild cactus fruits.[1] "You better not let him get away from you again, or he will kill you," they said to Coyote. Coyote started off and looked for the place where the prickly pear fruits were getting ripe. He went where the best fruits were and there he waited for Gray Fox. Pretty soon Gray Fox came along. He was singing about how he had gotten Coyote into the basket and then killed him. He was looking for prickly pear fruit. The best ones were by Coyote and he came over and started eating them. Then Coyote jumped out and grabbed him. Gray Fox tried to talk nicely with Coyote and promised many things, but Coyote paid no attention and killed him right there.

53. *COYOTE HERDS SHEEP FOR A WHITE MAN[2]

Coyote started traveling. After a while he came to a White man's house. The White man said he would give him some work. "I want you to herd my sheep for me," he said. So Coyote started in working, herding the sheep. He herded them all day till sundown.

After a while Coyote saw that some of the sheep were getting fat and he thought to himself, "I would like to eat some of them. Tomorrow I will herd them out, and then I will eat some." The next morning he herded the sheep out to a lake, about which many bulrushes were growing. When he got there he went after one of the sheep and killed it. Then he cut off its tail and stuck this into the mud at the edge of the lake. He killed lots of sheep. Each one's tail he cut off and stuck in the mud, all about the place. This way he killed them all.

Then he went back to the White man's house and called to the White man, "Gray Eyes, while I was herding your sheep they all sank into the ground." "Then let's get some shovels and go and dig them out," said the White man. So they did and went back to the lake. The White man saw the tails of the sheep Coyote had eaten, sticking out of the mud. He believed his sheep had really all sunk into the ground. Then Coyote told him, "Don't try to grab

[1] A favorite food of coyotes and foxes.
[2] Told by Bane Tithla.

their tails and pull them out because if you do you might pull the tail right off." In spite of this the White man thought he would try to pull them out by the tails, so he grabbed hold of one tail and pulled. Out came the tail, but nothings else. Coyote said, "I told you not to do that. Now you have pulled the sheep's tail off." But the White man kept pulling out one tail after another. Finally when he had them all pulled out, he still thought that the sheep were in the ground. He didn't know Coyote had eaten them. He had no more sheep. "Now all my sheep have gone in the ground. I have none left," he said.

My yucca fruits lie piled up.

54. THE TWO THIEVES[1]

One time, to the east, there lived a great thief. To the west, there was also living a great thief. Then the thief from the east started off towards the west. The thief in the west started towards the east. On their way they met each other in the middle of the earth. When they met, the thief from the west said, "Where did you start from?" The thief from the east said, "Over there to the east, I live and so I came this way. Where did you start from?" "I live in the west, and from there I came." Then the thief from the east, said, "What place did you come from and of what people are you?" The thief from the west answered, "I am a great thief. But what people are you and what kind of a place did you come from?" "I am also a great thief," the thief from the east said. Then the thief from the west said, "Let's go to the west." And the thief from the east said, "All right, let's go." But he thought that he would try out the other and after a while when they came to a tree in which was a red-tail hawk's nest, he said to the thief from the west, "You say that you are the greatest thief, so let's see you steal the eggs from under that old hawk on the nest, before she can move." The thief from the west went up to the nest, pulled out the eggs from under the hawk and the hawk never knew it. Then he took them to the thief from the east, and said, "You see, I am a great thief," and he showed him the eggs. "Yes, that's the time that you were a great thief," the one from the east said.

They went on their way and after a while they came to an old raven's nest. There were eggs in it. Then the thief from the west said, "Let's see you try to steal the eggs out from under that raven before she moves." "All right, I will get them," the thief from the east said, and he climbed up the tree. When he got to the top, he stuck his hand under the raven and took out the eggs. The raven didn't even know they were gone. Then he came down. "I also am a great thief," he said and he showed the eggs to the thief from the

---

[1] Told by Bane Tithla.

west. Then they said, "We are the same so let's become brothers and travel around together." Thus they traveled together all over the country till they came to a place where White people were living.

Here a White man had a store and the two thieves went to him. One of the thieves told the other to go in the store and steal some cans of food and bring them out where they could eat them. So the thief went to the store and stole some cans of food and took them out without the White man ever knowing they were gone. Then the two thieves went a long way off to the edge of the river, opened the cans in the shade, and ate. They stayed there all night. In the morning they were hungry again and the thief who had stolen the food the day before, said to the other, "Go and get some food and bring it back here. Get it in the store. You say that you are a great thief, so let's see you do it." They went to the store, one sitting outside while the other went in. Inside, the thief stole all kinds of good things to eat and brought them out. The storekeeper never knew they were gone. Then they went to the river and ate at the same place. When they were through, one said to the other, "There is a bank here. Let's see you go and steal some money. You say that you are a great thief. Let's see you do it. So they went to the bank and one of them stole out some money and no one knew it. They returned to the same place. When they got there, the one said to the other, "I said that I was a great thief and I am," and he showed the money that he had stolen to the other. Pretty soon the two wished that they had a drink. There was a saloon close by and one thief said to the other, "You say that you are a great thief. Let's see you go to the saloon and get some whiskey and bring it here." So they went to the saloon and one of them took out the whiskey, but this time someone found out about it. They also found out about the other things stolen from the store and the money taken from the bank. But no one knew who had done the stealing.

A shaman was living with the White people, and he could find out anything. He could see it in his mind immediately. After a long time during which lots of stealing had been going on, the White people went to the shaman and said to him, "We want to find out who has been doing all the stealing. We don't know who it is." Then the shaman started to think and pretty soon he said, "There is one man going about who is doing all this stealing. He is the thief. This man will go to a certain woman's house. The man who is there will be the one who is stealing everything." Early the next morning all the people went to the woman's place and hid themselves. When the thief came, they caught him and took him to jail. But the other thief was still going about and stealing a great deal. The people thought they caught the thief, but there was still someone going around stealing, and so they went to the shaman again and asked him to find out who it was. The shaman thought about it and immediately said, "There is one man who has a cross of red flicker tail feathers in his hat. He has made it so. I want everyone to come here tomorrow." The next day all the people came together and the thief got right in the midst of them. Then they started to look in everyone's hat. When they came to the thief's hat, they found the cross of red-flicker tail feathers. Another man stood in front of the thief and when he took off his hat to let them look, a cross of red flicker feathers was in it also. Then all the people took off their hats to have them looked in and everyone had a cross of red-flicker feathers. Even those who had already taken their hats off in back of the thief and had no feathers before, now had them. Thus they had to let the thief go and all the people went home.

The thief was still going around stealing. "This is not good," the people said. "There is someone still stealing." So they went to the shaman once more and asked him to find out who it was. The shaman said, "Bring the thief here who is in jail. Hitch up two mules and tie him behind them and drag him all about among the people's homes. If you see someone cry for him, it will be the man you are looking for." So they went to the jail, took out the thief, and dragged him about town behind a pair of mules. They had not gone far when one man started to cry. They caught him. The thief they had dragged behind the mules died, because he had had a rope around his neck. For the man who had cried, they brought a wild mule and they tied to it a rope which they fastened around the thief's neck. Then they turned the wild mule loose and he ran off dragging the man behind him. They had whipped the mule to make him run away. Thus they never knew what became of the second thief.

My yucca fruits lie piled up.

55. THE GOOD AND THE BAD BROTHERS[1]

One time there were two brothers traveling along. It was in their minds that they were going where other people were living. But no other people were living near there. On their way, they came to Red-tail Hawk sitting beside the road. The older brother said, "Let's kill him." But the younger brother said no. Then the older brother said, "Let's kill him," and he picked up a rock to throw at him. "No," said the younger brother, and caught hold of his arm. So the elder brother threw the stone down and the two went on their way. After they had traveled for a while, they came to Rattlesnake. The older brother said, "Let's kill him." But the younger brother said no. Then the older brother picked up a

---

[1] Told by Bane Tithla.

rock and said, "Let's kill him." The younger brother said, "No," ·and caught hold of his arm so that he could not throw the stone. The older brother let go of the rock and they went on their way. After a while they came to a horse. This horse was poor and old and just about to die. The older brother said, "Let's kill him so he won't go around any more." But the younger brother said, "Don't do it. The horse is very poor." "Then I will kill that horse right now," the older brother said and he picked up a rock to hit him on the head. "Don't do it," the younger brother said, and he caught hold of his arm and stopped him. The older brother dropped the stone and the two journeyed on.

After they had traveled a long time, they approached a place where White people were living. When they came near, they said, "Let's go to the White people. Maybe they will give us some bread." So they went there and came to one of the houses where they asked for bread. The White people gave them some and they ate it. After they had eaten, the White people told the older brother to wash some clothes for them. He started in to do the washing. Then they told the younger brother to go and cut some wood, and so he did. Thus the two worked for the White people, one washing and the other cutting wood. The White person for whom the younger brother was working said he was a good worker.

The older brother hated the younger and so he talked about him to some of the White people. There was a great cottonwood tree growing nearby. No one could cut this tree down, because as soon as it was cut it grew out again. The older brother knew this. He said that his younger brother claimed he could cut the cotton-wood tree down so that it would never grow up again. Then the chief of the White people heard this at the place he was living, and so he went after the younger brother. When he found him, he said, "I hear that you claim you can cut the cottonwood down so that it will never grow up again." "No, my brother told a lie. I never said that. He is making that up," the younger brother said. But the chief told him, "You have already said this thing and so you must go to the cottonwood and cut it down." He gave him an axe and the boy went to the cottonwood. When he got there, he sat down and thought to himself, "Why did I ever come here," and he started to cry. Then Rattlesnake came to him, the one whose life he had saved. "Why are you crying?" he asked. The younger brother told him all about it, "My brother told a lie about me. He said that I claimed I could cut this tree down. But I never said it." "That's all right, you go ahead and cut the tree down. I will go under the tree and cut all the roots and then go inside the tree trunk and thus to the top of the tree. When you see the leaves start to fall from the tree, begin to cut it down," Rattlesnake said. Then he went under the tree and inside the roots, while the boy sat there. Then he went inside the tree and up it to the top. Now the leaves started to fall and the boy began to cut. This way he cut the tree down and went back to the house. Next morning there was the tree lying on the ground.

The younger brother was still working for the same man, cutting wood. His brother hated him. He thought he would make more trouble for him. He said to the man for whom he was working, "My younger brother said if he married the chief's daughter, he could make her have a baby in one night." The man told the chief what the older brother had said. When the chief heard this, he sent for the boy again. The younger brother arrived and the chief said to him, "I heard that you said if you married my daughter you could make her have a baby in one night." "No, I didn't say that at all. It is my brother who has been lying about me," the boy answered. But the chief said, "You have already said this thing and so you will do it. If my daughter does not have a baby in the morning, I will kill you," and he went back to his home. The boy walked off a little way and sat down. He started to think to himself, "Why did I come here? I ought never to have come to this place," and he cried about it till sunset. Then Redtail Hawk came to him and sat on a tree close by. This was the one who the boy had helped before. "What are you crying about?" he said. Then the boy told him about what had happened and said, "My brother told a lie about me. He said I claimed that if I married the chief's daughter, I could make her have a baby in one night." "That's all right. Go ahead and marry her and I will help you out," Red-tail Hawk told him, "Sleep with her and in the morning scratch her hard between the legs till she bleeds. Then I will leave a baby there between her legs." At sunset, the boy went to sleep with the chief's daughter. He stayed with her all night and in the morning he scratched her between the legs till the blood came. He made lots of blood come out. About dawn, Red-tail Hawk came and put a baby between her legs. Soon after all the people woke up and heard the baby crying. Thus they let the boy go and didn't kill him. He went back to work for the man he had been working with before.

For a long time, the older brother thought about what he could say to put the younger in bad and make trouble for him. Then he told the White people that his younger brother had said he could kill du'ilgid. Now du'ilgid was a great animal who lay out in the open country where there were no bushes or trees. All the people had gone out to try and kill him before, but he had killed everyone he got hold of. Even the soldiers were afraid of him. Thus the older brother lied about the younger brother. Then they told the chief what the older brother had said and so the chief said, "Bring him here." When the boy came, the chief said to him, "du'ilgid is lying out in the open country. You said that you could kill him, but I know there is no man who can kill him. You said that you could kill him right away, I heard." "That is my brother who lies about me. My brother must hate me. I never said such a thing," the boy answered. But the chief said, "You have already said that you could kill him, so go ahead and do it." He gave him a a xaɬ[1] and told him to kill with it. The next morning, the boy went to the place where du'ilgid lived. It was a great, open, level plain and on this du'ilgid was lying. The boy went out on it a little way and then stopped. There he sat and began to think. He didn't know what to do and so he stayed there till noon, crying about it. Then the old horse he had helped before, the one who had been so poor, came to him and said, "What are you crying about?" "My brother has told a lie about me. This is du'ilgid out here and if you go near him he runs at you and kills you. No one can meddle with him," the boy said. du'ilgid was lying out there on the plain, stretching his neck and looking around. "My brother said that I claimed I could kill this monster and take him home with me. That is why I am crying. If I don't bring him back with me, all the people will see that I have not done this thing," the boy said. The boy didn't know what he was going to do and he cried some more. Then the horse said, "I will help you to kill him." The horse had nothing with him; no rope or anything to tie him with. He told the boy, "Go and get some yucca leaves and tie the pieces of them together. Put the rope that they make in my mouth, get on my back and ride me with it." "You might fall with me. You don't look strong," the boy said. "Go ahead and get on me," the horse answered. "But I am afraid that you will fall down with me if I do. That's why I don't want to get on you," the boy said. "Go ahead and get on me," the horse told him and so the boy did as he was bidden. He had his sword in his hand. Then the horse said to him, "I am going to run right under du'ilgid with you and if he gets up when I do this, you must stick him in the heart twice with your sword, right behind the shoulder." Then the horse started with him. As he got ready to run he jumped around. When the boy got on him, he turned to a fly and thus flew with the boy right under du'ilgid. As they flew under him, he got up and the boy stuck the sword into his heart. du'ilgid fell to the ground and his head fell also. He was truly dead and as he lay there on the ground, he was very large. The boy started to butcher him. He skinned him on one side, but he could not roll the body over to skin the other side. The horse told him, "Tie a rope of yucca round one of his legs and tie the other end about my neck. I will pull him over for you." "You are too thin and poor to do that. You couldn't pull him over," the boy said. "That's all right, go ahead and tie the rope around my neck," the horse told him. So the boy tied one end around one of the legs of du'ilgid, the other end about the

---

[1] The Apache equates this mythical weapon with a sword.

horse's neck, and drove the horse to one side. The body was rolled over and the boy butchered it on the other side. He was through butchering, but the boy told the horse that he didn't know how he was going to get the animal home. The horse told him, "Go and get pieces of yucca leaf. Then make a hole through the middle of the meat and tie it on my back with the yucca." "You are too thin. If I did that you would fall down. I don't think that you could carry the meat," the boy said. "Go ahead and tie it on. I can carry it for you all right," the horse told him. So the boy looked for a piece of yucca. He got it and tied the meat on. This way he loaded all the meat on the horse. "Sit on my back also," the horse said. "No, never mind, I don't want to ride on you. You might fall over with me," the boy answered. "That's all right, go ahead and get on me," the horse instructed. The boy got on his back. Thus they rode to town. When they came near, they stopped and the boy took all the meat off the horse. There was a great deal of meat and all the people came to get some, taking it away to use. Still there was lots of it left. After a long while, the meat was all gone. The people had taken it to eat. Then the younger brother went back to the White man he had been working for.

The older brother was still there. He hated his younger brother as before and wanted to get rid of him. So he told another lie about him to get him in trouble. This time he said, "My brother said that he could jump into a pot of boiling lead and come out unhurt." The chief heard about this. He said, "Why did he say this? Bring him here." So the younger brother went to the chief. When he got there, the chief said to him, "I hear that you said you could jump into a big pot of boiling lead and come out unhurt." "I didn't say that at all. It is my brother who said it. He doesn't like me and that is why he talks this way," the younger brother told the chief. But the chief answered, "You have said this thing already, so you will have to do it as soon as we melt the lead for you." Then they started to gather wood to make fire for melting the lead. The younger brother went aside and sat down. He thought his brother must hate him and he wondered why he told lies about him. "No one will help me now," he thought and he started to cry. Then the same horse that he had helped before came to him and said, "Why do you cry?" "My brother has told a lie about me and said that I claimed I could jump into a pot of boiling lead and come out safely. That is why I am crying," the boy answered. The horse told him, "I will help you, but this will be the last time. A trash pile is over there. Go to it, get eight cans, and bring them to me." The boy went and got eight cans, brought them back, and lined them up as the horse told him; four on each side. "Now go and get some yucca leaves and put them in my mouth," the horse said. So the boy went for some yucca leaves, brought them back and tied them in his mouth like a bit. "Now I am going to run back and

15

forth with you. When I get sweaty and lots of water starts to run off me, save it and put it in these four cans. After you run me back and forth and these cans are full of sweat, kill me immediately. Stick a knife in my throat and cut my belly open. Then cut my head off and carry it to the east. Take my blood and put it in the cans, the four that are left," the horse told him. "But I don't want to kill you. That would not be right," the boy said. "Go ahead and kill me just the same, so you can fill the four cans with my blood. Then you must cut off my head and carry it to the east," the horse said. So the boy got on him and rode him back and forth. Pretty soon the sweat started to run off him and the boy filled one of the cans. He kept on and after a while he filled another one of the cans. He ran the horse back and forth some more and filled another can. Now he had three cans full. He rode the horse back and forth till he had filled the last can. Then he killed the horse, sticking a knife in his throat. A lot of blood came out. This blood he caught in the belly which he had already cut open. He poured the blood from it into the other four cans. Last of all, he cut off the head and carried it to the east, where he placed it. Before he killed him, the horse said that when he was ready to jump into the boiling lead, he must wash his whole body with the four cans of sweat and likewise with the four cans of blood.

Then it was time to go to where they had the lead ready for him. When he arrived, he washed himself all over with the four cans of sweat, his head as well. He did the same with the four cans of blood. He used up all the eight cans and then he went to the boiling lead and jumped in. He stayed in the lead a long time. There was a trap door in the bottom of the big pot to drain the lead. They opened it. After the lead was drained off, he stood in the pot. His body was all yellow. He looked nicely. When it was over, he went back to the place he was staying. The next morning before his brother had time to tell another lie about him, he decided to tell a lie about his brother. Then he said to the White people, "My brother said that he could do the same thing as I did, and come out of the lead safely." They told this to the chief and the chief sent for the older brother. "Let him come here, the one who said this," the chief said. The older brother came to the chief and when he got there, the chief told him, "I hear that you said you could jump into boiling lead like your brother and come out safely. Is this true?" "No, that is not true. My brother has lied about me," the older brother answered. But the chief said, "You have said this thing and so we will melt up the lead for you." Then they started to gather wood to put around the pot and to build a fire to melt the lead. The older brother thought he would do as his brother had. He bought a horse, a blue one, and brought it to that place. Then he got four cans and lined them up on one side, and four other cans and lined them up on the other side. He started to run the horse back and forth. He did this till he had filled only part of one can, and then he killed the horse. He stuck a knife in the horse's throat and got the blood out with which he partly filled another can. Next, he took off all his clothes and started to wash himself with the sweat. There was not much of it and it didn't go very far. Then he washed completely with the blood. There was very little of this also. He went to the boiling lead and jumped into it, but he burned and only the bones floated up on top of the lead.

My yucca fruits lie piled up.

56. THE MAGIC RING[1]

One time there was a woman. She had a grandson. This woman was very poor and the two were living, eating anything that they could get. Then they set out and came to a place where lots of White people lived. They stopped at this place because they had nothing to eat. They had nothing of their own. So the old woman went to a White man's to get something. The White man told her if she washed some clothes for him, he would give her twenty-five cents. The old woman did the washing for him and got the twenty-five cents. She took the money to her grandson and gave it to him, telling him to go to the store and buy some bread with it. So the boy went to the store. When he got there, he saw a man standing on the corner holding a cat in his arms. The man said to the boy, "Buy this cat from me with your twenty-five cents." The boy bought the cat and took it home to his grandmother. When he got there his grandmother said to him, "Where is the bread?" The boy showed her the cat and said, "I bought this cat with the twenty-five cents." "We have nothing to eat and that is why I sent you to the store to get the bread," said his grandmother. The next morning the old woman went to the White man's place, did some more washing and got another quarter for it. Then she went home and told her grandson, "Now take this money and go and buy some bread. We are hungry, so don't buy anything else with it." The boy started off to the store again. As he went by the corner, a man was standing there with a puppy in his arms. The puppy was called ḷi·na·diltle'e꞊ (fluttering pet).[2] The man told the boy to get the puppy from him and give him the quarter for it. So the boy gave him the quarter, got the puppy from him, and took it home with him. When he got there his grandmother said to him, "Where is the bread?" "I bought this," he said, and he showed her the puppy. "I told you to buy some bread. We are hungry and we have nothing to eat," said the old woman. The next morning she went to wash clothes for the White man again. Thus

---

[1] Told by Bane Tithla.

[2] The term for a certain type of small dog whose movements are fluttering because of his short legs.

she earned a quarter once more. She took this and gave it to the boy when she got back, telling him, "You take this and go and buy some bread with it, and don't buy something else as you did before." So the boy started off to the store. When he got there, a man was standing by the house on the corner again. He was holding Yellow Snake[1] in his hands. The man said to the boy, "Give me your quarter for this snake." The boy gave him the quarter and got the snake. When he took it in his hands, the snake jumped out of them and ran under the house. The boy ran around to the other side of the house to try and find the snake. When he got there, he saw a little boy standing close; all yellow. He said to him, "Did you see something preety run by here? I had something preety and it ran away." "That is me. You have bought me, so take me with you," the little boy said. The grandson took the little boy home with him to his grandmother. When they got there, the old woman said to him, "Did you get the bread this time?" "No, I bought this little boy," the grandson said. "You mustn't do that again. We have no food," said the old woman.

Then Yellow Boy was sorry for them and so he said to the boy, "Go to the chief and ask him if there is anything that has been taken from him. If the chief says that nothing has been taken from him, keep on asking if anything has been taken from him. Ask him if someone took something away from him when he was a little boy. After a long time, the chief will tell you that when he was first married, his first child, a little boy, was taken from him. I am the son the chief lost when he was first married." The man who had sold the snake to the grandson, had done so to help him and to help the old woman.

The boy went to the chief and asked him if anything had been taken from him. The chief said no, that nothing had been taken from him. But the boy kept on asking if anything had been taken from him, as Yellow Boy had told him to do. Finally, the chief said that when he was first married, his little boy had been taken from him. Then the boy told him that he had the little boy at his house. The chief said to him, "I have lots of cattle and horses and I will give them to you if you will bring my little boy back to me." But the boy said no. Then the chief said to him, "I have a store over there and a saloon also. I will give these both to you if you will give me back my boy." But still the poor boy said no. Yellow Boy had told him to make the chief give him the ring on his finger before consenting to return the chief's son. So the poor boy said to the chief, "Let me see your hand," and when he saw the chief's hand, there was a ring on it. Then he said to the chief, "Give me the ring on your finger and I will give you back your son." But the chief said, "No. These, my cattle and horses, my store and saloon, I

---

[1] The sand rattlesnake.

will give to you, but not my ring." Still the poor boy said no. "Give me your ring and I will give you back your boy." After quite a while, the chief agreed and took off his ring and gave it to him. Yellow Boy had told him the ring that the chief had could do anything you wanted it to. The poor boy took the ring, went for Yellow Boy and gave him to the chief as the chief had told him to do. Then he went home with the ring.

That night he prayed to the ring, mentioning what he wished there to be for him and his grandmother in the morning, "In the morning when I wake up, there will be a good house all made of gold for me and my grandmother. There will be a good striped blanket and clothes and all kinds of things for us." The next morning when he woke up, that's the way it was, golden house and all. Then the poor boy was glad and he had lots to eat. The next night, he wished on the ring again and this time he prayed that he might have all the chief's horses and cattle. The following morning when he woke up, it had come true and he had lots of horses and cattle and also the store and the saloon that he had asked for. The next night he wished on the ring and prayed that in the morning when he woke up, there might be a man standing in front of the house holding a horse hitched to a buggy, and that someone should wake him up so that he might eat lots and after eating that he might go for a drive all over town in the buggy. When he woke up, that's the way it was and after he had done eating, he went out, got in the buggy, and drove about to see his horses and cattle. He drove to his store and to his saloon also. They kept on driving all day. When he got back to his house, a man took the horse to the barn for him.

The boy had seen that the chief's daughter was very pretty and so when he went to bed that night, he prayed to the ring that he might marry the chief's daughter and that someone would wake him up in the morning to get him ready for the wedding. He wished that he might lie with this girl. The next morning, that is the way that it was and some one woke him up. He got ready and was married to the chief's daughter. After he was married to the chief's daughter, he lived with her a long time in his house. Then one day he told the man who worked for him to harness up the horses and bring around the buggy to the house, that he was going to town. So this was done and he drove off. Now the wife had another friend, a man whom she used to go to and flirt with when her husband was away. This man had asked the wife to find out how it was her husband became rich so quickly and where he got his power.

The husband drove down town with the man who was working for him. He went to the store and after that to the saloon. At the saloon he started in to drink and after a while, he was drunk. Then he and the man working for him drove home. When he got there, he went into his house, still drunk. There his wife came to him and started to talk with him. "Tell me how it is that you got so rich.

You used to be poor before," she said. "I got rich by thinking," he answered. Then his wife said, "You couldn't get rich by thinking, as quickly as you have." The man took the magic ring and threw it on the floor so that she saw it, and told her, "I got all that I have from this ring." Then he put the ring on again and went off to take a sleep. While he was asleep his wife slipped the ring off his finger. Then, by herself, she made a prayer on the ring. She wished that she and the other man, her lover, might both be on the other side of the sea where no one would bother them, and that they had this golden house over there also. She wished that her husband might wake up the way he was before, poor and with nothing, that he would be sleeping in bed with his grandmother with only an old blanket to cover them.

When the man woke up the next morning, there was nothing left that he had had, only the cat and the puppy he bought. He had nothing else and he was living with his grandmother as he was before he had the ring. The chief saw he was living in a poor way and so he told him to come to him. When the poor man went to the chief, the chief asked him, "What have you done with my daughter?" "I don't know where she is. I went to bed with her last night and this morning she was gone," he answered. "You will have to find where she is in four days, or I will have your head cut off," the chief said. The poor man went home. There his cat and puppy were sitting, and he told them, "You two will have to go all over the world and find my wife and house, and also my ring." So the cat and the puppy set off to search the world for these things. On the morning of the first day, they came back. "Did you find my ring?" the man asked. But the cat and the puppy said no, that they had not. The man sent them out again to search the earth. On the morning of the second day they came back once more. "Did you find my ring?" he asked them. But they said no, they had not. He said to them, "Go to the edge of the sea, and look there for it." Then on the morning of the third day they came back to him. "Did you find my ring?" he asked them. But they said they had not. He told them to go across the sea and search. "Visit the Mice people there. Their soldiers know every place," he said. So the cat and the puppy went to the edge of the sea. The man had told them if he didn't have the ring back, he would have his head cut off by the chief and that they must find it for him. So now they were trying to get the ring for him. When the two got to the edge of the sea, the puppy said to the cat, "Do you know how to swim?" The cat said no, that he did not know how to swim. "But if there is a little stream, I can jump over it," the cat said. Then the cat got on the puppy's back and the puppy started to swim over the sea with him. Thus they swam across and when they got near the other shore, the cat jumped off the puppy's back to the land. When the cat jumped he kicked the puppy under the water and the puppy got all wet. When he got to the shore, he said to the cat, "You ought not to have jumped off me like that. You kicked me right under the water."

Then the two went on to where the Mice people were living. dɫusts'ǫ·setse'igudn (mouse with his tail cut off) was the Mouse chief. This name meant that the chief's tail was short. The cat and the puppy talked to the Mouse chief, and said, "Your soldiers have been all over. Maybe they have seen a house of gold." The Mouse chief got all his soldiers together and asked if any of them had seen a house of gold. But the soldiers all said that they had seen no such thing. Then the puppy said to the Mouse chief, "Give us six of your soldiers to eat." When the six soldiers had been given to them, the puppy ate three and the cat ate the other three. Then the Mouse chief said to the two: "dɫusts'ǫ·setsela·t'a'da'iska·dn (mouse with tuft at end of tail) has soldiers all over. Why don't you go and ask him if he knows about this thing you are looking for." So the cat and the puppy went to Tuft-tailed Mouse and asked him, as his soldiers had been everywhere, if any of them had seen a house of gold. All the soldiers were told to come, but when they got there they all said they did not know of any gold house. Then one of the soldiers said he had seen a house of gold over by the edge of the sea and that he had never seen it there before. So the chief of these Mice people told this soldier to go with the cat and the puppy, and show them where the place was. The cat and the puppy started off with the Mouse soldier for the golden house. About dark, they arrived. They had picked out twelve Mice soldiers to go along, and now they sent them in under the golden house. They got up through the floor of the house by a crack in the boards. When they were in, the man and the woman in the house saw them and the woman got scared. She said, "Where will I put the ring? There are lots of mice here and it was never like this before." The man thought a good place to put the ring would be in a white jar standing there, in which water was kept. But the woman said no, that something wrong was going on, because all the mice were there and that the jar was not a good place. "On top of the cupboard is a bowl of chili; why don't you put it there?" said the man. But the woman said no again. "Then put it in your mouth and close your mouth when you go to sleep," the man said. "No, I might cough in my sleep and the ring would come out," the woman answered. "Well, where will you hide it then?" said the man and then, "Put it in your vagina," he said. So the woman agreed and hid it between her legs.

Then the mice gathered together and went out of the house, back to the cat and the puppy. There were lots of mice and even Tuft-tailed Mouse was there. "What will we do now?" the mice said. "That woman has put the ring in her vagina. The man told her to hide it some place, but she wouldn't do it. He told her to put it in

the water jar, but she said no. Then he said in the chili bowl, but she
said no. Then he said to put it in her mouth, but she said no. Then
he said to put it in her vagina and she did it," they said. So none
of them knew what to do and they talked about it for a long time.
"We will have to get it some way," they said. Then Tuft-tailed
Mouse said, "Let's go and see about it," and so they went in the
house. When they got inside, Tuft-tailed Mouse went to the jar of
water and stuck his tail in to feel for the ring. Then he went to the
bowl of chili and stuck his tail in that also. Then he went to the
woman as she was lying asleep on the bed and touched her nose
with his tail. Now he said, "If I can make her sneeze, the ring might
fall out from between her legs." So all the mice went to the woman
and stood, ready, between her legs, to catch the ring in their outstretched hands if it should drop out.[1] All night the mice had been
going and coming about the house, but both the man and the woman
slept on soundly. Then Tuft-tailed Mouse went to the jar of water
again and wet his tail in it. Then he went to the bowl of chili and
stuck his tail in it. When he was ready he went to the woman lying
asleep on the bed, and put his tail to her nose. When she breathed
in the chili, it made her sneeze. All the time the other mice were
standing ready to catch the ring in their hands, should it pop out.
The woman kept on sneezing, but for a long time the ring did not
come. The mice were singing between her legs, and hollering,
"Ring come out, ring come out." Finally the ring popped out and
the mice caught it in their hands. They took it out to the waiting
cat and the puppy and gave it to them. Then they all started back.
The puppy said, "Let me carry the ring." But the cat said, "How
are you going to carry it?" "I will carry it in my mouth, around
one of my teeth and I will keep my mouth tight shut," the puppy
said. "No, I know that you always open your mouth when you are
going along. I have seen you do it. It will be better if I hold it in
my paw," the cat said.

After a while they came to the edge of the sea and there the cat
got on the puppy's back and the puppy started to swim across with
him. When they were almost to the other side, the cat jumped off
the puppy's back to the shore. As he jumped off, he kicked him
under the water as he had before. Thus when the puppy got to the
shore, he was all wet and he said to the cat, "Don't do that again.
You kicked me under the water and got me all wet." He got mad
at the cat. Then the two started to their home and arrived there in
the morning. When the poor man saw them, he asked if they had
found the ring and if they had it with them. "Yes, here it is," they
said, and they gave it to him. That night the poor man prayed on
the ring and wished that he had the golden house back and was
living with his grandmother as before; that his wife might sleep

---

[1] This part is the high point of the story and causes immense amusement both to narrator and listeners.

with him again. The next morning was the day they were going to cut off his head if he did not have the chief's daughter, but when he woke up he had the golden house back again and his wife was in it with him, as well as everything else he had had before. The chief came to see the golden house; inside he saw his daughter, so he was satisfied.

My yucca fruits lie piled up.

57. MAGIC FLIGHT[1]

Long ago, this story happened. There was one man, an Apache, who gambled a great deal. This way he won lots of things. Then he kept on gambling and lost all that he had. After this, he started out to travel all over. He came to where White people were living, and they were living in a square house. The man sat down at the corner of the house and waited. Pretty soon, there came a White man with a black horse. The White man spoke to him and said, "Do you want to work for me?" "All right," the man said. He thought this was a White man, but instead, it was really the Devil. Then the White man said, "If you want money, I will give it to you." "All right, I would like some money," the man said. He said this because he had none and wanted to get some. So he asked for twenty dollars and the White man gave it to him. Then the White man said that he was going back to his home on the other side of the hill. "Well, tomorrow I will come to your place," the man said, "not today." This one on the black horse could change himself to anything and that was how he was able to change himself to the form of a White man.

The same day the man gambled away all of the twenty dollars that he had been given by the White man. The next day, he went back to the White people's house where he met the White man for whom he was going to work. That White man had said he lived on the other side of the hill and so he went there to look for him. But when he got there, he could find no house, so he took the tracks of the black horse and started to follow him. After he had gone a way, Raven came to him and said, "Where are you going?" "I met a man yesterday who told me that he wanted me to work for him and so I am trying to find him," he said. Then Raven said to him, "That is a bad thing you are saying. That man is no good and no one ever bothers with him." "All the same I promised to go to his place today and so I don't want to tell a lie," he said. Raven kept on telling him not to go to the White man, that he was not really a White man at all. "But I have promised to go to him, so I will have to go. I can't tell a lie," the man said. Then Raven asked him if he knew where this one lived and said,

---

[1] Told by Bane Tithla.

"I don't think that you know where he lives." This one he was trying to find could change himself to Wind of Darkness, to a horse, or to anything that he wanted. Then Raven said to the man, "This one you are trying to find lives far off where you can't find him." "I promised to go to him and so I am going to him," the man said. Then Raven said to him, "Go to find him if you have to then, and I will help you out." So he gave him two pieces of bread, round ones. It was noon and he cut the bread. At that place, there was growing sulphur wheat and Raven told the man to pull it up. When the man pulled the plant up, there was a hole underneath and down below he could see what looked like another world, with a blue sky. The tracks of the man on the horse had lead right to this bush. Raven told the man to blindfold himself so that he could not see. Then he told him to get on his back, that he would carry him to the home of the one he was looking for. With the man on his back, he flew down into the hole. The man had tied something around his eyes as Raven had told him to do, and this way they went down. Raven had said to him, "While you are on my back you may think that I am carrying you off some place, but you must not try to lift that blindfold from your eyes. If you do, you will fall down." After a while, they came to the ground. The one they were looking for lived close to a hill and the two stopped on top of this hill. Here Raven told the man, "This one you are going to has four daughters. The first one gets the water," and he showed him where willows were growing round the water. "The second one comes for the water next, and the third one comes for the water after her. Last of all will come the fourth girl. She is good and polite. If she should come for water, go to her and she will tell you something that will help you. If you see her coming, hide in the willows until she gets there. Then go to her. The other three girls are just the same as that one, their father. They are bad, so don't go to them. I am going back now," and Raven left him.

Pretty soon, the first girl came for water. The man hid himself from her. Then the girl got the water and went back with it. After her came the second girl for water and he hid himself again. Then she went back with the water. Afterwards, the third girl came for water and when she had it, she went back. Now the fourth girl came for water. Before she got there, the man went to the willows and hid in them. When the girl got to the water, she sat down and the man went to her. Then the girl said to him, "How did you get here?" and she told him that no one ever came here. The man said to her, "One man came to me up above yesterday and told me to come here to work for him." "That one is my father and no one ever bothers with him. Don't go to his place. You better go back," she said to him. But he told her, "I have already promised to come and so I will have to go to him now." The girl had warned him to help him out, but he only would say that he had to do as he had promised.

The girl tried to make him go back, but he would not and so she said to come with her to the house. They went. When they came to the house, the man stopped by the door and the girl went in. When she got inside she said to her father, "A man is outside whom you told to work for you. That is why he has come." "Yes, that's right, I told him to come here. Tell him to come in," the father said. The man came in the house. When he got in, the White man told him, "There is a table. Go and eat," and the man did. After he was through, the White man talked with him. He told him, "Early in the morning, you will start to work. A little house is over there. You can stay in it." The little shack was not much good, but the man went inside it. He slept there that night.

Early the next morning, the White man had breakfast fixed and sent one of the girls over to call the man. He came and ate. After he was through, he went outside. Then the White man gave him an old, dull axe, a dull old hoe, and an old pick. These tools were so old that they were no good. He told him to go out in the field and work; that he must plant corn which would grow and ripen this same day. "The next day you will bring this corn in to me," the White man said. The man looked at the place the field was supposed to be and there were a lot of small hills. It would be impossible to make any farm there. He went out to two hills in the field and stood there. He didn't try to work, but just stood. "Why did you come here," he thought to himself and he sat down. Then he started to cry and felt sorry that he had come. He sat this way all morning till noon. Just about noon the fourth girl came to him. She had told her father maybe the man was hungry and that he would like some food, so she would take it to him. The father said all right and so she brought him some food. But the man just sat and cried when she got to him. Then the girl said to him, "Why do you cry? I thought that you came here to make a field. I told you to go home." Then he ate a little. When he was through eating, the girl told him to put his head in her lap and she would look for lice in his hair. So he did this. While she was working on him, he went to sleep. When he was asleep, the girl prepared the field. Then she planted the corn and immediately it was ripe. She woke the man up and told him, "While you slept the field became this way." The girl went back to the house and the man went also. It was sunset then. The White man told him to come and eat and so he went in. Then the White man said to him that tomorrow he would work again in the morning. He went back to his little shack to sleep.

The girl made some cornbread out of the corn that grew in the field, and in the morning the man took it to her father. Then he went back to his shack again. The girl said to her father, "Let me go and see that man," and she came over. When she got there, she said, "Today you will get the hardest job." When he got home, the Devil, the girl's father, was glad because he had had the corn-

bread to eat, he said. Then he went in his house. The Devil's wife
was very old. He said to her, "When we first got married, we flew
to the ocean and while we were there, I lost my ring." Then he told
the man to go over to the ocean and find the ring. "That ring has
been lost a long time, but I think it is still there. I want you to go
and find it and bring it back here to me, because I like it very
much." The ocean was not far off. The man went to its edge and
stood there looking at the waves coming in. Then he sat down and
just looked. The waves were like mountains and he was afraid of
them. So he just sat there and cried and said, "Why did I come
here? I could have stayed at home and been all right." This way
he sat till noon. Then the girl said to her father, "That man went to
the ocean. Maybe he is hungry. I will take some food to him," and
so she put some food in a basket and took it to him. When she
came to the edge of the ocean, she found the man sitting there,
crying. Then she said to him, "I told you to go home." Now the
man ate the food up and when he was through, the girl said to
him, "How are you going to find the ring?" and she sat down. The
man told her, "I don't think that I will be able to find the ring and
so I am just sitting here." The girl said to him, "If you want to, cut
me up in little pieces." But he said, "No, I dont' want to do that."
The girl said, "Then how are you going to find the ring if you don't
cut me up in little pieces?" She said this to help him out. She had
brought a cloth along with her. The man said, "Why should I cut
you up? You wouldn't be any good to me then." But the girl said,
"Cut me up and I will help you that way," and so he said all right.
"Cut me up into little pieces and throw me into the ocean. Don't
leave any pieces. Then take this cloth and cover your head with it
and lie down. Don't look. When it is time for me to come back,
when the tide rises to you, uncover your head. There will be a lot
of little fish and you must take them all out with your hands. Don't
let any of them get away." Then the man cut the girl up into little
pieces and threw the pieces all into the water. He lay down and
covered his head with the cloth. When it was time for the girl to
come back, he uncovered his head and looked at the edge of the
ocean. There were a lot of little fish and he scooped them out with
his hands. But one little fish got away between his fingers. Then
he lay down and again covered up his head with the cloth. In a
while the girl came back and woke him up, showed him the ring
that she had found, and gave it to him. Then she went home and
he did also. When he got there he gave the ring to the Devil. Then
the Devil said, "I had that ring for a long time when I was a boy.
Then I flew with my wife over the ocean one time and lost it. Now
I have it back," and he was very glad. After supper he said to the
man, "Tomorrow you will work again in the morning." As the man
was all through eating, he told him to go his shack and stay there.
When it was just about dark, the girl said to her father, "Let me go

and talk to that man," and so she went to him and talked with him. "There is another very hard job that my father is going to give you tomorrow. He is a very bad man and he can change himself into anything. Tomorrow will be the worst and he will get you a wild horse to break. This wild horse will be him."

This man had come from far off to do these hard jobs and that was why the four girls were helping him. All four of the daughters had come this night to the shack, to talk with the man and to help him. Then they said, "There will be a big black horse in the stable for you. You cannot touch him he is so wild. The saddle that you will have to ride will be the Devil's wife." The first girl said, "I will be the bridle." The second girl said, "I will be the stirrups." The third girl said, "I will be the crupper." Then the fourth said, "I will be the cinch." This way all the girls said they would help him out. The first girl said, "I will be the bridle and hold the horse's nose tight." The second girl said, "I will be the stirrups and hold your feet in tight." The third girl said, "I will be the crupper and twist the horse's tail up tight." And the fourth girl said, "I will be the cinch and I will hold on tight for you." They told him to get himself a stick, a big one about two feet long and have it ready in the morning. Before they left him, they said, "He will have you ride in the morning," and then they went to the house and he went to sleep.

The next morning there was some food for the man and they called him to come and eat. After he was through eating, he went outside and waited. The horses were kept in the barn and so the Devil told him, "There is a horse in the barn that no one can break. Maybe you're the only one that can break him. I want to try him. When you go to the barn, the door will open for you." Then the man went to the barn and when he got to the door, it opened for him by itself and he went in. Inside he stopped and saw a big black horse. Then the horse ran at him with his mouth open showing his teeth. The man had his stick and when the horse was just about to bite him, he hit him hard on the nose. When he hit him, the horse turned a little and right then the man jumped on his back. Then the horse started to buck with him. He bucked with him over black metal in four places. There were four hills sticking up like blades and the horse ran over these with him. On the sides of the hills, there was black metal sticking out. If he fell off, it would cut him. All four girls were helping him. The first was holding on to the horse's nose tightly, the second was holding his feet in the stirrups, the third was holding the horse's tail up tightly, and the fourth was holding on the saddle. The man hit the horse with the stick and the horse bucked. The horse kept on this way and finally he was about to jump in the ocean, but then he stopped and said, "My children, he has almost killed me," and so he turned back. The man hit him with the stick on both sides, but the horse did nothing.

When they got back to the house, the man took off the saddle and the bridle. The horse was all in and had no more fight in him. After this, he went to his shack and the saddle, bridle, crupper, cinch, and the horse turned back into the Devil, his wife, and the four girls and all went to the house. About sunset, they called him to eat, so he went in the house and ate. When he was through eating, the Devil said to him that he would talk to him in the morning and so the man went back to his shack.

About dusk the girl said to her father that she wanted to go and talk with the man. Then she went to him and told him, "Tomorrow, if my father talks to you, he will ask you to marry one of his daughters. When he does this, you must pick me out. If you should pick out one of the other girls, it will be a bad thing for you. My father will line us up and blindfold you and tell you to pick one of us. When he does this, if you take our hands in turn and you find one hand that has the first joint of the little finger gone, then pick her. The time you let the one little fish get away, that was the first joint of my little finger." Then the girl left him and he went to sleep. In the morning, the food was ready and so the man went to eat. When he was finished eating, the Devil said to him, "You have worked for me and so you can marry one of my girls." They all came outside and the girls lined up. Then the Devil told the man to tie something about his eyes and go to the girls. The one that he caught would be his wife. He told him that he must take hold of the girls' hands. The man did this. He took hold of the girls' hands and he was careful to feel for the end joint of the little finger. He had tried all the girls except the last one. Then he took her hand and felt there was no end joint to her little finger. So he lead her out from the line. He went to the house and sat down. The Devil said to him, "I like you, my son-in-law. You will not have to work on hard jobs for me any more. You will only go around and have a good time from now on."

The man and the woman had been married for a long time. Then the woman said to the man, "Where did you used to live? Let's go back to that place." "I have forgotten where I used to live," he said. But the woman answered him, "I know this place. It's not far off." "No, I don't know where it is and if we went, I might get lost and go the wrong way," the man said. "Over there is your home, just a little ways," his wife said. "All right, let's go there," the man said. Then it was sunset and a little later on it was dusk. When it was about time to go to bed, the woman said, "In the barn there are lots of big horses, but don't take them. There is one little pony who is poor and you must take him. He is mine." So the man went to the barn and there he saw lots of big horses, but he kept on till he came to one poor, little pony. He was very thin. When he saw it, he thought to himself that he wouldn't go home with such a poor horse and that he would take one of the big ones. So he got one of the big horses and took it to the house. When he came, the woman said, "I told you not to get one of the big ones, but to get my little, poor horse. If you take him, we will get home right away. You have made a mistake." But the man said to her, "I don't think that the poor horse could take us home at all and that is why I have one of the big strong horses." "That little yellow horse of mine is Wishing Horse and wherever you want to go, he will take you. He knows in his own mind where you want to go. This big horse, if you ride him for one mile, he will go all right, but from then on, you have to kick him all the way. Anyway, let's start before my father wakes up," the woman said. Then they got on the big horse and started off. After they had gone about a mile, the big horse slowed down and they had to kick him along. They got about halfway by morning. When it was sunrise, they could see behind them a great rain coming. Immediately the woman made an adobe house close by. In front of the house she made stand an apple tree. Then she turned herself into an old woman and sat down under the tree. The man turned into an old man and went to stand in front of the house. The big rain coming behind them was the woman's father and his wild horses. "If we had brought Wishing Horse, we would be home now," the woman said. The big rain was close to them and the Devil was coming, so the girl said to her husband, "When he gets here, even if he says lots to you, you must not answer him. But take three apples in your hand and say, "Three for a quarter." So the old man was holding three apples in his hand when the woman's father got there. The Devil said to him, "My daughter ran away from home. Did you see her pass here?" "No one has passed here," the old man said. Then a horse was coming. This horse stopped close to the house, jumped over it and was gone. That was all they heard. The horse was the Devil himself, for every step that he took, he went one mile, so it must have been him. The man went to look for the horses tracks but there were none. He came back to the house. He thought they would go on their way and so he started off with his wife. After they had gone a little way, they saw behind them male rain (a heavy rain) coming and so they changed themselves into the old woman sitting under the apple tree and the old man standing in front of the adobe house with three apples in his hand. "Three apples for a quarter. Just say that, if he says anything to you," the woman said to her husband. So the male rain came up to them and it was the woman's father. He said to the old man, "My daughter ran off. Have you seen her go by? It was last night that she left." "Three apples for twenty-five cents," the old man said. The Devil talked on but the old man just said, "Three apples for a quarter." "I'm not talking about apples. I'm asking about my daughter," the Devil said. But all the old man would say was, "Three apples for twenty-five cents," and so the Devil just left them and went back, because he couldn't do anything with them. After he had gone they started on their way again. But they had not gone far when from behind them they saw male rain coming. It was a great rain. They stopped and the woman made a boat and put it on the lake at that place; in the middle. Then she said to her husband, "If we had Wishing Horse, we would be at your home already." The big rain was coming close and Wishing Horse was with it. The woman said to the man, "No matter what my father says to you, you must not talk to him. If you do talk to him, we will be right back at my home where we started from." When the storm got to them, the Devil was there also and when he stopped, he saw the two out on the lake. Then he told his daughter to look at him just once and he asked his son-in-law, to do the same. "I like you and that is why I chose you for my son-in-law," he said. But the woman said to her husband, "Don't look at him." The Devil talked a long time and then he said, "My daughter, you can go any place that you want," and then he turned and went home.

After the Devil had left them, they went on again. When they were pretty near the man's home, they stopped, unsaddled the horse, and chased him back towards his home. Then the woman said, "Go to your family now and I will wait for you here. But if you go near your mother, father, brothers, sisters, and grandparents, do not let them touch you. Just go around among them. If one of them should touch you, you will forget all about me for good. When you have seen them, come back here to me." So the man started off to his relatives. His family thought that he had died long ago, because he had been away so long. But now they saw him coming and when he got to them, they started to cry over him and tried to catch hold of him. But he said, "Don't touch me. Don't come near me," and wouldn't let any of them come close. Then his grandmother came up behind him and grabbed him with her arms. This way she caught and touched him. Right then the man forgot all about his wife and how he had married her. She went back to her home instantly.

The man stayed on with his family for quite a while. Then there was one chief among the White people who had a nice daughter. The man became friends with her. After a while they decided to get married. The girl suggested it and the man agreed. So they went to a house and there the priest talked to them. They were about to be married. The man had a white ribbon in his hand by which he held the girl, but he could not touch her yet. Then a white dove flew in the house and lit on one of the beams over the people's heads. The people looked up at the dove, but didn't say anything. Then the white dove said, "Don't you remember me? It was I who helped you out one time." No one answered and so the dove said again, "Don't you remember the time that I made the adobe house and I made you into an old man and myself into an old woman?" But still no one answered. "Don't you remember the time that I made the boat when my father ran after us and talked to us?" the dove said. But no one answered her. "Don't you remember how we started off from where the boat was and came on near to your home, how I told you not to let anyone touch you? Do you still remember?" the dove said. No one answered her. "Do you remember how you went to your relatives and your grandmother caught hold of you from behind?" the dove said. Now the man remembered everything and said to her, "Let's go back again." Then he became a white dove also and flew up and perched beside her. The two flew out together and left all the people sitting there. The man never came back to marry the chief's daughter and so the people all left.

My yucca fruits lie piled up.